LORDS of
POVERTY

LORDS of POVERTY

The Power, Prestige, and Corruption of the International Aid Business

GRAHAM HANCOCK

THE ATLANTIC MONTHLY PRESS
NEW YORK

Also by Graham Hancock

Journey Through Pakistan

Ethiopia: The Challenge of Hunger

AIDS: The Deadly Epidemic

First published in Great Britain in 1989 by Macmillan London Limited

First Atlantic Monthly Press paperback edition, January 1992

Printed in the United States of America

Library of Congress Cataloging-in-Publication Data

Hancock, Graham
  Lords of poverty.
  1. Economic assistance—Developing countries.
2. Non-governmental organizations—Developing
countries—Corrupt practices. I. Title.
HC60.H278   1989   338.9'1'091724   89-6893
ISBN 0-87113-469-1(pbk.)

The Atlantic Monthly Press
19 Union Square West
New York, NY 10003

FIRST PRINTING

Contents

Acknowledgements ix

Introduction   The Rain Kings   xi

PART ONE   Masters of Disaster?   1

PART TWO   Development Incorporated   35

PART THREE   The Aristocracy of Mercy   77

PART FOUR   The Midas Touch   111

PART FIVE   Winners and Losers   153

CONCLUSION   Aid Is Not Help   185

References 195

Index 227

The Development Set

Excuse me, friends, I must catch my jet –
I'm off to join the Development Set;
My bags are packed, and I've had all my shots,
I have travellers' cheques and pills for the trots.

The Development Set is bright and noble,
Our thoughts are deep and our vision global;
Although we move with the better classes,
Our thoughts are always with the masses.

In Sheraton hotels in scattered nations,
We damn multinational corporations;
Injustice seems so easy to protest,
In such seething hotbeds of social rest.

We discuss malnutrition over steaks
And plan hunger talks during coffee breaks.
Whether Asian floods or African drought,
We face each issue with an open mouth.

We bring in consultants whose circumlocution
Raises difficulties for every solution –
Thus guaranteeing continued good eating
By showing the need for another meeting.

The language of the Development Set,
Stretches the English alphabet;
We use swell words like 'epigenetic',
'Micro', 'Macro', and 'logarithmetic'.

Development Set homes are extremely chic,
Full of carvings, curios and draped with batik.
Eye-level photographs subtly assure
That your host is at home with the rich and the poor.

Enough of these verses – on with the mission!
Our task is as broad as the human condition!
Just pray to God the biblical promise is true:
The poor ye shall always have with you.

Ross Coggins

Lords of Poverty is dedicated to those senior staff at the World Bank who illegally acquired and read my original synopsis in the early days of this project. By attempting from the outset to limit my access to inside information they convinced me that the aid business does indeed have much to hide.

Acknowledgements

In gathering the extensive documentation from a wide range of sources, which was necessary before a single word of this book could be written, I am grateful for the hard work and long hours put in by my research assistants Stan Winer, Ruth Thorlby and – latterly – Fiona Bibby. I would also like to express my thanks to Teddy Goldsmith, editor of *The Ecologist* magazine, who gave me access to his extensive library on development and aid-related issues and who was kind enough to read and comment on my text. Thanks also to Edward Milner for his advice and encouragement and to my parents for their frequent and helpful readings of the various drafts of the manuscript. Needless to say, none of these people should be held responsible for any of the book's failings – which, along with the views expressed in it, are entirely my own.

From inception to completion *Lords of Poverty* took up much of my time over a period of more than two years. My warmest gratitude is thus reserved for my wife Carol and for my children Luke, Leila and Sean, who bore with me throughout.

Graham Hancock
March 1989

THE RAIN KINGS

This book is an attack on a group of rich and powerful bureaucracies that have hijacked our kindness. The bureaucracies I refer to are those that administer the West's aid and then deliver it to the poor of the Third World in a process that Bob Geldof once described as 'a perversion of the act of human generosity'.[1]

I want to make it clear at the outset that my attack is principally focused on *official* aid organisations. Other than passing references to the disaster-relief operations of some charities in Part One, I have deliberately refrained from mounting an offensive against the *voluntary* agencies – for example, Oxfam, Save the Children Fund and Band Aid in Britain, or Catholic Relief Services, Operation California and Africare in the United States. I do have criticisms of the long-term development work of almost all of these smaller 'non-governmental' organisations; however, by and large, I believe their staff to be well motivated and their efforts worthwhile. Furthermore, they are funded on a voluntary basis by contributions from the general public and thus are under considerable pressure to use properly the money they receive. They rarely do significant harm; sometimes they do great good.

The same, however, cannot be said for official aid agencies. Whether 'multilateral' – like the World Bank – or 'bilateral' (USAID or Britain's Overseas Development Administration), such agencies are financed involuntarily by tax-payers who are then allowed absolutely no say in how their money is spent. Official aid also involves the transfer of very *large* sums of money – so large, in fact, that the resources of the voluntary sector look puny and insignificant by comparison. It would thus seem sensible, at the very least, for the official agencies to be directly accountable to the public – to be 'transparent', open and honest in their dealings.

This, unfortunately, is not the case. Indeed, critical study is sharply and effectively discouraged. Those of us, for example, who wish to evaluate the progress, or effectiveness, or quality of development assistance will soon discover that the aid bureaucracies have already carried out all the evaluations that they believe to be necessary and are prepared to resist – with armour-plated resolve – the 'ignorant', or 'biased' or 'hostile' attentions of outsiders. Even the few apparently independent studies in this field turn out in the majority of cases to have been financed by one or other of the aid agencies or by institutes set up with aid money. And, where there is no such direct link, more subtle influences are generally at work. Academics at schools of development studies, for instance, often aspire to highly-paid jobs in the United Nations or the World Bank and can be forgiven for not biting too hard a hand that may be about to feed them. Western journalists investigating projects in poor countries usually do so under aid-agency auspices and tend to come away with a partisan view of what they have seen. Likewise appeals for disaster-relief, which have played a particularly important rôle in shaping public perceptions of aid issues in recent years, portray the agencies and their staffs in a light that is entirely positive – if not actually saintly.

At a more general level, foreign aid – now worth almost $60 billion a year – has changed the shape of the world in which we live and had a profound impact on all our thinking. Consciously or unconsciously we view many critical global problems through lenses provided by the aid industry. When we come to analyse these problems we draw on a vast data-base that the aid industry has generated – and that the aid industry controls. If, as individuals, we choose to act to solve these problems then we will find that the aid industry has already defined and determined most of the directions in which we may move.

What we have here, therefore, is a publicly-funded enterprise, charged with grave international responsibilities, that has not only been permitted to wall off its inner workings from the public view but that also sets its own goals, establishes how these goals are to be attained and, in due course, passes judgement on its own efforts. Perhaps inevitably in such a hermetically-sealed universe, these judgements tend to be favourable and seek to reassure us that all is well, that formidable difficulties are slowly but surely being overcome and that aid is fundamentally good. Indeed, the promotion of such anodyne, cheerful and uplifting messages has become a massive international exercise employing thousands of people and absorbing public-relations budgets worth hundreds of millions of dollars a year.

It is a tribute to the success of this PR campaign that foreign aid is now a sacred cow. In all Western countries, irrespective of their wealth, and irrespective also of their ideological stance, 'overseas development' has been elevated above political debate to become the 'least questioned form of state spending'.[2] Perhaps this lack of examination explains why foreign-aid budgets always increase. The *rate* of expansion may be relatively slow here, relatively fast there; in all donor countries, however – even in times of general austerity – *more* gets spent on overseas development every year.

Thus, while we may cut our military spending, pare our education systems to the bone, and put our health services under the microscope, foreign-aid allocations regularly escape cost-benefit analysis and efforts are seldom made to link further funding to the achievement of *results* in the field. As Professor Bauer of the London School of Economics accurately observes: 'Whatever happens in the recipient countries can be adduced to support the maintenance or extension of aid. Progress is evidence of its efficiency and so an argument for its expansion; lack of progress is evidence that the dosage has been insufficient and must be increased. Some advocates argue that it would be inexpedient to deny aid to the speedy (those who advance); others, that it would be cruel to deny it to the needy (those who stagnate). Aid is thus like champagne: in success you deserve it, in failure you need it.'[3]

There is, of course, criticism of the aid industry – but such criticism tends to be confined within a rather narrow range. Most commonly we hear the voices of those who say that aid is insufficient and that it should be increased. Some detractors single out specific types of aid as being inappropriate (food aid, for example, or programme aid, or aid for the development of heavy industries). Others focus on particular instances in which aid has been used wastefully, or corruptly, or has gone to governments that are not politically popular in the West. All these different criticisms have one thing in common: they fail, as Professor Bauer puts it, 'to question aid as such'.[4]

In writing *Lords of Poverty* it has been my explicit purpose to do just that – to question aid as such. In consequence, this is not a book that campaigns for *more* aid; in my view, more of a bad thing can only be a worse thing. Neither is this a book that argues for a *redirection* of aid – for example, to better-designed projects or to more worthy countries. I do not accept that aid can be made to work *if only* method X is used in place of method Y, *if only* this is done instead of that, *if only* the political or commercial strings attached are forthwith removed, *if only* the poor are properly 'targeted' rather than the better-off – and so on. Such formulas, much loved by the aid industry, have about as much intellectual validity as the facile excuses of tribal rainmakers who deny the basic absurdity of dancing beneath the breathless sky and seek instead to explain the failure of their efforts in terms of obscure but correctable errors in their performance of the ritual. Like rainmakers, too, the high priests of foreign aid are always ready to claim the credit if, by some freak coincidence, things end up going *right* for a change instead of wrong.

In tribal society it is such dexterous dodging of the real issues that allows the rainmakers to stay in business even though they don't make rain; likewise, in Western public-spending, the same tricks of the trade ensure that huge sums of our money continue to be transferred to aid organisations that seldom – if ever – produce any tangible results. Despite the fads, fancies, 'new techniques', 'new directions' and endless 'policy rethinks' that have characterised the development business over the last half-century, and despite the expenditure of hundreds of billions of dollars, there is little evidence to prove that the poor of the Third World have actually *benefited*. Year in year out, however, there can be no doubt that aid pays the hefty salaries and underwrites the privileged lifestyles of the international civil servants, 'development experts', consultants and assorted freeloaders who staff the aid agencies themselves.

Because I single out these personnel for particular vilification in *Lords of Poverty* it is inevitable that some will see this book as an unprincipled attack on a basically caring and worthy group of people. Equally, I am well aware that in deliberately drawing attention to the unsavoury, greedy, stupid and dangerous aspects of the aid industry's behaviour I am swimming against the tide of received wisdom – and in some ways being 'ungentlemanly'. What I have to say will bitterly offend many people. I make no apologies for that. In democratic societies, we have the right to know the whole truth about publicly-funded institutions – rather than just the partial truths that the bureaucrats who staff those institutions *want* us to know.

PART ONE

MASTERS OF
DISASTER?

And you must know this law of culture: two civilisations cannot really know and understand one another well. You will start going deaf and blind. You will be content in your own civilisation . . . but signals from the other civilisation will be as incomprehensible to you as if they had been sent by the inhabitants of Venus.

Ryszard Kapuscinski, *The Emperor*

THE WHITE WOMAN, tired but pretty, the one in the blue paisley frock, what exactly is she doing? Beneath the hot foreign sun, a trickle of perspiration on her brow, busy and wan, harassed and concerned, what *can* she be up to?

She's measuring the circumference of black children's arms, she's weighing marasmic babies in a sling, she's distributing high-energy biscuits to listless and demoralised kids, she's mixing a life-saving solution of oral-rehydration salts, she's supervising the share-out of a grain ration, she's digging a pit latrine. She's a nutritionist or a nurse, or a construction engineer, she's a volunteer with no particular skills or a professional with many, she's an evangelist or an atheist, she's with Oxfam or UNICEF, with World Vision or the Red Cross. In 1989 she was in Mozambique, in the Sudan, in Ethiopia, and in refugee camps along the border between Kampuchea and Thailand. She'd been in all these places in 1988, too, and in 1987. She'll still be in them in 1990 and in 1991. The personification of faith and hope, delivered to developing countries by *our* charity, she's to be found wherever and whenever disaster strikes. She's the one the camera focuses on briefly ministering to cholera victims in a field-hospital, the one the reporter gets a quote from in front of the feeding station, the one whose weary eyes tell you that she's seen it all before and that she expects to go on seeing it again and again and again.

FRIENDS IN DEED?

Western relief workers in Third World disasters have become potent symbols of the fundamental decency and rightness of international aid. Of course we must help when people are suffering, when lives are in terrible jeopardy, when the sky falls or the earth dries up. Tight-fisted though we may be at other times, a sudden crisis makes us kind.

Charities established to do good works amongst the poor know that they can benefit from this powerful but transitory altruism and go into public-relations overdrive when there is a relief operation in prospect. It's a simple fact of life in the voluntary sector: with appropriate media hype, famines, dramatic influxes of refugees, floods, earthquakes and other such catastrophes can be real money-spinners.

A look at the accounts of Oxfam bears this out. After several years of relatively slow expansion, the world-renowned British voluntary agency doubled its takings over the period 1978–80; it achieved this through high-pressure fund-raising for victims of famine and war in Kampuchea following the Vietnamese invasion of that South-East Asian country in 1979. Thereafter public donations remained fairly static until 1985 when appeals on behalf of the starving in Ethiopia multiplied Oxfam's earnings again – to an all-time high of £51.1 million, up from less than £20 million in 1983–4.[1]

Clearly, emergency relief work has a much greater capacity to mobilise public generosity than Oxfam's more routine long-term development activities. The same holds true for other charities as well. In 1985, for example, Band Aid raised £76 million for the starving from the British public.[2] Americans each year hand over slightly more than $1 billion to private voluntary organisations engaged in the Third World, largely spurred on to do so by poignant televised appeals for famine and disaster relief. All in all, voluntary agencies like War on Want, Oxfam and Christian Aid in Britain, World Vision, CARE Incorporated and Project Hope in the United States, and Médecins Sans Frontières in France, can count on a total of $2.4 billion a year in charitable donations to finance their projects and programmes in the developing countries.[3] The international media ballyhoo surrounding the Ethiopian famine raised this figure, albeit briefly, to almost $4 billion in 1985.[4]

Our support for the humanitarian endeavours of the voluntary agencies is also reflected in opinion polls. A recent survey conducted in the United States for the World Bank concluded that 'scepticism about government efficiency in handling aid leads to a preference for non-governmental channels in the distribution of aid'.[5] Likewise, in Europe, people in ten countries were asked the question: 'Which agencies provide the most useful help to developing countries?' Only 12 per cent of the respondents said 'the government'; 25 per cent said 'private organisations'.[6] Another US survey concluded, 'Americans clearly favor aiding the poor countries for moral and humanitarian reasons,' and added: 'public support is strongest to alleviate such basic problems as hunger and malnutrition, disease and illiteracy'.[7] A United States Presidential Commission on World Hunger established that when assistance was described as 'aid to combat hunger' 77 per cent of Americans were in favour of maintaining it or increasing it; however, when the question was put in terms of 'economic aid' to developing countries, support dropped to 49 per cent.

The emotional demand of mass suffering is strong and direct. It compels us to reach for our cheque books in response to disaster appeals by the voluntary agencies. Also – through us – it influences the behaviour of our elected governments: although Britain and the United States have imposed a political ban on long-term development assistance to socialist Ethiopia, both were generous with 'humanitarian' assistance during the 1984–5 famine and again during 1987–8.

Governments control the purse-strings of official aid budgets that dwarf the resources available to the charities.[8] It should not be forgotten, however, that these budgets, too, are provided by 'us' – all official aid, whether earmarked for 'long-term' or 'emergency' purposes is financed out of tax revenues. It is then channelled to the Third World through two rather different types of organisation: 'bilateral' (for example, Britain's Overseas Development Administration and the United States Agency for International Development) and 'multilateral' (for example, the EEC's Directorate General for Development, the World Bank and the various agencies of the United Nations system like the Food and Agriculture Organisation, the World Health Organisation and the United Nations High Commissioner for Refugees).

Generally speaking, the more that an official agency's work can be packaged as humanitarian and charitable in focus, the more likely it is to receive the mandate of popular approval. One senior staffer at UNICEF (the United Nations Children's Emergency Fund) told me that he found it both exciting and fulfilling to be employed by an agency that had such a 'sexy' subject matter. 'Of course most of our finances come directly to us from member governments of the UN,' he said, 'but Joe Public gets worked up and concerned about children in trouble; that's why people buy our Christmas cards. We're seen as being amongst the good guys.'

The charitable impulse at the root of much aid-giving is at its most potent during disasters and emergencies. It is, however, a double-edged sword. On the one hand it raises lots of money. On the other it stifles questions about the uses to which this money is put – and makes those who ask such questions look rather churlish. Criticising humanitarianism and generosity is like criticising the institution of motherhood; it is just not 'the done thing'. One observer has expressed the problem particularly well:

> Humanitarians ask individuals and governments, out of charity, to give funds to allow them to bind up wounds, comfort the weak, save lives. Compassion expects everyone to agree on the method. Since they are guided by a moral virtue, compassion, any obstacle in the path of carrying out humanitarian objectives must be *immoral*. And since the objective is so good, it is inconceivable that recipients will fail to be grateful.[9]

But what is it, precisely, that the recipients are expected to be grateful *for*?

In some cases it is a good deal less than donors and tax-payers are led to expect. In August 1988, for example, Sudan (previously drought-stricken) was hit by severe flooding of the River Nile and, overnight, more than a million people were rendered homeless in Khartoum, the capital city. As the waters continued to rise, epidemics of diseases like cholera and typhoid posed an ever-increasing threat. In addition many of the flood victims were completely destitute and without any kind of food or shelter. Aid agencies in the industrialised countries responded to this disaster with strident newspaper and television appeals for help and millions of dollars were quickly donated. Two weeks after the flooding, however, almost no tangible signs of the relief effort could be seen on the ground: a dozen or so plastic sheets here, a few blankets from the Red Crescent Society there, and a grain-distribution station with just twelve sacks of flour in hand. Visiting reporters were proudly shown a newly erected camp of 300 tents provided by Britain: for reasons that no one on the spot could explain, all the tents turned out to be empty and under armed guard – even though tens of thousands of homeless people were milling about on mudflats nearby.

By this time no fewer than eighty-five relief flights had arrived from Europe and the US bringing 1,200 tonnes of supplies. What was unfortunate was that these consignments had included just 400 tonnes of food (against a UN estimate of 12,000 tonnes to cover the immediate need). 'That's why, if we go to any corner, we will find that the majority of people have received nothing,' said Al Haj Nugdalla Rahman, a local MP. Amongst the food that *was* sent was a large container-load of fresh meat which – in the absence of refrigeration – quickly began to rot. By the time it was distributed it was 'really smelling' according to one relief worker. By contrast much more durable – and necessary – items like clothing, soap and hospital tents were almost completely missing from the relief deliveries during the first two weeks.[10]

Despite such failings in the crucial early days, genuine efforts were subsequently made during the Sudan floods to help those in need. All too often, however, appeals for money are *not* followed up by action of any practical kind. One agency that has mastered the art of saying much and giving little is The Hunger Project, a massive international undertaking which raises funds in the United States, Britain and many other countries with the claim that it is dedicated to the 'eradication of the persistence of hunger and starvation' in the Third World;[11] in fact it sends almost no money to the starving at all. According to the US National Charities Information Bureau, The Hunger Project received donations totalling $6,981,005 in 1985. Out of this, $210,775 was passed on in the form of grants to other organisations involved in relief work in hungry countries. All the rest was spent in the US under such headings as 'enrollment and committee activities', 'communication, information and education services', 'publications', 'management and general' and 'fund-raising'. Telephone expenses for the year approached half a million dollars.[12] In 1984 The Hunger Project's British office raised £192,658 from the public of which just £7,048 went to the Third World.[13]

In 1985, International Christian Aid, a large US voluntary organisation, was accused by officials at the UN and at the State Department of failing to send a single cent to Ethiopia out of $18 million raised for famine relief in that African country.[14] ICA denied the allegations: according to its own accounts 28 per cent of its income is spent on fund-raising and administration in the United States; all the rest, i.e. 72 per cent, goes to the Third World.[15] However, an investigation of the charity by an agency of the US Better Business Bureau had previously concluded otherwise: a close analysis of ICA's expenditure for 1983 showed that just 41 per cent of its income in that year went to support the programmes cited in its fund-raising solicitations.[16] A similar example is the Dallas-based relief organisation, Priority One International; in one year it sent overseas just 18 cents out of every dollar that it received in donations.[17]

Fortunately, humanitarianism is not always the last refuge of the scoundrel.

Figures from the Charities Aid Foundation show that most of Britai'
twenty-one voluntary agencies only divert about 10 pence out of each pound
raised to pay for their overheads, administration and fund-raising. Band Aid
did particularly well during the Ethiopian famine of 1984–5; it kept its costs
down to just 7 pence in every £100 received. War on Want, which came under
attack in October 1986 with charges that its then Director, George Galloway,
had spent £20,000 in eighteen months staying in luxury hotels, in fact spent
only 1.7 per cent of its income on administration and fund-raising in 1984–5.
Save the Children Fund, with costs running at 7.42 per cent of moneys
received in the same year, says: 'We have a policy of keeping our overheads
down to below 15 per cent of our income . . . We want maximum income to
give maximum aid.'[18]

FREELOADERS, FOOLS AND THE GOD-SQUAD

Whether the aid is charitable or official, however, whether it is funded out of
direct public donations or out of taxes, the employees of all the agencies
concerned inevitably play a crucial rôle in the field and bear a tremendous
responsibility. They must interpret correctly the needs of the poor and they
must meet those needs quickly and competently.

It is generally taken for granted that they do both of these things, and do
them well. Press and television reports tend to play up relief workers as
hard-pressed saints. Some recipients of emergency assistance have, however,
been heard to express ungracious doubts about those who come to help. As one
African refugee asked petulantly: 'Why is it that every US dollar comes with
twenty Americans attached to it?'[19]

In many Third World disasters, a great deal of aid money is spent purchasing
the expertise that Americans – and Europeans – provide. According to a
detailed study of refugee relief in South-East Asia:

> The agencies' 'operating', 'logistics' and 'miscellaneous' costs are enor-
> mous and almost impenetrable. Each agency calculates them on a
> different basis. Somewhere among them are the considerable costs of
> personnel. The International Commission of the Red Cross treats its staff
> superbly. In Phnom Penh much of their food was imported from
> Europe; in Thailand UN officials constantly complained that the Swiss,
> with their air-conditioned cars, their weekends on the beach, lived far
> better than anyone else . . . One World Health Organisation official
> asked for a fee of $50,000, a generous per diem, and a ticket for his wife,
> to come for a short assignment to Phnom Penh. Eventually he compro-
> mised on $16,000, the per diem, and no wife . . . UN officials would get
> more in two days' allowances than the relief programme would provide
> for the average Cambodian over a twenty-seven-month period.[20]

The aid personnel who consume these resources come in all shapes and
sizes, all kinds and varieties. Some are very good indeed – and undoubt-

edly earn their pay. Others are extraordinarily bad, their motivation is questionable and their input is negligible or even harmful. All too often, during Third World disasters, staff, experts and consultants are not subjected to any kind of careful scrutiny before they are sent into the field; common sense gets abandoned in the rush to help.

It should be said at the outset that much of this help is barely tangible to the victims of the catastrophe. Many Western 'disaster experts' turn out to be merely on expensive fact-finding missions. What this means in practice is that they arrive with empty hands and leave with their heads full of information which may, or may not, later be translated into action. At the height of the Sudanese drought in February 1985 the Khartoum Hilton (where a single room costs $150 a night without breakfast) seethed with delegations which had come 'to assess the situation'. Despite critical water shortages in many parts of the country, and despite the fact that the devastating extent of the emergency had been thoroughly assessed over the preceding four months, not one additional drilling rig had by then arrived.[21]

Worse than this, as an anthropologist who spent several years living amongst African refugees has observed: 'During an emergency, whatever their background, almost any white face which arrives on the scene has the chance of a job.'[22]

I came across an example of the accuracy of this remark during the famine that afflicted the East African country of Somalia in 1987. In charge of one highly reputable British voluntary agency's emergency feeding operations there I found a bronzed globe-trotter whose only qualification for the position appeared to be the fact that he had an African wife (she was not a Somali but he employed her in the field anyway, causing massive resentment amongst locally recruited staff who rightly believed they could do her job better). He told me that the agency had first taken him on to its payroll in Ethiopia, which he had been visiting as a tourist in 1985 ('piece of luck, that'). Later he had been transferred to a more senior position in Tanzania – where he was keen to return as soon as possible since that was where his wife came from. When I expressed my doubts that he could be of much use to anyone in Somalia – which he had never visited before and claimed to dislike intensely – he reassured me that he was only there on a short-term secondment. His absolute lack of any relevant technical experience (he'd studied philosophy at university) was thus compounded by a sublime ignorance of Somali conditions and customs.

In Somalia again, but some years earlier, International Christian Aid, World Vision and a number of other US charities wasted valuable donor dollars by recruiting Christian zealots to manage their programmes in the refugee camps that had been set up following fighting along the border with Ethiopia. In addition to antagonising and outraging the Muslims amongst whom they worked, these people were generally young, untrained and inexperienced. Robert Smith, a born-again World Vision official in Somalia, caused puzzlement – and some hilarity – amongst suppliers of equipment and materials by signing all his requisition telexes with the words 'God Bless Robert'.[23] The extent to which God complied is not known. What is clear, however, is that requisitions from the US charities were frequently wasteful and badly thought out. ICA had a penchant for constructing shelters with imported materials that were not properly treated with insecticides – most of them collapsed on their occupants after being weakened by termites. According to one ICA nurse, who resigned in disgust: 'The camp managers were completely untrained in this kind of business. Some of them appeared to place a higher priority on evangelising than on administering to the refugees' physical needs.'[24]

Many other crass errors were made as a result of putting evangelism before good management. For example, one of the American agencies ordered $100,000 worth of equipment and supplies for the camps, and then cancelled when – rather belatedly – it was realised that the relevant budget was badly overspent. What was much worse was that the Christian staff involved in this snafu chose to make additional savings by suddenly cancelling their ongoing work in the health sector – including all the vital booster shots in the second stage of an inoculation campaign which had made initial rounds in eleven camps. Thousands of children in whom the immunisation process had been started but not completed were thus rendered more susceptible to deadly epidemics than they would have been if they had simply been left alone.[25]

Whenever religion is mixed injudiciously with relief work there are human costs to be paid. Despite ample evidence of this, however, the onward march of Christianity remains an abiding concern of many voluntary agencies. According to Ted Engstrom, who was President of World Vision until 30 June 1987: 'We analyse every project, every programme we undertake, to make sure that within that programme evangelism is a significant component. We cannot feed individuals and then let them go to hell.'[26]

During 1980–1 this policy led to grave charges being levelled against the giant American charity's refugee programme in Honduras, which was being carried out under the overall direction of UNHCR (the branch of the United Nations mandated with international responsibilities for refugees). The charges, most of which were strenuously denied, came from other relief workers on the spot. According to these witnesses, World Vision employees frequently used the threat of withholding food supplies to coerce Salvadorean refugees into attending Protestant worship services. It was also alleged – and again denied – that World Vision employed several ex-members of the local secret police (DNI) and had a policy of allowing the Honduran military free access to the refugee camps that it administered. The most serious accusation was that, on the night of 22 May 1981, two Salvadorean refugees who sought sanctuary at the Honduran village of Colomoncagua were picked up by World Vision, installed in a vehicle and told that they were being taken to the refugee camp at Limones. Instead they were handed over to the military. A few days later the same two refugees were found dead at the border.[27] World Vision once again denied involvement in these events.

A VERY HIGH COMMISSIONER

In refugee relief, as illustrated by the Honduran example, UNHCR co-operates with and finances the activities of a host of private voluntary organisations. Although this is not widely understood, HCR is *not* itself an implementing agency; it simply raises money from UN member governments which it then passes on to charities contracted to do the actual fieldwork.

Thereafter, standards of supervision are often very slack, or completely absent, and abuses can easily occur. Recently, for example, one voluntary organisation carrying out HCR programmes in Beirut used UN funds to buy tents, beds, blankets and bedsheets through four fictitious companies at mark-ups of as much as 300 per cent. In most cases, as auditors subsequently discovered, 'the quantities purchased were considerably more than the number of refugees and there were substantial differences between the quantities paid for and those actually received'. The loss resulting from these transactions was in the region of half a million dollars.[28]

Sometimes HCR's money never even reaches the country hosting the refugees – let alone the refugees themselves. One American voluntary agency working in East Africa received $400,000 from the world body payable *entirely in the USA* as 'relief staff support costs'. The relief staff concerned were mostly recent graduates of Columbia University, still wet behind the ears;[29] none of them had been in Africa before and they had no relevant experience. Nevertheless they were sent into the field at the UN's expense (for UN read Western tax-payers) and there given power and authority as camp managers over the lives of hundreds of thousands of 'helpless refugees' – many of whom were far better qualified than they were. In a similar fashion, in Sudan in 1985, an expatriate with no appropriate skills was employed at UNHCR's expense to recruit medical staff to work on refugee programmes. Some of the refugees themselves – they were Ugandans – *did* have medical qualifications. However, neither the expatriate concerned, nor the voluntary agency for which he worked, bothered to consult them. As a result many errors were made.[30]

UNHCR's own officials are not immune to this kind of arrogance and stupidity. In 1987 Bishara Ali, a Somali living in Canada (where he had obtained economics, sociology and social work degrees), applied for the job of Field Assistant at HCR's office in the central Somali town of Belet Weyne. He was turned down by Robin MacAlpine, HCR's Assistant Representative in Somalia, on the astonishing grounds that he was too well qualified. 'With your broad experience in Canada,' MacAlpine wrote, 'it is considered unlikely that you would be able to spend years in such a post without considerable frustration.'[31] Bishara told me in 1988:

> After receiving that letter I felt angry, humiliated and rejected. It proved to me that whatever we [Third World] people do in achieving academically, professionally and technically we would still not be acceptable to the white bureaucracies who enjoy the good life at our expense.[32]

It is interesting to note the kind of people that HCR *does* consider suitable for jobs in Belet Weyne. Sydney Waldron – a construction engineer who was employed by an American charity implementing HCR programmes in Somalia – recalls once being summoned to deal with a 'sanitary emergency' in the central Somali town. At that time Waldron was extremely busy on HCR construction work near Mogadishu, the capital; since his orders came from no less a person than UNHCR's regional head in Belet Weyne, however, he thought he had better respond. Besides, the town stands on the banks of the flood-prone Shebelle River, close to several refugee camps, and cholera is an ever-present risk. 'Sanitary emergency' was thus most likely the UN's diplomatic euphemism for a killer epidemic. Fearing this to be the case, Waldron hastily consulted with a Somali sanitary engineer about 'basic slit-trench and pit construction, labour recruitment, payment plans, tool availability, and other plans essential to the provision of sanitary facilities for some 200,000 refugees'. He then records:

> After a seventeen-hour trip of memorable discomfort (six persons and support equipment in a short wheelbase Toyota), I arrived in Belet Weyne to discover the nature of the sanitary emergency which had called me away. The regional head of UNHCR had been forced to relocate his residence to a temporary encampment after the town of Belet Weyne had flooded out. My task, in its entirety, was to provide him with a latrine pit and enclosure, and a shower enclosure. He had, in essence, diverted me from responding to construction needs which he, himself, had outlined in the UNHCR construction requirement report, in order to satisfy his personal comforts. My approach to this construction problem was a model of efficiency: I conveyed a packet of shillings from his hands to those of four Somali labourers, who dug the necessary pit.[33]

That night Waldron slept in an unusual place – on top of two refrigerators in the house that had been rented in Belet Weyne by the voluntary agency for which he worked. The refrigerators, he observes, had been 'flown in from the United States at considerable expense' but were 'useless except for sleeping on since they had been purchased with 110-volt electrical systems; like most of Africa, Somalia operates on a 220-volt electrical current'.[34]

JUNK, WASTE AND STUPIDITY

Refrigerators were not the only costly and useless items that were freighted to Somalia at this time as a result of bad management and bad planning by humanitarians involved in refugee relief. Perhaps the most grandiose white elephants were a number of all-purpose health centres, prefabricated in Finland at an initial budget appropriation of $1 million each. Waldron again:

> By the time they were ready for shipment the cost of these health centre buildings had purportedly doubled, i.e. to the staggering price of $2 million each. The additional cost was associated with the decision to include two flush toilets rather than only one. There was no plumbing or

water source to which these might have been connected in the camps. When, finally, the health centres began to arrive in Mogadishu, another problem in design became apparent: their disassembled components were twice as wide as the available trucking could handle. I was offered the job (in all seriousness) of cutting these components in half on the docks of Mogadishu. The only such health centre to be erected during my stay in Somalia was virtually unusable since it was horribly hot inside. There was no electricity in the camp for its air-conditioners.[35]

The folly, irrelevance – and sometimes dangerous idiocy – of much that passes as humanitarian assistance is not publicised by the aid agencies at all, for understandable reasons. On the contrary, their press releases paint a rosy picture. Disaster victims, however, must live with the realities of relief. Perhaps because they do not read the press releases, some of them are beginning to be choosy about what they will accept.

At about the same time that Sydney Waldron was confronting the daunting challenge of sawing health centres in half in Somalia, Detroit newscaster Beverly Draper was en route for that same benighted country aboard a US air force Hercules filled with food, pharmaceuticals and clothing she had collected for the refugee camps. The drugs, most of which were salesmen's samples donated by well-meaning doctors and pharmacists, were in due course destroyed by Somali public health officials who rightly considered them 'garbage'.[36] Other than useless drugs designed to remedy the ailments of affluent patients, the poor and hungry in what is one of the hottest countries in the world have also received frostbite medicine shipped from Minnesota,[37] electric blankets, and huge consignments of Go-Slim soup and chocolate-flavour drinks for dieters.[38]

Even when appropriate in terms of content, emergency aid can still sometimes turn out to cause more trouble than it is worth. On Christmas Day 1986, for instance, a relief convoy left Khartoum, capital city of the Sudan, for the town of Wau in the far south where fighting and drought had led to famine. The convoy was carrying 200 tonnes of food when it set off; by the time it arrived in late January 1987, however, 22 tonnes had mysteriously disappeared. A generator for the local hospital had been brought on one of the trucks but was found to have had so many parts removed from it that it was unusable. Adding a final insult to injury, it was then discovered that the fuel needed to get the convoy back to Khartoum had also been stolen; almost all the remaining food had to be sold to cover the cost of replacing it and to pay the wages of the troops who had made up the convoy's escort. Joseph Nykindi, Bishop of Wau and Chairman of the town's relief committee, subsequently wrote to donors: 'We appreciate your efforts, but if this is what you call food aid we don't want it.'[39]

Food from the European Economic Community is another gift horse that is frequently looked in the mouth, with complaints on record from a host of beneficiaries. According to Euro-MP Richard Balfe: 'It is completely unacceptable for us to export food that we would not eat ourselves.' Following widespread fall-out from the nuclear accident at the Chernobyl power plant in Russia in 1986, however, some badly contaminated Community food, illegal in Europe, has turned up in aid shipments. In 1987, for example, a pasta factory on the Red Sea had to be closed down after taking delivery of irradiated Italian flour made from Greek wheat. A year later, in 1988, a number of impoverished African countries were forced to reject EEC food because it was found to be dangerously radioactive.[40]

'During a disaster, all sorts of junk comes rolling in,' says Larry Simon of Oxfam-America. He is right. Food for Hungry Inc., an American private voluntary organisation, arranged a shipment of 19 tonnes of 'survival food and drugs' to Kampuchea during the great famine there in 1979–80. The food was so old that San Francisco zoo-keepers had stopped feeding it to their animals and some of the drugs had expired fifteen years earlier.[41] One British charity's response to an African emergency included packs of tea, tissues and Tampax, while a West German voluntary agency sent 1,000 polystyrene igloos which proved too hot for the intended recipients to live in. Since the igloos could not be dismantled they had to be burnt.[42] Famine victims in India were sent blankets which they neither needed nor used; in due course the Indian government donated the same blankets to Nepal which, subsequently, donated them back to India.[43]

Laxatives and anti-indigestion remedies are other favourites amongst agencies that provide humanitarian relief to the starving. According to Mary de Zuniga, a public health official in Nicaragua, 'Whenever anybody donates a medicine, there just seems to be an overdose of milk of magnesia. We said we could probably use it to whitewash the building.'[44]

Recently, relief agencies shipped nearly 800 cases of outdated baby food and food supplement to a Honduran refugee camp.[45] Likewise, despite the well-known health risks posed to small malnourished children by unvitaminised dried skimmed milk,[46] this commodity remains a popular relief item in emergencies. According to a 1987 special report of the EEC Court of Auditors, 'Botswana received a delivery of 500 tonnes of non-vitaminised skimmed milk powder, which was contrary to the most basic dictates of common sense. Since the milk was intended for direct consumption by children in schools and small clinics, it should have been vitaminised to prevent the risk of serious gastric disorders.'[47]

Mauritius, too, got 500 tonnes of the unvitaminised DSM. In this case the auditors note:

> The addition of vitamins was essential – since the powder was for immediate distribution to more than 100,000 people from vulnerable categories. The supply agreement reached with the government definitely stipulated that the vitamins should be added, but the Directorate General for Development at the Commission omitted to mention this requirement in the mobilisation request which it sent to the Commission's Directorate General for Agriculture.[48]

Other notable examples of EEC 'humanitarianism' gone wrong include 15,000 tonnes of maize loaded at Le Havre bound for famine-stricken Mozambique. On arrival the consignment was found to be old, full of broken grains, impurities and mould – and was, as a result, totally unfit for human consumption. A shipment of 26,000 tonnes of maize sent as food aid to the people of Niger was also examined by the auditors, who concluded sadly: 'It was not even acceptable as animal fodder.' In 1982 the tiny drought-stricken African republic of Djibouti actually had the temerity to refuse delivery of an emergency shipment of 974 tonnes of European wheat flour, which it declared unfit for human consumption! The EEC, however, was determined to impose its food on hungry Africans somehow and finally got the same consignment of flour accepted by Zaïre – albeit two years later, in 1984.[49]

In 1983 Morocco ended up using 240 tonnes of EEC butter oil to make soap – the oil was found to contain four times the maximum level of aerobic germs permitted under European regulations. In the same year Tunisia received 345 tonnes of butter oil of even more dangerous quality – it contained a high level of peroxide and was, in addition, contaminated with faeces.[50] There was, on the other hand, nothing wrong with the 4,500 tonnes of EEC butter that Libya, a wealthy petroleum exporter, was allowed to buy at the heavily subsidised price of 16 UK pence a pound during 1986. The deal, worth more than £7 million, also included 700 tonnes of subsidised beef – no doubt a popular item on the dinner tables of the Libyan people, who have amongst the highest disposable incomes in the world. Defending its action, the Commission argued that it was cheaper to subsidise sales of first-class butter and meat to Libya than it was to store these surplus items in Europe. However, as British MP Tony Marlowe commented: 'What about the poor? What about the starving in the Third World?'[51]

The sad truth, as the auditors themselves regretfully conclude, is that the record of the EEC's humanitarian aid to the poor is just a 'catalogue of disasters', with bureaucratic errors and inefficiencies, wastefulness, inappropriateness and unforgivable lateness very much the order of the day. In June 1983 the Commission received a request for help from Indonesia, which had suffered a poor harvest. In response to this request, 15,000 tonnes of wheat were shipped – but not until August 1984, even though the next harvest was by then over. Following hurricanes in Mauritius the Commission granted 2,000 tonnes of cereals as 'immediate food aid' on 25 March 1981; the consignment actually arrived fifteen months later – on 20 June 1982. A March 1981 request from China for urgent help after drought in Hubei province did not produce any food shipments until July 1982. Likewise, although the EEC knew that local stocks of Zambian maize would run out in April 1983, deliveries of food aid did not begin until July of that year.[52]

In Mozambique in 1988, emergency food aid from all sources, including the EEC, was found to be taking up to nine months to be delivered. Another phenomenon was also apparent: when a consignment did eventually arrive, the donor concerned would frequently insist that it be sent to the province it had originally been earmarked for – even if that province was by then oversupplied and other areas were in need. This caused serious problems for Mozambiquan farmers who, against all the odds, had succeeded in producing a crop: donors appearing with food to give away ruined the market for them and put them out of business.[53]

In the hands of well-meaning but ignorant humanitarians, food aid frequently does more harm than good. According to a study by the US Agency for International Development, Guatemala received 41,000 tonnes of food from sympathetic outsiders after it had suffered a devastating earthquake. Very little of the Central American country's own food supplies had ueen destroyed by the quake, however, and local farmers had just brought in a record-breaking harvest. The most visible result of the humanitarian largesse dumped on Guatemala was thus the complete collapse of prices in the domestic grain market and greatly increased privation for rural producers.[54]

Band Aid, the dynamic charity set up in Britain by Bob Geldof with the avowed intention of responding to the real needs of the Third World and avoiding such snafus, wasted more than $4 million of donated money on the purchase of eighty second-hand lorries for Sudan. The lorries, which were bought in Kuwait, proved to be in such bad condition that they were virtually unusable. It took five months – and many more dollars – to repair them.[55] In Ethiopia, Band Aid's determination not to allow local political problems to pollute its humanitarian endeavours led to a decision to get assistance directly to the people of Eritrea and Tigre through the rebel movements which control the countryside in those provinces. A lorry was sent on a ship going to Port Sudan so that it could be taken into Tigre overland. Unfortunately the ship stopped first at Assab, an Ethiopian port. With the provocative legend 'To the people of Tigre from the people of Watford' emblazoned on its side, the lorry stood on deck in full view of Ethiopian Customs officials who quickly requisitioned it – on the entirely reasonable grounds that Tigre is part of Ethiopia.[56]

Despite such mistakes, however, Band Aid's efforts were generally effective and life-saving. By contrast, some humanitarian aid can kill. For example, Map International Inc., of Wheaton, Illinois, received a donation of $17 million worth of heart-regulating pacemakers from the American Hospital Supply Corporation. The donation solved a problem for AHS by giving it a hefty tax write-off from an area of its operations that it had anyway decided to close down. The pacemakers, which duly went to the Third World, quickly began to give the recipient countries other problems, however: most of the units were susceptible to battery leakage and other life-threatening malfunctions.[57]

FUND-RAISING

The fund-raising methods that generate Western charity can be as reprehensible as the uses to which that charity is put. All too often what underlies the strident appeals, the images of starving babies and shell-shocked refugees, turns out not to be a genuine concern for the wretched of the earth but, rather, a kind of capitalism of mercy in which aid organisations compete to boost their own size and prestige – with precious little reference to those who are meant to benefit from their programmes. It is doubtful in the extreme whether the end justifies the means, but this, in a sense, is irrelevant; what we have here is a situation in which the means has become an end in itself.

In late 1984 a French television company organised a 'Trucks for Hope' convoy which sped across the Sahara Desert from the Mediterranean bringing medicines, equipment and food to the needy countries of the West African Sahel. Viewers were not told that almost as much money was spent on keeping the convoy in live satellite contact with France as was spent on the relief supplies. Most of the medical equipment carried was smashed to bits en route because of the dramatic requirement to maintain a fast pace for the cameras despite bad or non-existent roads. 'We chose the marathon format in order to keep the public in suspense,' explained the organiser of what was described at the time as the 'humanitarian equivalent of the Paris–Dakar rally'.[58]

World Vision, which runs a successful operation in Britain as well as in the United States, regularly makes powerful and emotional appeals to our humanitarianism. Its high-pressure sales techniques often seem to be based more upon the law of the jungle than upon anything else. Operating a survival-of-the-fittest philosophy in a competitive market-place, and apparently defining 'fitness' not in terms of the work it does amongst the poor but, rather, in terms of the quantity of funds raised, World Vision is not above sabotaging the efforts of other charities in order to fill its own coffers.

A classic example of this sort of strategy dates back to the early 1980s when Operation California, a relief agency based in Los Angeles, organised a pop concert to raise money for Kampuchean refugees. The concert was televised by CBS and, at the end of the programme, Operation California flashed its telephone number for viewers wishing to donate. What it did not at first know was that World Vision had purchased commercials – for screening outside the Los Angeles viewing area – to coincide with the concert, during which, at regular intervals, it flashed its own toll-free 800 number. According to Operation California Executive Director Richard Walden, many callers were not told that this toll-free number was World Vision's. Indeed, when Los Angeles Deputy District Attorney Edward Feldman called the 800 number and asked, 'Is this Operation California, the same people who had the concert on tonight?' he was told, 'Yes.'

In Feldman's opinion this was not merely unethical: 'It was wire fraud. It was a federal crime – the use of the airwaves and the phones to put out a phony message for the purpose of getting money . . . from our viewpoint it involved deceptive exploitation of the fund-raising concert.'

Operation California, which was then working out of a one-room headquarters in Beverly Hills, quickly expressed its outrage to the larger and infinitely richer charity and threatened to go public with its complaint. World Vision's response was quietly to pass over a cheque for $250,000. It did not make clear whether this was intended as compensation for the revenues that Operation California had lost as a result of the commercials or as hush money.[59]

On 21 December 1984, unable to resist the allure of Ethiopian famine pictures, World Vision ran an Australia-wide Christmas Special television show calling on the public in that country to give it funds. In so doing it broke an explicit understanding with the Australian Council of Churches that it would *not* run such television spectaculars in competition with the ACC's traditional Christmas Bowl appeal. Such ruthless treatment of 'rivals' pays, however: the American charity is, today, the largest voluntary agency in Australia.[60]

World Vision's competitive use of the media has been less successful in Britain where it has been frustrated on a number of occasions. In 1985, for example, the charity's Northampton-based British office paid $25,000 to Mohamed Amin, the cameraman who, in October 1984, had shot the first news footage of the Ethiopian famine. The money was a subsidy for a tear-jerking thirty-minute documentary that Amin was making called 'African Calvary', and was given on the understanding that viewers of the film would be asked at the end to make their donations to World Vision UK. The funds would no doubt have come in useful to finance the agency's lavish aid programme in Ethiopia which, at that time, was spending large sums on running what was effectively a private scheduled air service in the northern provinces of Wollo and Tigre; the World Vision fleet of five planes included a Twin Otter with a price tag of more than $2 million. Unfortunately, however, the BBC – which screened the film in Britain – did not approve of the idea of a single charity getting all the benefit and wanted instead to direct the audience's money to the Disasters Emergency Committee, a non-partisan umbrella organisation set up by a group of British voluntary agencies including Cafod, Christian Aid, Oxfam, the Red Cross and Save the Children Fund. An hour before the show went on the air the BBC found itself threatened with legal action and was forced to reinstate the World Vision appeal; rightly, however, it also included details of the Disasters Emergency Committee – thus allowing viewers to make up their own minds.[61]

Another World Vision scam is gross over-exaggeration of the extent of Third World disasters. An advertisement that the charity's US headquarters placed in the *National Catholic Reporter* on 2 October 1981 claimed that twelve million people in East Africa were 'on the verge of death. It's the greatest human-need crisis of our time.' The statement was not true – as World Vision admitted after officials from the UN complained to the publisher. In 1982 the giant charity remained apparently unrepentant: it screened emotional television commercials across the USA breaking news of a massive refugee influx into Somalia from neighbouring Ethiopia. What the commercials failed to mention was that the pictures and information were almost three years old.[62]

World Vision was not the worst offender in this respect, however. At the same time International Christian Aid was running its own ads about Somalia's refugees. According to Arthur E. Dewey at the State Department's Bureau of Refugee Affairs, an ICA film 'erroneously claimed that 1.5 million refugees lived in Somalia, when the actual number was one-third that amount; fighting had increased, when it had decreased; children received 600 to 800 calories a day, when much of the refugee population actually was receiving too much food'.[63] Likewise, the Dallas-based relief group Priority One International successfully parted humanitarians from their money with the claim that its missionaries in the South American country of Colombia were so poor that they had to exist on popcorn. Contacted by telephone, however, the missionaries themselves were more honest. Asked why they were eating popcorn they replied, 'Because we like it,' and added that they received regular deliveries of US-style food flown in from a nearby city.[64]

Perhaps the worst aspect of charitable advertising, however, is the temptation, which few voluntary agencies can resist during disasters, to make ever more mawkish appeals. Undoubtedly these do raise money but they also humiliate the supposed beneficiaries and misrepresent them as passive victims incapable of doing anything for themselves. Thus on television in the United States Maurice J. Mosley, the President of Priority One International, once unshrouded a dead Somali baby for the benefit of the camera while the baby's relatives held a wake in the background. 'No gift is too big,' Mosley told viewers.[65]

Neither is such schmaltzy and degrading sensationalism confined to the charitable sector of the aid industry. Similar examples from other areas include posters produced by UNHCR. What the posters all show is refugees in attitudes of submission or helplessness. Commenting on what he calls the persistent 'psychological reaction to refugees as people for whom "we must do something"', Martin Barber, Director of the British Refugee Council, had this to say about the subjects of the UNHCR campaign: 'They were waiting for something to happen. They were holding out their hands. The photographer was standing up and they were sitting down.'[66]

Bob Geldof, to his credit, has consistently refused to be photographed clutching the hand of a starving child. But even Live Aid, which started out at least with undertones of a more analytical and positive approach, could not in the end avoid getting in on the act. As Steve Bonnist of the Intermediate Technology Development Group puts it:

> The success of Live Aid was the result of a constant barrage of negative images in the media engendering support. The following year, the same negative mechanism was at work. Sport Aid announced that they were raising money for long-term, self-help development. Yet, by the time the event rolled around, instead of positive images of people getting on with the job of building their own future, we again had a stream of pictures of famine victims appearing everywhere in the media. The infamous promotional video, made in a film studio, with rats crawling over the feet of extras, portraying shuffling zombies scrabbling in the dust for grains

of corn, merely reinforced the prejudices of many – that Africans are incapable of doing anything to help themselves.[67]

Disaster appeals of this sort pander to – and reinforce – the widespread belief that the impoverished peoples of the Third World are fundamentally helpless. Victims of nameless crises, disasters and catastrophes, they can do nothing unless we, the rich and powerful, intervene to save them from themselves.

The notion that we can do anything of the sort is both patronising and profoundly fallacious – particularly since our record in this field is blotted with failures, deceits and follies. Far from being isolated incidents, the fiascos of humanitarian relief that I have described hint at an entire substratum of persistent structural problems which confound virtually all other forms of aid as well.

Some Solvable Problems

I will concede at once that a number of the difficulties which are specific to emergency relief could be dealt with relatively easily. For example, UNHCR could much more thoroughly vet and screen the voluntary agencies to which it subcontracts its responsibilities in the field, thus hopefully weeding out some of the worst abuses inflicted upon refugees. So far it has instituted no such system, however.[68] For the present, as Sydney Waldron rightly observes: 'any group capable of writing proposals is eligible to participate in UNHCR-co-ordinated relief efforts'.[69]

Another serious problem, also not beyond the bounds of human ingenuity to solve, is the sheer *number* of different kinds of organisation that flock like benign vultures to the scene of each and every Third World catastrophe. Leaving aside for a moment the private charities which, by definition, are a diffuse and scattered bunch with widely differing skills and concerns, it is a little-known fact that there are *at least* sixteen specialised United Nations agencies which can become involved in disaster relief activities;[70] frequently they all do so at the same time. Thus, treading heavily on each other's toes, bickering violently amongst themselves and competing in sometimes unseemly ways for ascendancy, we find UNICEF and the World Health Organisation, UNHCR and the United Nations Development Programme, the Food and Agriculture Organisation of the UN, the World Food Programme, the World Meteorological Organisation, the United Nations Environment Programme, and the United Nations Office for Emergency Operations, to name but a few. In addition to their often strained inter-familial relations, all these agencies also have to relate to the charities, to the International Commission of the Red Cross, and to governmental organisations like USAID and Britain's Overseas Development Administration. Inevitably this causes a nightmare of co-ordination, ruffled feathers all round, and much wasteful duplication of effort.

Part of the difficulty here is that all the agencies, whether voluntary, bilateral, or multilateral, have their own areas of specialisation. This can lead them to respond to catastrophes subjectively – in terms of what they are good at doing – rather than objectively, i.e. in terms of what actually needs to be done. As Oxfam's Hugh Goyder has observed: 'In many disaster relief operations there is normally a dispute between those agencies that feel that medical treatment should have priority and those agencies that see food as a priority.'[71] Such disputes have had fatal consequences. A 1987 study of a famine-relief camp in the Sudan, for example, found that donors emphasising the nutritional needs of recipients had managed to silence those emphasising medical and sanitation needs. In the end, however, more lives were lost because of preventable epidemics of measles and other diseases than because of malnutrition.[72]

It would help if the disaster victims themselves were consulted about their own priorities. This usually does not happen, however. Following the Israeli invasion of Lebanon in 1982 many Palestinian refugee camps suffered severe damage and this created an urgent need for new shelters to be built. Although this was a priority for the refugees, it was not seen as so important by those who came to help, many of whom were not in the shelter business. An on-the-spot observer comments:

> No one was hungry, there was no malnutrition, but one agency which specialised in nutrition arrived and demanded that they set up a thera-peutic feeding centre. There was no malnutrition at all, but they insisted that they must start a therapeutic feeding centre. Other organisations may want to supply things like ambulances or orphanages because this is what they specialise in; perhaps in the States they support an orphanage and they want to help in Ethiopia or Somalia, so – let's support an orphanage. There are not many orphans in refugee camps.[73]

Because conflicts between agencies, and badly planned or inappropriate responses like these, occur during every famine, refugee influx, or similar disaster in the Third World, each such event is followed by desperate calls for better co-ordination in the future. The calls are rarely answered, however, even when structures are put in place precisely to ensure this co-ordination. Since 1971, for example, and at a cost of more than $30 million to Western tax-payers, the UN has funded a fully fledged Disaster Relief Office with a specific mandate 'to mobilise, direct and co-ordinate international relief efforts and promote disaster prevention, planning and preparedness'.[74] According to a damning confidential report by its own auditors, UNDRO has failed almost entirely to fulfil this mandate:

> Involvement in relief co-ordination has been only modest, and other co-ordination activities have not evolved as planned. Despite many missions, neither a coherent technical co-operation programme nor major projects have been developed. Most planned research activities have been delayed or never undertaken, and information dissemination and sponsorship of meetings have been limited . . . Other UN system organisations have not accepted UNDRO's leadership and few signifi-cant joint activities have taken place.[75]

UNDRO has itself been involved in wasteful expenditures of precisely the kind that were supposed to be reduced or eliminated by its co-ordination efforts. In 1975, for example, as part of the broader programme to improve the communications capacity of the UN, it spent $90,000 on two portable high-frequency radio sets for immediate disaster relief and emergency use in the field. 'The transceivers', the auditors note, 'have only been used once (unsuccessfully) in 1976, and have since been in storage. UNDRO has discussed selling them to the UN Field Service, but no sale has taken place.'[76]

Likewise, as long ago as 1976, UNDRO established a library intended to produce and update a reference catalogue and provide information to all types of user. 'These objectives have not been attained,' according to the auditors. The library has

> no supervisor, no systematic organisational structure, no catalogue (beyond index cards), and is rarely used by UNDRO staff members. More seriously, while other smaller disaster units actively exchange information with the research community, and proposals are being developed for worldwide disaster research information networks, UNDRO is not serving as a research catalyst: outside enquiries are rarely received and UNDRO has no clear procedure for responding to those that do arrive.[77]

UNDRO is also not spending its substantial budget for staff travel in the ways originally intended. In 1975, when it was young, the organisation estimated that it should spend $97,000 a year on travel costs for relief co-ordination – with about 92 per cent of this for travel to disaster sites. Despite a dramatic increase in the budget since then, however, the auditors found that only 27 per cent of staff travel was actually to disaster areas. 'The majority of UNDRO trips – 73 per cent – have been for attendance at seminars and meetings, and "liaison" or "representational" travel to donor countries and organisations.'[78]

It is little wonder that UNDRO is unable to contribute much to co-ordination of relief efforts in the Third World when its staff spend most of their time at conferences in the First. Something could be done to improve on this unhappy state of affairs, however, and on UNDRO's so far rather unhelpful service. Indeed, with the experience gained in the multiplicity of disasters that occurred during the mid- to late 1980s it is fair to say that the aid community has learnt at least some lessons about co-ordination and has begun to put these lessons into practice.

The extraordinary delays which sometimes occur in the delivery of emergency food during famines likewise need not be regarded as inevitable. Such delays, as documented earlier, are at their most spectacular in the case of the EEC – which still takes an average of 400 days to respond to urgent appeals for help.[79] Similar problems, however, occur across the whole spectrum of international relief agencies. For example, a study of the UN World Food Programme's response to eighty-four emergencies showed that it took an average of 196 days for requests for assistance to be processed and the food delivered.[80] A lot of people can die in 196 days. It should be possible with better management and the build-up of strategic stocks at various locations to reduce this fatal time-lag; WFP is, furthermore, now working actively to achieve this end.

ARROGANCE AND PATERNALISM

But other difficulties persist which defy simple managerial solutions. At the root of these is the humanitarian ethic itself in which aid becomes something that the rich compassionately bestow upon the poor to save them from themselves. Britain's Prime Minister Margaret Thatcher best summed up this patronising attitude when she said of Ethiopian peasant farmers: 'We have to try to teach them the basics of long-term husbandry.'[81]

The truth is that there is very little we can teach these tenacious and courageous people about the basics of their trade that they do not already know far better than we do; they have been extracting a living – and often a surplus – from the harsh eroded mountainsides of their homeland for millennia. What they do need, if they need anything, is the *means* to maintain their productivity in the face of escalating ecological disaster. Mrs Thatcher's thinking on the subject, however, is indicative of the manner in which aid becomes transformed by the strange alchemy of mercy from mere neutral material help into something that 'we', the rich, *do* to 'them', the poor.

Between the rich and poor constituencies are 'our' representatives in the field, the middle-men – the voluntary, governmental and multilateral organisations that mobilise and deliver the aid. These organisations are riddled through and through with notions of compassion that are, as one observer has put it, 'inherently ethnocentric, paternalistic and non-professional'.[82] Their staff are outsiders in the unindustrialised countries in which they work. They hail from societies which believe themselves to be more highly evolved than others (that is, from developed as opposed to *under*developed societies) and which are deeply convinced of the superiority of their own values and of the supremacy of their technical knowledge.

Precisely because of such attitudes, a medical programme for Ugandan refugees in southern Sudan was run during 1984 by a European nurse while a fully qualified Ugandan doctor (himself a refugee) was given only minor responsibilities. A former principal of a Ugandan agricultural college was also among the refugees. He was unemployed, according to Oxford anthropologist Barbara Harrell-Bond who was then conducting research in the camps. However:

> The agencies drafted in a number of inexperienced and less qualified personnel from the US and Europe to *run* the agricultural programme *for* refugees. The advertisement for one position of agricultural adviser illustrates the point. The advertisement asked for applicants who would be able to *teach* Ugandan farmers how to grow sorghum, sweet potatoes,

and cassava, whereas the most serious problem the refugees faced was lack of hoes and seeds.[83]

In one African country I met an anthropologist from Manchester University who had been contracted by Britain's Overseas Development Administration to do a survey amongst settled farmers in a tropical area that was about to be extensively sprayed to eradicate tsetse fly (and in which limited spraying had already begun). What he discovered, after conducting detailed interviews, was that the local people were bitterly opposed to the project. Many of their chickens, which contributed an important part of their diet, had been killed by the initial spraying and they did not want to lose any more. In addition, they were apprehensive that once the tsetse flies were gone nomadic herdsmen would move livestock in and destroy their crops (cattle cannot graze in areas of tsetse infestation because of trypanosomiasis). The anthropologist's findings were ignored by ODA, which went ahead with the spraying anyway (indeed, it is difficult to see why the survey was commissioned in the first place; the decision to bombard the area with insecticide had been made some time before and was, according to the anthropologist, irrevocable).

This is, unfortunately, typical of the way in which 'aid' decisions are made – without reference to those whom they will most immediately affect. Only a very few researchers from the industrialised countries (they are predominantly anthropologists or ecologists, who have no influence upon what happens) listen to the opinions of the supposed 'beneficiaries' of the processes of development and have any degree of access to what one observer has called 'the rich and detailed system of knowledge of the poor'. Aid workers, on the other hand, who are directly engaged in development, 'are ignorant of and *conditioned to despise that knowledge*'.[84] In general the bigger, the more prestigious and the more bureaucratised the agency the more inclined it will be to despise and thus ignore the wishes and opinions of its clients.

Once again, the negative and often murderous consequences of the wide prevalence of this state of mind amongst expatriates who administer aid programmes become most tragically apparent in the delayed, inadequate and inapposite responses that they make to catastrophes. Their responses to other kinds of aid challenge – those concerned with long-term development rather than with short-term emergencies – are conditioned by the same attitudes of cultural and technical superiority and are thus equally wrong-headed, as other parts of this book will show. But disasters, by their very nature, tend to bring things out into the open with the result that the failures of the aid agencies in this particular setting are more *conspicuous* than elsewhere – and thus are more frequently exposed by the mass media.

THE SOMALI DROUGHT

In 1987, while doing field research in Somalia,[85] I came across just such a failure on the part of a large group of aid organisations. This failure did not result from any particular malice on their part, or from any conspiracy (indeed, they were much at odds with one another), but simply from the attitudes of mind of the key expatriates on the scene and from the routine work methods of the agencies they served. What happened in Somalia in that year was a text-book example of aid gone badly wrong and, for this reason, I shall recount it in some detail in the pages that follow.

There is a certain equation, called the 'debt-service ratio', which is of great importance to all developing countries and which, in Somalia, plays a crucial rôle in defining the relationship between donors and government. On one side of this equation is placed the amount of hard currency that a given country earns in a year from its exports; on the other is placed the amount of hard currency that it must pay out annually in interest and principal on its foreign debts. If export earnings exceed debt-service – happiness. If debt-service exceeds export earnings – misery. Somalia is in the latter camp; in 1987 its debt-service obligations were estimated to be 167 per cent of export earnings, then running at about $135 million a year.[86] By contrast, foreign aid in cash and in kind was worth approximately $400 million a year.

What these figures mean is that Somalia's economy is dominated by foreign aid, to which it must resort to finance all of its official imports and a big chunk of its debt-service liabilities as well. In a very real sense, the government of Somalia *depends* on aid for its survival, and must rely heavily on aid funding for any development initiative it wishes to undertake. Accordingly, it is not surprising that almost every international aid agency is represented in one form or another in Mogadishu, the Somali capital. Most of the better-known private charities have well-staffed offices here as do many multilateral and governmental organisations.

Since Somalia benefits from America's largest aid programme in sub-Saharan Africa, the United States Agency for International Development is a particularly prominent member of the donor community. Operating out of a huge fortified enclosure near the suburb of Medina, USAID is in every sense an imposing presence. Visitors to the compound must pass through a rigorous and rather intimidating series of security checks. When – and if – they are allowed in, they cannot fail to be convinced that they have been given access to a very important place. This impression was enhanced in 1987 by the personality of USAID's country representative. A brusque angry-looking pipe-smoker with beetling brows and a no-nonsense manner, he occupied a luxuriously appointed office of which the two principal features were a stars-and-bars flag and a massive wooden desk. Seated behind this desk, like the headmaster in his study, this gentleman had a habit of appearing to be deeply engrossed in paperwork when visitors were ushered in. Sometimes he would read and sign letters for as long as ten minutes before turning his attention to his guest who, by this stage, would often be too overawed to state his business coherently.

The United Nations family of specialised agencies are also important members of the donor community. Their principal offices are located in an extensive compound at the end of the scenic seafront corniche known as the Lido. Here, protected by a high wall, an iron gate and a regiment of uniformed security guards, the United Nations Development Programme (UNDP) and UNICEF have their country headquarters. Other UN agencies like the Food and Agriculture Organisation, the World Food Programme and the World Health Organisation are to be found in other parts of Mogadishu, but their staff all attend regular meetings at UNDP, which acts as the co-ordinating agency.

Although Somalia is classified as a 'hardship posting' – thus automatically entitling USAID staff there to a level of remuneration 25 per cent higher than they would earn in other more favoured countries[87] – expatriate lifestyles seem to want for nothing. UN employees, for example, benefit from lavish duty-free allowances of imported alcohol and other items and enjoy salaries that *average* approximately $55,000 per annum.[88] By contrast the most highly paid Ministers of the Somali government would have to work for almost fifty years to earn the same amount.[89] Aside from the staff of voluntary agencies like Oxfam, who are not paid well by international standards, and who must, accordingly, live in modest and shared accommodation, the majority of aid officials in Mogadishu occupy large houses and villas; most employ two or more domestic servants; all have imported cars for private as well as official use.

Recreational amenities available to expatriate aid workers are also exceptionally pleasant. The principal attraction is the International Golf and Tennis Club, strategically sited across the road from USAID headquarters. Here, in addition to the golf course and tennis courts, a well-appointed restaurant serves prime steaks, hamburgers and iced drinks to sunbathers at the side of a swimming pool that would not look out of place in the gardens of a Hilton or Intercontinental hotel. Club membership is open to all expatriates in Mogadishu, who gather here in great numbers every afternoon of the week (working hours for most are from 7 a.m. until 2 p.m.). Alternatives include the Anglo-American Beach Club[90] and the Italian Club, both on the Lido. International restaurants abound, with fresh seafood, including lobster and shrimp, being specialities of Mogadishu. At weekends the opportunities for adventurous fun expand, with sailing and scuba-diving being particularly popular.

At the time of my visit in 1987, Somalia's Central Rangelands – accessible within ten hours by car from Mogadishu – were afflicted by a severe drought. This drought, which followed three years of inadequate rainfall, was allowed to become famine because expatriate aid workers and development experts from a wide range of different bilateral and multilateral agencies were not prepared to leave their offices in the capital to find out what was going on elsewhere and were, in addition, arrogant, over-confident of their own judgements and unwilling to listen to local viewpoints. The Somali famine was neither large nor spectacular by comparison with those that occurred in Ethiopia in 1984–5 or in Kampuchea in 1979–80. Nevertheless it was to cause considerable – and entirely avoidable – human suffering in one of the world's poorest countries.

During the crucial months of February, March and April 1987, the dominant opinion within the donor community was that the problem was not a serious one – that what Somalia was experiencing was a 'prolonged dry season', *not* a drought. Regrettably, this view prevailed over the government's own much more accurate analysis – namely that, irrespective of whether the rains came or not, the problem would soon be very serious indeed.

My own investigations in Mogadishu showed that as early as December 1986 Somalia's Ministry of the Interior and Ministry of Livestock were in touch with UNDP about the gravity of conditions in the Central Rangelands and elsewhere. By February 1987 the government had begun formally to notify its main aid partners that it believed an emergency was imminent, and it had lodged detailed requests for relief feeding by the beginning of March – before any deaths had occurred. The government's assessments and early warnings were in this case supported throughout by Oxfam and UNICEF, both of which also tried to draw the attention of large donors to the need for preparedness. All these appeals fell on deaf ears.

Part of the problem stemmed from inter-agency bickering. One incident of this sort was a row between UNICEF and the World Health Organisation (WHO), both of which have responsibilities for primary health care in different districts of Somalia. Asked in early April by the Ministry of the Interior to investigate twenty-six deaths from diarrhoeal diseases in Wanle Weyn district in lower Shebelle region, UNICEF first notified WHO, who were the responsible agency in this district. However, WHO, apparently in a fit of pique at not itself being notified by the Ministry of the Interior, refused to co-operate with UNICEF, which then went ahead anyway and examined the fatalities. Subsequently, UNICEF's investigators concluded that 'the underlying cause of death is lack of food . . . the area has experienced drought for the last three years and the current food level in the villages is extremely low. There appears to be insufficient food for the population to survive on its own resources . . . Many hundreds of cattle have died.'

The World Health Organisation refused to act on this analysis when it was presented at the regular donors' meeting, denied its significance and accused UNICEF of 'making mountains out of molehills'.

At the same meeting WHO also criticised a report produced by Oxfam on the nutritional status of two central regions of Somalia: Hiraan and Galgaduug. The Oxfam report, which followed a more impressionistic but equally worrying document circulated to donors in February, was the result of a detailed nutritional survey carried out in March. It showed large numbers of children to be below the crucial 80 per cent weight-for-height indicator and observed that the nomadic populations of the two regions were suffering dangerously high livestock losses. The report concluded that: 'The prospect of drought, destitution and malnutrition-related deaths is imminent . . . The lesson of ignoring suggestive signs until widespread human starvation becomes camera fodder for the Western media should be too recent to be forgotten.'

WHO rejected all of Oxfam's findings and said that the concluding comments in the report were 'alarmist'.

WHO, however, was not the only big aid organisation in Somalia to refuse to listen to warning voices. USAID – the world's largest single source of food aid –

26

was equally deaf. At one meeting, staff of the Central Rangelands Development Project (a long-term programme that is in fact funded by USAID) made an attempt to describe to other donors the deteriorating situation in their catchment area and suggested there might be a case for emergency intervention. They were interrupted during their presentation by a senior USAID official. 'You're here to do development, not relief work,' he is reported to have said, 'so shut up and mind your own business.'

USAID's apparently determined rôle in discouraging responses from other donors and in stonewalling government requests for help was one of the most bizarre aspects of the drought – all the more so because of the agency's enormous economic influence and political weight in Somalia.

The first appeal on record from the government to USAID was made on 7 February 1987 in a letter written by the Ministry of Livestock. The letter requested emergency assistance in the form of grains for supplementary feeding of livestock, grains for human consumption, medicines 'for intestinal problems faced by local inhabitants' and veterinary drugs 'for control of lice and ticks currently causing problems to animals in poor condition'.

USAID's reply, which took ten days to draft, was a short note dated 17 February requiring 'quantification of the needs in each of the commodities you requested'. In this letter the agency emphasised that it would expect the government to meet the needs from its own stocks but added that the United States might be prepared to finance this operation. The financing would not take the form of new assistance but would come from 'counterpart funds' – i.e. revenues already earned by the government from the sale in local markets of previously delivered US food aid (such revenues are held in suspense accounts and can only be released with USAID's written consent).

In late February a second government letter was sent to USAID, this time from the Ministry of Finance, again drawing attention to the impending catastrophe in the Central Rangelands and again requesting emergency assistance. The reply, dated 2 March, reiterated the agency's view that the government should propose a distribution plan for its own food stocks and that, subject to acceptance of this plan and cost estimates, USAID might release counterpart funds to cover the costs incurred.

On 5 March the Ministry of the Interior wrote to USAID with a cost estimate and a detailed distribution plan for what were then the three worst-affected regions: Hiraan, Galgaduug and Mudug. This estimate, which, just two months later, looked conservative rather than alarmist, was based on the assumption that 880,000 people would be in need of emergency feeding for one month and that the immediate requirement was therefore 13,200 metric tons of sorghum. With ancillary items like dried skimmed milk and food oil, plus transportation and handling, the whole operation was costed at 75 million Somali shillings (about $750,000).

USAID's reply, sent ten days later, was a derisive rejection of the government's estimates and costings. Far from 880,000 people in need, the agency insisted that the true number was between 25,000 and 30,000 and suggested

450 metric tons of sorghum would be quite sufficient to cover the requirements of such a small group for one month. The agency put the purchase and distribution costs of 450 metric tons of sorghum at 9.5 million Somali shillings (about $95,000) and offered to meet these costs out of counterpart funds subject to presentation by the government of an acceptable distribution plan.

The Ministry of the Interior's reply, sent by return, queried with some amazement USAID's figure of just 25,000 to 30,000 affected people. The Ministry asked how it was possible to arrive at such a low estimate for three major regions in which 75 per cent of the population were seriously affected by drought.

USAID did not reply to this query but, on 5 April, wrote again asking for a detailed distribution plan for 450 metric tons of sorghum. In the same letter the agency advised government of its understanding that the World Food Programme might be prepared to organise food-for-work schemes in the affected areas. With something of a 'let them eat cake' attitude, USAID concluded: 'It would appear, with all due respect, with what has been pledged by various parties together with the government's own resources, that the matter is well in hand.'

On 13 April the Ministry of the Interior wrote to express its shock at USAID's hard-line approach. The letter went on to advise that the Ministry had withdrawn not 450 but 1,000 metric tons of sorghum from government stores for distribution in the affected regions and that, in addition, it had managed to obtain a donation of 600 metric tons of wheat from the Saudi Arabian Red Crescent Society, which was now also being distributed. The letter closed with a request that the agency clarify its own position vis-à-vis the drought emergency without further delay.

USAID's next letter, dated 15 April – two days later – had a unique Alice-in-Wonderland quality in that it yet again asked for a detailed distribution plan for 450 metric tons of sorghum. It also advised that, in the agency's view, the nutritional status of the people of the Central Rangelands was serious but 'not critical' (by this time several hundred children had died of malnutrition-linked conditions).

On 21 April, however, USAID wrote again, hastily releasing counterpart funds to cover the cost of the 1,000 metric tons of sorghum already distributed from government stores to famine victims. The tone of this last letter differed markedly from that of the earlier correspondence in that it praised the government's distribution efforts and concluded that USAID was 'proud to be able to support the government's initiative'.

I visited the drought-affected areas myself between 22 and 26 April 1987 and published an eyewitness account in a British national newspaper, *The Independent*, on 27 April. Travelling some 2,000 kilometres overland in the regions of Hiraan, Galgaduug and Mudug, I came repeatedly across appalling scenes of malnutrition, notably amongst children and the elderly. The carcasses of dead livestock were scattered everywhere across the rangelands and a famine migration of destitute nomads had begun, with families camped on the outskirts of every settlement – frequently roofing their temporary shelters with the skins of their last camels.

When I returned to Mogadishu I interviewed USAID's country representative and asked how it was that his agency had been so late to act. In essence, his reply was that the government had not made it clear to him how severe the drought was. Like other donors subsequently, he criticised Somalia for the delay in announcing an emergency.

In the event, Somalia made a formal declaration of a state of emergency on 29 April 1987. Appealing for international assistance, Interior Minister Ahmed Suleiman told assembled diplomats and aid agency chiefs that more than five million people were affected by severe drought in twelve of the country's regions, and that 600 had already died. He listed total livestock losses as 55 per cent of sheep and goats, 15 per cent of camels and 35 per cent of cattle. Noting the extremely poor condition of the remaining herds and the large numbers of people already destitute, he said that relief feeding would be necessary for at least six months. Shortly afterwards USAID headquarters in Washington issued a statement supporting these findings and announced that it was holding emergency meetings and would be sending experts to Somalia to help the government assess its needs.

Given the blatant hostility and scepticism on the part of USAID during February, March and April 1987, it is hardly surprising that the drastic step of declaring an emergency was not taken sooner by the government. The tone of the agency's letters, and the scornful dismissal by the larger donors of Oxfam's and UNICEF's field reports, were taken as clear indicators of the kind of reception that an early emergency declaration would have received. As Interior Minister Ahmed Suleiman put it in an interview with me: 'We had reason to believe that some of the donors thought we were just crying wolf.'

Even after the declaration of the emergency, the arrogance of the large donors and their apparent inability to absorb the realities of conditions in the Central Rangelands remained a crucial factor in shaping the international response that was mounted. Early in May the government estimated that, out of the five million people affected by drought, some 1.6 million were by then in urgent need of a full-scale relief operation. Donors rejected this estimate and countered it with a much lower figure of their own – 265,000 in urgent need of feeding.

Regrettably the donors' figure was not the product of careful field research. It was devised by six 'information collecting teams' which made a whistle-stop tour of regional and district capitals in the first two weeks of May, conducted interviews with local officials, and then did some highly suspect sums on the basis of these interviews. The teams rarely went far off the main road that runs through the Central Rangelands and made no effort to contact and interview nomadic groups, let alone conduct nutritional surveys amongst them.

Half-baked though it was, however, this information-collecting exercise was the baseline for the distribution of 3,400 tonnes of grain that was started in May under the auspices of the World Food Programme. The first half of the distribution, according to the Ministry of the Interior in Mogadishu, 'created a lot of confusion and unrest. The distribution was not even. Some villages in the affected areas received assistance while others were denied.' In addition there was a dispute over the transportation costs, which – in slavish accordance with normal operating practices – were only met partly by WFP. As a result, the second half of the distribution scheduled for early June 1987 was postponed by the Somali government pending agreement on a more sensible distribution plan and agreement also on who would pay for the balance of the fuel costs. Meanwhile, Somalia went ahead as best it could with distribution of bilateral donations of wheat and other commodities from friendly Third World countries like India and Kenya.

I visited the Central Rangelands for a second time during June in order to make a television documentary for Britain's Channel 4. I was horrified to find that the already bad nutritional status of the people had deteriorated dramatically since my earlier visit and that the only food available for them to eat was Indian wheat being distributed by the Somali government. The famine migration that I had seen beginning in April had become a mass movement of the population into ad-hoc squatter camps with no sanitation and with inadequate shelter. Although the delayed spring rains had by then begun to fall they had come too late to save the nomads' livestock herds, all of which had already perished. Neither were the rains of any comfort to the famine victims; the net effect was to add cold and damp to their chronicle of misfortunes and to spread deadly water-borne diseases amongst them. Our cameras recorded a high incidence of severe marasmus in infants.

The hospital in Galkaio, regional capital of Mudug, was swamped with terminal cases. Many children were suffering from catastrophic diarrhoea brought on by drinking polluted water; others had pneumonia – a common complication of malnutrition, now exacerbated by the rains. No injectible antibiotics were available in the hospital and medical staff could only stand by hopelessly. WHO, which has a responsibility for primary health care in Mudug, had sent no appropriate drugs to the regional medical officer.

By this time Western donors in Mogadishu had set up a structure to improve co-ordination of the aid effort. This structure was known as the Drought Action Committee and counted amongst its members the British Ambassador (representing the Overseas Development Administration), USAID's country representative, and staff members from Oxfam, UNICEF, WHO, FAO and several other agencies. The Chairman was a senior official who was given a central rôle in decision-making on behalf of the entire group. In his well-pressed blue shirts, and sporting a handlebar moustache, the individual concerned reminded me strongly of the classic image of the gung-ho RAF officer about to take to the skies in his Spitfire to repel the Hun during the Battle of Britain. Neither was this image inapposite since he seemed to interpret his rôle in the Somali capital as an adversarial one vis-à-vis the Somali government. He told me frankly that, in his view, Somali officials were 'trying to use the drought to extract the maximum amount of aid from us', and he made it clear that he did not intend to let them get away with this vicious subterfuge. 'We're all bloody tired of their constant demands for more,' he confided.

While his desire to defend the Western purse from the piratical depredations of avaricious Somalis was something that I could understand – although not approve of – I was surprised to learn on my return from the Central Rangelands in June that he *had not been to the drought-affected areas at all* during the whole of 1987. This seemed to be a strange oversight for the Chairman of the Drought Action Committee. It was an oversight that enabled him to persist stubbornly in the belief that the country was confronting only a short-term and minor problem that could be solved with a few thousand tons of food. A factor that added to this conviction was the onset of the rains, which had been particularly heavy in Mogadishu. Out jogging one morning during a torrential downpour he reportedly pointed to the skies and told another aid agency official: 'Well, that's the end of the drought, then.' If that was indeed his view, then it is possible that he did not realise the extent to which the rains had made things worse, rather than better, in the far-off Rangelands.

I and my camera crew brought him up to date on the situation there by showing him the raw footage of our film, after which a number of further information-collecting missions were hastily dispatched to the field. A long-delayed nutritional survey begun at the same time was abandoned as pointless after only a few days since it was evident that almost everyone was malnourished and that there was no longer any point in waiting for statistical evidence of this manifestly obvious fact before deciding what action to take. Many children died needlessly before medical and feeding teams could reach them.

I have cited this example of delayed and inadequate donor response to Somalia's 1987 emergency at length because it provides a detailed illustration of the ways in which expatriate aid workers have the power to make arbitrary decisions that may mean the difference between life and death for thousands of poor people. They cannot be relied upon to make the *right* decisions; throughout the Third World they frequently make the wrong decisions. The 'humanitarian' character of their mission encourages them to avoid examining the efficiency of their own work methods and leads them to resent those who question their generosity. Many of them (USAID and United Nations employees) enjoy diplomatic status. Most live in privileged circumstances with salaries and a quality of accommodation that are unimaginably lavish by local standards. They have vast resources at their disposal – to bestow or withhold during an emergency as they see fit. All these factors conspire to render them liable to a deadly kind of *folie de grandeur*.

Déjà Vu

It is a folly that persists through time and that, again and again, causes the international system of humanitarian relief to fail in its essential mission. The same thing happened in Ethiopia in 1983 and early 1984; although the writing was on the wall for a famine that television reporter Michael Buerk was later to describe as being of 'biblical proportions', the aid agencies missed, ignored or downplayed the warning signs and only lumbered ponderously into action when tens of thousands had already died.[91] The Ethiopian government was subsequently widely accused of failing to alert donors to the impending disaster. The truth, however, was that it had done so, repeatedly; the problem lay with the agencies themselves, which simply refused to listen. Seven months *before* Buerk issued his emotional televised appeal from the devastated area outside Korem, Dawit Wolde-Giorgis, then Ethiopia's Chief Commissioner for Relief and Rehabilitation, told assembled aid agency chiefs: 'Ethiopia is facing a potential disaster of considerable magnitude in which, this year, around one-fifth of the country's population will need assistance in some form or another. If those affected do not receive relief assistance, the consequences will be frightening.' He backed this statement up with a detailed statistical account of the numbers of people in desperate need ('1,790,000 out of 2,500,000 in Wollo; 1,300,000 out of 2,400,000 in Tigre'). Damningly, as one confidential internal report produced by Oxfam puts it: 'Virtually no one, including Oxfam, took the request very seriously.'[92] They only began to give it credence after the intervention of television; the cost of the delay, as is now only too well known, was the needless loss of more than a million Ethiopian lives.

Plus ça change. The devastating famine that killed millions in the West African Sahel during 1972–3 had been signalled *since 1967* by clear warning signs which, though unmistakable indicators of what was to come, were ignored by aid agency staff on the spot.[93] Explaining this failure to anticipate the crisis a senior American official observed delicately: 'It sneaked up on us over a five-year period.'[94] Once again it was the mass media that exposed the disaster and that asked the painful questions which eventually forced the relief mechanism into action.

'What tends to happen is that nothing happens,' says Dr John Seaman, a senior medical officer with Save the Children Fund, 'the donors tend not to believe what is going on. They need to see people dropping in their tracks before they will act.'[95] It seems inevitable that this should be so when, at every level in the structure of almost all our most important aid-giving organisations, we have installed a tribe of highly paid men and women who are irredeemably out of touch with the day-to-day realities of the global state of poverty and underdevelopment which they are supposed to be working to alleviate. These over-compensated aid bureaucrats demand – and get – a standard of living often far better than that which they could aspire to if they were working, for example, in industry or commerce in their home countries. At the same time, however, their achievements and performance are in no way subjected to the same exacting and competitive processes of evaluation that are considered normal in business. Precisely *because* their professional field is 'humanitarianism' rather than, say, 'sales', or 'production' or 'engineering', they are rarely required to demonstrate and validate their worth in quantitative, measurable ways. Surrounding themselves with the mystifying jargon of their trade, these lords of poverty are the druids of the modern era wielding enormous power that is accountable to no one.

PART TWO

DEVELOPMENT INCORPORATED

For every problem there is a solution that is simple, direct and wrong.

H. L. Menken

O NE WARM SEPTEMBER evening I flew into Washington, DC, to investigate the problem of poverty. I'd been in Ethiopia the week before and in the Philippines and Pakistan before that; it did not, however, seem to me in the least bit paradoxical that I should now be visiting the federal capital of the richest nation on earth in order to learn more. I had come simply to attend the joint annual meeting of the Boards of Governors of the World Bank and the International Monetary Fund – two institutions that play a central rôle in mobilising and disbursing funds for impoverished developing countries.

I spent the night in the pleasant home of friends who both work in the aid business – she's a consultant, he's employed by the Agency for International Development – then, next morning, I went along to finalise my accreditation as an observer at the meeting. Strolling down the sunny side of 19th Street admiring the rows of stretch limos drawn up outside the headquarters buildings of the Bank and the Fund, I bumped into an aid official I have known for some years. She regarded my jeans and short-sleeved shirt with a disparaging eye. 'You can't go around looking like that,' she said finally, 'nobody will talk to you.'

She was right – as I would myself have realised earlier if I had not still been so jet-lagged. There were quite a few delegates milling about and they were all dressed in dark suits and shiny shoes, white shirts and silk ties. Feeling suddenly as out of place as a peasant-farmer in the stock exchange, I got my laminated photo-identification pass issued as quickly as I could and hurried off to smarten up my act.

GOING FOR THE INTERNATIONAL CHAMPAGNES

The Bank–Fund annual meeting is a rallying point for everybody who is anybody in the poverty business: for aid donors and aid recipients, for private Western financiers who have lent money on commercial terms to Third World nations, for academics and researchers, for UN bureaucrats, for company directors, for experts, for onlookers and for fellow travellers of all kinds. It is an important forum for the discussion of development issues but it is also a sort of trade fair of international creditors and debtors. It is a serious professional get-together but it is also a social event with its own unique hierarchies and rituals. VIPs normally scattered to the four corners of the world and shielded from visitors by ramparts of fawning retainers are, for this brief period, gathered together in one place, wined, dined and rendered accessible. Over mountainous piles of beautifully prepared food, huge volumes of business get done; meanwhile staggering displays of dominance and ostentation get smoothly blended with empty and meaningless rhetoric about the predicament of the poor.

Barber Conable, the former US Congressman who became President of the Bank in 1986, was in full oratorical flow at the meeting I attended. Balding and bespectacled, he took the podium to say this:

> Our institution is mighty in resources and in experience but its labours will count for nothing if it cannot look at our world through the eyes of the most underprivileged, if we cannot share their hopes and their fears. We are here to serve their needs, to help them realise their strength, their potential, their aspirations . . . Collective action against global poverty is the common purpose that brings us together today. Let us therefore re-dedicate ourselves to the pursuit of that great good.[1]

The 10,000 men and women attending the conference looked extraordinarily unlikely to achieve this noble objective; when not yawning or asleep at the plenary sessions they were to be found enjoying a series of cocktail parties, lunches, afternoon teas, dinners and midnight snacks lavish enough to surfeit the greediest gourmand. The total cost of the 700 social events laid on for delegates during that single week was estimated at $10 million[2] – a sum of money that might, perhaps, have better 'served the needs' of the poor if it had been spent in some other way. Xeropthalmia, for instance, a disease caused by vitamin A deficiency, blinds 500,000 African and Asian children every year and permanently impairs the sight of millions of others. With $10 million it would be possible to provide a full year's supply of vitamin A tablets to 47 million children at risk in the developing countries, thus undoubtedly helping them 'to realise their potential'.[3]

Such calculations, however, seemed far from the minds of the glittering and well-heeled people gathered by the Bank and the Fund to review the problems of world development. They clearly had no objection to the small fortune that was being spent on pampering their own stomachs. 'They've booked up the whole city,' commented William Holman of Design Cuisine Inc.

Ridgewells, a well-known Washington catering company, prepared twenty-nine parties in one day alone, according to executive Jeff Ellis who added: 'This year the hosts want more expensive menus, and they're inviting 30 per cent more people. No one is stinting – but, then, they never have.' A single formal dinner catered by Ridgewells cost $200 per person. Guests began with crab cakes, caviare and *crème fraîche*, smoked salmon and mini beef Wellingtons. The fish course was lobster with corn rounds followed by citrus sorbet. The *entrée* was duck with lime sauce, served with artichoke bottoms filled with baby carrots. A hearts of palm salad was also offered accompanied by sage cheese

soufflés with a port wine dressing. Dessert was a German chocolate tu.
sauced with raspberry coulis, ice-cream bonbons and flaming coffee royale.

The Shoreham Hotel estimated its revenue from the ninety-six parties held
there during the conference at $1 million. According to Harriet Schwartz, a
partner at caterers Washington Inc., 'The Taste of America' party laid on by
her company at the Shoreham was designed as a Cook's tour of the best in US
cuisine, specially planned to enthral foreign guests. More than 1,500 delegates
attended an equally stunning event at the Foundry, hosted by the World Bank.
On offer were thirty different foods, ranging from gravadlax to steak tartare to
jambalaya. 'The name of the game now is catering to people who go for
high-quality imported wines,' commented Herb Rothberg, general manager at
Central Liquor. 'The IMF has been coming in here, doing a lot of entertaining,
and they're going for the international champagnes.'

Appropriately, the conference itself was not held in some dour auditorium
but, rather, in a first-class international hotel – the sumptuous and exclusive
Sheraton-Washington. Here 550 guest rooms had been converted into temporary offices, eleven miles of special telephone lines installed, a twenty-four-hour
print shop opened and 54,000 watts of floodlights added at IMF and World
Bank behest. Mary Noel Walker, the hotel's Director of Public Relations,
admitted that she had no idea what the floodlights were for. 'It's their house
during this time,' she said with a shrug. Indeed, the Sheraton, which has
served as the principal venue for the conference since the 1940s, is so much
'their' house that when its new extension was planned in the late 1970s the
Fund and the Bank were consulted for suggestions, and phone installations
were designed to their specifications.

The mammoth hotel, however, is plainly no longer big enough to cope with
the expanding needs of conference delegates. At peak hours it is even difficult
to get into a lift. Waiting in the lobby to go up to the sixth floor for a meeting
with Dr Chedly Ayari, President of the Arab Bank for Economic Development
in Africa, I found myself in a jostling queue of more than twenty distinguished
but evidently irritated people. Amongst them, in a charcoal-grey suit, was
Nigel Lawson, Britain's Chancellor of the Exchequer – a man not used to being
kept waiting.

I was not able to establish where Lawson was heading, but when I reached
my own destination I quickly got into another queue – this one consisting
exclusively of African Ministers of Finance. All were from countries that have
benefited from the $1 billion-plus of development loans that the Arab Bank has
provided on soft terms to the world's poorest continent since 1974, all were
impeccably attired (Gucci shoes and Louis Vuitton attaché cases much in
evidence), and all were waiting either to explain to Ayari why exactly it was that
they were not yet in a position to meet interest payments then due, or else to
proposition him for yet more money.

Looking at the kinds of car delegates were going around in I could
understand why they might need to get their hands on some extra cash. At
times the queue of costly gas-guzzling limousines occupied the full length of

the driveway of the Sheraton-Washington, extended into Woodley Road and ran on from there into Connecticut Avenue. Indeed, the congestion was so severe that delegates were frequently to be seen leaving their vehicles in exasperation and sprinting towards the hotel, hot and sweaty in their pin-stripe business suits, photo-cards flapping against their elegant lapels. 'A good driver wouldn't let his client walk two feet,' said one chauffeur in despair.

Despite such aggravation, however, Washington limousine companies were doing a roaring trade. John Goldberg, the general manager of Dav-El Livery, said that bookings outnumbered the available cars in his fleet by a factor of three to one; he'd had to bring in more cars from New York to make up the difference. 'Incredibly long hours, seven-days-a-week working,' said Embassy Limousine manager Steve Murphy, who was renting out his plush vehicles at $44 an hour with a ten-hour minimum. 'You have to scramble a lot. It's a combination of playing chess and poker at the same time.' According to Sean Surla, another chauffeur, the IMF–World Bank conference ranks second only to presidential inaugurations when it comes to limo-mania. 'They pour a lot of money into this,' he said. 'They each have to have their own car.'

A movable feast, the Bank–Fund meeting takes place every third year in a developing country. Back in 1985, when I was first starting to research this book, the venue was the Hilton International in Seoul, capital city of South Korea. In order to make space for a parking lot big enough to accommodate the fleet of limos used by delegates, the Korean government helpfully razed to the ground the poverty-ridden red-light district adjacent to the hotel – demolishing a total of 128 buildings.[4]

A little later that same year, with the meeting in Seoul over, members of the development set gathered in North America once again, this time in New York City where, I recall, the streets were jammed solid for several days by slow-moving processions of huge motor cars. The situation got so bad that the *Times* coined a phrase for it – 'limo lock' – which summed things up pretty neatly. You could barely move anywhere in any direction without coming across a line of monster machines with smoked-glass windscreens and strange boomerang-shaped antennae on their boots. Why? Because the United Nations was celebrating its fortieth anniversary and because thousands of delegates were suffering from the 'my car is bigger than yours' syndrome.

Thus, like Siamese twins joined at the hip, aid bureaucrats and their limousines are never far apart. Indeed, pomp and ceremony of just about every possible kind, gourmet dinners, and five-star hotels are integral components of the day-to-day existence of those employed by international organisations to solve the problems of global poverty. Whether they are from the United Nations Development Programme, or from the World Bank, few of the officials concerned see their costly addiction to the trappings of status and wealth as indications of deeply ingrained hypocrisy; rather, they take their privileged lifestyles for granted as inalienable rights, as self-evidently legitimate rewards for the 'great sacrifices' that they somehow believe they are making.

Unsurprisingly, these same pampered and over-paid bureaucrats have organised things so that they can continue to prosper even if they are *fired*: redundancy payments at the World Bank, for example, average a quarter of a million dollars per person. When Barber Conable took over as President in 1986 he vowed that he was a new broom who was going to sweep clean. Out of the institution's total staff of more than 6,000, some 700 executives lost their jobs in the year that followed; the money spent on this exercise, $175 million,[5] would have been enough to pay for a complete elementary school education for 63,000 children from poor families in Latin America or in Africa.[6]

THE DEVELOPMENT INDUSTRY

'The Bank's reorganisation is now completed,' Conable reassured his literate and well-fed audience at the annual meeting in September 1987. 'Looking ahead, I am confident that we have greatly improved our institutional ability to provide sensitive, effective and timely support to each of our borrowers and to offer intellectual leadership in the understanding of development.'[7]

In order to make such a claim, Conable must have a fairly clear idea of what 'development' actually is. This certainly seems to be the case when he identifies measures 'to promote economic growth' and 'combat poverty' as the 'fundamental tasks of world development', and when he goes on to describe the institution that he heads as the 'world's principal development agency'.[8]

But what exactly does he mean? A housing project, after all, is a 'development', as is any new event that changes a current situation. The logical sequence of a thought can be described as 'development' but, then, so can the awakening of a child's mind or the budding of a teenager's breasts.

Dictionary definitions of this much-used, much-abused word vary; in one way or another, however, all incorporate ideas of growth – as in 'well-grown state', 'stage of advancement', 'the process of making fuller or bigger'. *Collins English Dictionary*, in a column which also defines 'deviant' and 'devilish', tells us that 'development' is the 'act or process of growing, progressing or developing'. Something that is 'developmental', according to the *Concise Oxford Dictionary*, is something that is 'incidental to growth' or 'evolutionary' in its rôle. The verb 'to develop' involves inevitable notions of making progress, of effecting a transformation from a primitive to a more elaborate form.

Applied to countries, the basic concept of development does not change. 'Underdeveloped countries' must in some sense be stunted and backward; 'developed countries', by contrast, are fully grown and advanced. Once you start using such language, you cannot avoid the value judgements that the words contain. Obviously it is better to be developed than to be underdeveloped. It would be crazy to suggest anything else. Can you imagine anyone preferring to be backward when they could be advanced, stunted when they could be fully grown? Of course not.

On the foundations of this kind of logic a giant international industry has been built. It is a fantastically complex, diversified and devolved industry, of which Mr Conable's Bank is just a single – though important – component part. Financed largely by the official aid of rich countries, mandated to promote 'development' in the poor ones, it is an industry that employs hundreds of thousands of people around the world to fulfil a broad range of economic and humanitarian objectives. The *Wall Street Journal* once described it as 'the largest bureaucracy in history devoted to international good deeds'.[9] I prefer to think of it as Development Incorporated.

Disaster relief, documented in Part One, is only a small aspect of the overall work in which Development Inc. is involved. Food, for example, would seem to be the pre-eminent 'disaster commodity' but only 10 per cent of all food aid is used for disaster relief and feeding refugees.[10] Excluding these food shipments, *barely 1 per cent* of all the money spent on aid each year is earmarked for emergencies;[11] the rest is ploughed into long-term projects and programmes in the Third World intended, as the UN Charter puts it, to create 'social progress and better standards of life in larger freedom . . . to employ international machinery for the promotion of the economic and social advancement of all peoples'.[12]

Thus, in every poor country where a huge public infrastructure scheme is under way – a dam, a trunk road or a power-station for example – Development Incorporated is likely to be involved. Sanitation, water and sewerage works, ports and airports, trains and boats and planes, crop spraying, irrigation, rural health centres, the construction of classrooms, the construction of hotels, mining, prospecting, range management, livestock centres, cement factories, resettlement schemes, family planning programmes, rural literacy programmes, the provision of seeds, the provision of experts, debt relief, balance-of-payments support, technical co-operation, building railways, building bridges, institutional reforms, national planning, the construction of hospitals, the drilling of wells, teaching foreign languages, eradicating tsetse flies, expanding fisheries – in one way or another Development Inc. plays a rôle in all of these things, and in many many more besides.

The poorer the country they take place in the more likely it is that all or most of these activities will be paid for by 'Official Development Assistance' – ODA for short – a concept that excludes finance provided by private voluntary organisations like Oxfam. ODA is public money, raised by taxation and disbursed by official agencies, including state or local governments. To be classified as ODA a transfer of resources (whether in cash, in kind, or in the form of expertise) must also meet the following tests: (*a*) it must be administered 'with the promotion of the economic development and welfare of developing countries as its main objective'; and (*b*) it must be 'concessional in character', containing 'a grant element of at least 25 per cent'.[13]

Thus, *loans* to Third World countries can only qualify as ODA if they are made on 'soft' (concessional) terms; loans to which commercial or near-commercial rates of interest apply are *not* aid. Likewise, any kind of military assistance, concessional or otherwise, is automatically excluded by the ODA definition, since such assistance obviously has nothing to do with the promotion of economic development. Humanitarian assistance provided by official agencies, however, and emergency relief (including food aid) – although not strictly 'developmental' in purpose – *are* included in all calculations of ODA.

Official aid-flows that meet all the above criteria now tend to vary between $45 billion and $60 billion a year. Some rich countries make very large individual contributions to this total, others give much less. In 1986, for example, world ODA stood at $46 billion; out of this, roughly $37 billion came from eighteen 'Western' industrialised nations. The breakdown was as follows: United States ($9.784 billion); Japan ($5.634 billion); France ($5.136 billion); Federal Republic of Germany ($3.879 billion); Italy ($2.423 billion); Netherlands ($1.738 billion); United Kingdom ($1.750 billion); Canada ($1.700 billion); Sweden ($1.090 billion); Norway ($796 million); Australia ($787 million); Denmark ($695 million); Belgium ($542 million); Switzerland ($429 million); Finland ($313 million); Austria ($197 million); New Zealand ($66 million); and Ireland ($62 million). In the same year, the Soviet Union provided $3.8 billion of ODA and oil-rich member states of the Organisation of Petroleum Exporting Countries provided $4.5 billion.[14]

It is extremely difficult to get these kinds of figure with their endless strings and columns of zeros, their commas and their decimal points, into any kind of useful perspective. Comparisons between ODA and other forms of spending help, however.

The USA and the Soviet Union together spend $1.5 billion *every day* on 'defence' – in other words the total annual value of world aid is equivalent to roughly one month's military expenditure by these two countries. Fifty MX 'Peacekeeper' missiles cost $4.54 billion – more than the ODA of the Federal Republic of Germany. Research on 'Star Wars' in fiscal 1988 cost $3.9 billion; for this amount – which is more than the ODA of Canada and the UK combined – you can also buy one Nimitz-class aircraft-carrier. A single Trident submarine, at just less than $1.5 billion, is worth as much as the combined aid programmes of Australia and Denmark.[15] Since 1962 the USA has spent almost $300 million on training *dolphins* for military purposes[16] – more than the annual aid budgets of Austria and New Zealand combined. In 1988 Britain spent about fourteen times more on defence than it did on aid.[17]

British women, meanwhile, spend roughly $480 million every year on fragrance and skin-care products[18] – more than Switzerland spends on aid. The booming international market for duty-free goods at airport, ship and in-flight sales outlets is now worth $5.5 billion per annum[19] – more than France spends on aid. Americans spend $22 billion a year on cigarettes[20] – more than is spent on aid by the three largest Western donors combined. Worldwide, consumers spend $35 billion a year on personal computers[21] – more than is spent on aid by the ten largest Western donors combined.

The United States has an estimated 832,500 millionaire families;[22] if their average net wealth were just $1 million each, then they would be worth collectively approximately eighteen times as much as entire world ODA. In fact average net wealth in this group is vastly more than $1 million. There are now twenty-six billionaires in the USA and there are 400 individuals whose wealth exceeds $180 million each.[23] Michael David Weill of the US company Lazard Frères earns an annual *salary* roughly equivalent to the combined value of the aid budgets of Ireland and New Zealand.[24] Meanwhile, the $10 billion disbursed each year under the US foreign aid programme represents rather less than half of the net wealth of the world's richest man: Yoshiaki Tsutsumi, Chief Executive of the Seibu Group, a Japanese property and railway company.[25]

Sweden spends just over $1 billion per annum on aid; it costs almost exactly the same amount of money to run the New York City Police Department.[26] The administration of the city of Hamburg in the Federal Republic of Germany costs $840 million a year[27] – more than Norway's annual ODA. Metropolitan Tokyo spends about $650 million a year running its fire department[28] – more than Belgium's ODA. The EEC spends $20 billion per annum just to *store* surplus food produced by European farmers[29] – more than the combined ODA of all the member states of the Community.

A conventional measure, used in all official aid statistics, is to express ODA as a percentage of the Gross National Product (GNP) of each donor country.[30] In order to encourage generosity, the United Nations General Assembly has established targets in this respect.

As early as 1960, for example, that august body adopted a resolution which expressed the hope that 'the flow of international assistance and capital should be increased substantially so as to reach as soon as possible approximately 1 per cent of the combined national incomes of the economically advanced countries'.[31]

By 1967 the idea had been to some extent redefined and the sights lowered; at the second United Nations Conference on Trade and Development which took place in that year the figure of 0.75 per cent of GNP to be given in official development assistance was widely accepted.[32]

Then, in 1970, the General Assembly adopted a Strategy for the Second UN Development Decade which stated: 'Each economically advanced country will progressively increase its official development assistance to the developing countries and will exert its best efforts to reach a minimum net amount of 0.7 per cent of its Gross National Product at market prices by the middle of the decade' – i.e. by 1975.[33]

More recently, in 1980, the Assembly resolved:

A rapid and substantial increase will be made in official development assistance by all developed countries, with a view to reaching and, where possible, surpassing the agreed international target of 0.7 per cent of the Gross National Product of developed countries. To this end, developed countries which have not yet reached the target should exert their best efforts to reach it by 1985, and in any case not later than the second half of the decade.[34]

In the event, only a few industrialised countries did manage to achieve the target by the mid-1980s. Top of the league in 1986 was Norway, with 1.20 per cent of GNP. Next came the Netherlands with 1 per cent exactly, then Denmark (0.89 per cent), Sweden (0.88 per cent) and France (0.72 per cent). Britain, on the other hand, had only achieved 0.33 per cent (a figure that fell to 0.28 per cent in 1987) and the United States of America, the richest country in the world, was near the bottom of the league with 0.23 per cent; only Austria gave a lower proportion – 0.21 per cent of its GNP. Ireland, Italy, New Zealand, Belgium, Australia, Finland, West Germany, Japan, Canada, and Switzerland were all also well beneath the 0.7 per cent horizon.[35]

In many respects, therefore, aid looks like quite an insignificant part of the international economic order. Viewed from other perspectives, however, it appears much more formidable. If Development Incorporated were an industrial company, for example, then it would have to be ranked amongst the largest and most powerful multinationals in the world. With roughly $60 billion to play with every year, it is a great deal bigger than, say, Standard Oil of California, IBM or Unilever, and vastly bigger than BASF, Bayer, Siemens, Phillips, Nestlé, Hitachi or Volkswagen.[36] Furthermore, unlike all these entities, Development Inc. has a licence to spend every cent of its revenues in pursuit of its mission. No profits need be set aside, no dividends paid out to shareholders. This is a business that cannot go bankrupt because, like the legendary Horn of Plenty, its resources are constantly replenished, topped up, restored.

Despite the growing contribution of the Soviet Union, and the relatively large amount of ODA provided by OPEC member states, this replenishing, topping-up and restoring is still done, overwhelmingly, by citizens in the 'Western' bloc of industrialised countries: for every $100 of tax revenue raised for public spending by our governments about $1, on average, is allocated each year as Official Development Assistance.[37] This money is then handed over to the bureaucrats who staff the various governmental organisations that we have established to disburse our aid.

MINISTRIES AND AGENCIES

Examples include Britain's Overseas Development Administration and the US Agency for International Development, Australia's Development Assistance Bureau, Belgium's Administration for Development Co-operation, France's Ministry of Development Co-operation, Norway's Agency for International Development, the Danish International Development Agency, FINNIDA of Finland, CIDA of Canada, the German Development Corporation, the Swedish International Development Authority, the Swiss Development Corporation, and so on. Altogether, as noted earlier, there are eighteen Western nations which are prominent aid-givers. All eighteen have seats on the Development Assistance Committee of the OECD – a kind of donor 'club' – and all eighteen have established their own self-contained aid bureaucracies.

Sometimes these are departments within the Foreign Ministry – USAID and

Britain's Overseas Development Administration, for instance; sometimes they are fully fledged ministries in their own right – this is the case in the Netherlands and in France; sometimes – as in Denmark and Sweden – they are semi-autonomous government corporations. In all cases, however, they *are* bureaucracies and usually fairly large ones. Even the Overseas Development Administration in Britain, a lightweight by comparison with its US or French counterparts, has more than 1,500 permanent employees on its payroll including administrators, economists, professional advisers and scientists. In common with other aid organisations it also has a revolving group of field staff working on development projects that it has financed overseas: 339 'experts' and 'managers' in Zambia alone, for example. Many of these people are not classified as 'permanent' but are hired instead under two- or three-year contracts.[38]

Governmental aid organisations spend rather more than half of the money that they receive from tax-payers in their respective countries on direct, 'bilateral' assistance to developing nations – giving priority to those with which they have historical links or which are important to them for other reasons. In the case of Britain, the share of bilateral aid has varied in recent years between 57 and 63 per cent of the total; India and Kenya, both former colonies, have consistently been amongst the principal beneficiaries.[39] In the case of Italy bilateral aid is approximately 60 per cent of the total[40] and Somalia and Ethiopia are favoured recipients. The percentages allocated to bilateral development assistance are similar for most other donors, as are the ways in which they prioritise recipients; the United States, for example, gives special consideration to the Philippines where it has several military bases, and to Egypt, which it sees as a conservative bastion against the spread of communism from neighbouring Libya.

The 40 per cent or so of official development assistance that remains after bilateral allocations have been subtracted is channelled through 'multilateral' development organisations which, in theory at least, give help where it is most needed rather than on grounds of political expediency.

THE EEC

Headquartered in Brussels, the European Economic Community is an important conduit for multilateral aid although, since it represents the particular interests of a regional lobby, it is probably better described as a multi*national* entity. Its development assistance programme – which benefits sixty-six countries in Africa, the Caribbean and the Pacific as well as a growing number in Asia and Latin America – is financed by contributions from European member states. To give an illustration, Britain each year passes almost half of all its multilateral aid through the medium of the EEC; in 1986 the figure involved was £223 million.[41]

The European Development Fund (which received £79 million of the British contribution in 1986) is one of the Community's principal instruments for financial and technical assistance. Its aid, worth about $1 billion per annum, takes the form both of outright grants and of long-term 'soft' loans (typically over forty years with interest at around 1 per cent or less). Agricultural and agro-industrial projects are favoured for financing but the EDF also provides emergency aid from time to time and gives some assistance aimed at stabilising poor countries' export earnings. Further concessional assistance worth about $1.2 billion per annum is provided to developing countries under Title 9 of the EEC's annual budget. About half of these funds are made available in the form of cash grants; the balance is food aid which is handled by two key departments: the Directorate General for Development (DG8) and the Directorate General for Agriculture (DG6). Britain's contribution to the EEC food aid programme in 1986 was £59 million. Finally, the Community operates the European Investment Bank which provides finance on near-commercial terms to several developing countries.[42]

THE UNITED NATIONS FAMILY

EEC institutions are on the borderline between bilateralism and multilateralism. A large number of genuinely multilateral development agencies, however, belong to the United Nations system. The world body now has some 160 independent member states and all of them, according to their means, contribute to its funding. Approximately $70,000 per annum comes from each of the seventy-eight poorest countries, while some of their richer neighbours give hundreds of millions of dollars. The result, in a typical year, is that the UN obtains 30 per cent of its money from just three wealthy nations – the USA, the Federal Republic of Germany, and Japan – and 80 per cent from just twenty-seven countries.[43]

Total funding now runs at around $6 billion a year; of this about one-third comes in as mandatory contributions 'assessed' against member states; the balance is made up of voluntary contributions which vary from year to year depending on the political mood in the donor countries and on the size of the cake available in national aid budgets.[44] Well over half of all the money spent by the UN qualifies directly as Official Development Assistance and almost all the rest – more than 90 per cent – is 'development-related' under the category of 'economic, social and humanitarian activities'.[45]

UN agencies which receive and spend ODA fulfil a wide variety of different functions.

The United Nations Development Programme, for example, headquartered in New York, describes itself modestly as 'the world's largest development service network . . . It provides a greater variety of services to more people in more countries and in more sectors than any other development institution . . . It is also the central funding and co-ordinating mechanism for technical co-operation by the entire UN development system.'[46] Its 'capacity-building ventures designed to enhance a country's abilities to plan and manage its own development' include: 'groundwater and mineral exploration . . . computer technology and satellite communication . . . seed production and rural extension services . . . industrial training, research and feasibility studies'.[47]

UNDP is financed almost entirely out of voluntary contributions – it gets about $800 million a year.[48] Although it has 115 fully staffed field offices of its own in the Third World, it is not structured to implement projects; this is done – in the main – by the twenty-nine 'executing agencies' of the UN system, all of which receive money from UNDP and all of which compete vigorously for their share of the cake.

The Food and Agriculture Organisation (FAO) is the largest of these executing agencies, with some 10,000 employees, the vast majority of whom are permanently based at headquarters in Rome.[49] Its field programmes receive substantial funding from UNDP, but it also gets money directly from member governments of the UN in the form both of voluntary and assessed contributions. All told, FAO receives – and spends – around $500 million to $600 million per annum.[50]

Describing itself as 'a development agency, an information centre, an adviser to governments and a neutral forum',[51] FAO participates in several thousand agricultural projects in the Third World each year. This participation takes the form mainly of technical assistance, which in practice means the provision of experts to 'strengthen local institutions, assist research and training, and develop and demonstrate new techniques'.[52] Typically FAO will have 3,000 of its experts in the field at any one time: some will be part of large teams working on long-term projects; others – the majority – will be on short missions, advising, for example, on the setting up of a national cereals marketing board, or on the best location for a fish-farm. FAO does *not* make capital investments to buy infrastructure or equipment (except on a very small scale); it does, however, run an Investment Support Programme which 'helps developing countries find the external capital they need to build up their agriculture'.[53]

Linked to FAO, and also headquartered in Rome, is the World Food Programme (WFP) which mobilises and delivers food aid designed to meet emergency needs and which also organises food-for-work schemes intended to promote 'economic and social development' in poor countries. Resources, worth in the region of $1.3 billion per two-year budgetary period, come in from member governments mainly in the form of food commodities, with cash and/or services also being provided in some cases. WFP food aid, unlike the EEC's, is delivered to recipient countries with the freight and insurance charges paid; in the case of the poorest countries, the Programme is also able to pay up to half the local transportation costs.[54]

The World Health Organisation, which has its headquarters in Geneva, is another important UN multilateral agency. It spends around $500 million a year[55] and – like FAO – gets some of its money from UNDP, some from the assessed contributions of member states and some from voluntary contributions. It claims to be working towards 'the attainment by all citizens of the world of a level of health that will permit them to lead a socially and economically productive life'.[56] In order to achieve what it calls 'Health for All by the Year 2000' it has set itself four principal sub-goals: developing and organising the manpower and technology needed for disease prevention and control; eradication of the main tropical diseases; immunisation of all the world's children against six of the major childhood diseases; and the establishment of health infrastructures to provide primary health care services to the majority of the world's population.[57]

WHO's annual budget is in fact less than that of any one of the four largest regions of Britain's National Health Service.[58] Nevertheless, the Organisation does not walk alone. Also immunising children throughout the Third World, also working to provide primary health care services, is UNICEF – the United Nations Children's Emergency Fund – which spends around $400 million a year. UNICEF concerns itself with seven major development sectors of which 'basic health care' is the most important. Others are water supply, nutrition, social services for children, formal and non-formal education, planning and project support, and emergency relief.[59]

Working through eighty-seven field offices in 118 developing countries – forty-two in Africa, thirty-three in Asia, thirty in Latin America and thirteen in the Middle East and North Africa – UNICEF's headquarters are split between New York and Geneva. The Fund also has important administrative establishments in Copenhagen, Sydney and Tokyo. Finances come mainly in the form of voluntary contributions from member governments of the UN – about 76 per cent of the total. Most of the remaining 24 per cent is raised through the sale of Christmas greeting cards. In addition there are some public donations channelled through the National Committees which UNICEF has established in many countries. No other UN body receives money directly from the general public.[60]

Overlapping to some extent with UNICEF in the areas of 'formal and non-formal education' is another agency – the United Nations Educational, Scientific and Cultural Organisation. According to its constitution, UNESCO's purpose is 'to contribute to peace and security by promoting education, science and culture in order to further universal respect for justice, for the rule of law and for the human rights and fundamental freedoms which are affirmed for the peoples of the world without distinction of race, sex, language or religion by the Charter of the United Nations'.[61] Practical concerns include combating illiteracy in developing countries, promoting the growth of social science facilities in Africa and Asia, and strengthening 'cultural identity, creativity and cultural development'.[62]

UNESCO's imposing headquarters are at place de Fontenoy in Paris where – despite its mission in the Third World – about 80 per cent of the biennial budget of around $370 million has traditionally been spent.[63] Dissatisfaction with excessive bureaucratisation and in general with the management policies of Director General Ahmadou Mahtar M'Bow led both the United States and Britain to withdraw their financial support from the Organisation in the mid-1980s. In late 1987 M'Bow was replaced by Federico Mayor of Spain.

Another UN multilateral agency, the International Labour Office, has also had to get by for some years without the support of the United States, which withdrew because of alleged 'socialistic' policies. Headquartered in Geneva, ILO operates a large number of technical assistance programmes in developing countries. These are aimed at 'the promotion of employment, development of human resources, vocational training, small industries, rural development, co-operatives, social security, and industrial safety and hygiene'.[64]

UNIDO, the United Nations Industrial Development Organisation, also concerns itself with industrial issues. Based in Vienna, it provides technical assistance and conducts seminars and meetings intended to raise the industrial capacity of developing countries. Its administrative and research activities are covered by the regular UN budget at a level somewhat below $100 million a year; its operational activities are heavily dependent on finance provided by UNDP and on fluctuating voluntary contributions from member states.[65]

Other multilateral agencies of note within the UN system include: the United Nations Environment Programme (UNEP), headquartered in Nairobi; the United Nations High Commissioner for Refugees (UNHCR), based in Geneva; the UN Conference on Trade and Development (UNCTAD); the Office of the United Nations Disaster Relief Co-ordinator (UNDRO); and the United Nations Fund for Population Activities (UNFPA). There are also many other organisations and entities ranging from Economic Commissions in Africa, Asia and Latin America to the UN Centre for Human Settlements which concerns itself with the plight of the homeless in the Third World. All in all the United Nations system now employs in excess of 50,000 people in the cause of world development.[66]

IFAD AND THE REGIONAL BANKS

There are a number of bodies, registered as UN specialised agencies, which look very different from all the others. Rather than providing expertise and technical assistance, these concentrate their efforts on capital aid and thus, effectively, function as development banks.

One such is the International Fund for Agricultural Development, which is based in Rome. Financed mainly by the voluntary contributions of OECD and OPEC member states, it was established in 1977 and, in its first six years of operation, provided long-term 'soft' loans worth almost $1.6 billion for 135 agricultural projects in eighty developing countries. IFAD went into a slump thereafter until January 1986 when negotiations for a replenishment of its core resources were concluded – giving it a further $460 million to lend over the period up to 1989. Of this, 40 per cent came from OPEC nations and 60 per cent from the eighteen members of the Development Assistance Committee of the OECD (Britain's share, for example, was $13.22 million). IFAD also operates a separate Special Programme which supports projects in some twenty-four sub-Saharan African countries suffering from drought and desertification. Again, finances for the Special Programme come from both OPEC and OECD sources.[67]

IFAD, as its name suggests, lends specifically for agriculture. Within and outside the UN system, a variety of other kinds of development bank and fund also exist and are able to make loans in support of projects of all kinds. Some focus their attentions on particular geographical regions – for example, the Asian Development Bank/Fund, the African Development Bank/Fund, the Inter-American Development Bank, the Caribbean Development Bank and the Arab Bank for Economic Development in Africa. These all attract a wide range of different types of finance, which they then 'lend on' for development purposes. In recent years Britain has contributed £72 million to the Asian Development Fund and has pledged £20 million to the Caribbean Development Bank's Special Development Fund which provides loans on concessional terms. These sums of money have come out of the UK's multilateral aid budget.[68]

Official aid, however, represents only a portion of the finances available to these institutions. Typically, wealthy countries subscribe to the capital of the banks and contribute to the periodic replenishments of the funds, but large amounts of money are also raised on international capital markets. The clearest illustration of the place of all this within the framework of Development Incorporated is provided by the institution on which all the regional development banks are modelled. This institution is the World Bank. With more money at its disposal each year than any other agency, bilateral or multilateral, it is the single largest source of development finance on earth and is thus worth looking at in some detail.

A GLOBAL LENDER

The World Bank, like IFAD, is registered as a UN specialised agency but, in fact, its relationship to the United Nations system is tenuous in the extreme. World Bank budgets are *not* included when one talks of UN agencies and organisations spending $6 billion a year. The management of the Bank does *not* answer to the United Nations but only to its own Board of Governors which consists of the Ministers of Finance of 151 member countries.[69] More important, the UN has traditionally been characterised by egalitarian decision-making: each nation has one vote and, in theory at least, little countries like Kiribati and Barbados have as strong a voice as big ones like the United States or Britain. At the World Bank, by contrast, votes are based entirely on the size of the financial commitment that each member state has made. There is no pretence of equality – the economic superpowers run the show.

Like a Hindu god, the World Bank has four arms. Of these the two strongest are the International Bank for Reconstruction and Development (IBRD) and the International Development Association (IDA), both of which will be considered in some detail below. The third limb is the International Finance Corporation (IFC), which lends mainly to support the expansion of private investment and private enterprise in the developing countries. Finally there is a Special Facility for Sub-Saharan Africa.

Total loan commitments made by the World Bank through these four linked but functionally distinct entities for fiscal 1987 were $19.207 billion.[70] However, only $920 million of this came from the IFC and only $613 million from the Special Facility.[71] It is the IBRD and the IDA that are the major lenders for development – the former committed $14.188 billion in 1987 and the latter $3.486 billion.[72]

When one talks of the 'World Bank', therefore, one is largely talking of the IBRD and the IDA. Appropriately, both are administered from the same building – World Bank headquarters in Washington, DC – and by the same staff. Both lend for the same types of programme and project and often do so in the same countries at the same time. They are funded in entirely different ways, however, and attach very different terms to the loans that they make.

THE INTERNATIONAL DEVELOPMENT ASSOCIATION

IDA is often described as the 'soft-loan affiliate of the World Bank'. This is because it provides interest-free finance and because repayments of principal – which do not begin until ten years after signature of loan agreement – are spread relatively painlessly over periods of up to fifty years.[73] Such concessional terms of course qualify all IDA loans as Official Development Assistance. In 1987, out of the $3.486 billion lent, more than 90 per cent – $3.177 billion[74] – went to the thirty-five 'least-developed countries' on earth.[75] During the eleven years from 1977 to 1987 IDA provided this group of countries with a total of $31.627 billion – serious money by any standards.[76]

IDA is funded, in the main, out of the multilateral aid budgets of World Bank member states. Britain, for example, gave £133.8 million in each of the three years 1985, 1986 and 1987 and has committed almost £525 million ($770.5 million) for payment in equal instalments over the years 1988, 1989 and 1990.[77] The periods in question (1985–7 and 1988–90) represent respectively the seventh and eighth 'replenishments' of IDA, with the total value of the latter – 'IDA 8', as it is known – being $12.4 billion. The share of the United States in this amount is $2.875 billion – about four times larger than Britain's. Japan's share is $2.150 billion and West Germany's is $1.322 billion.[78]

Since IDA was established in 1960, the voting strengths of member nations have varied considerably, reflecting amongst other things the rise of West Germany and Japan to the rank of industrial superpowers. Such fluctuations can be expected to continue. Throughout, however, because of the scale of its contribution, the United States has had the dominant voice and has at all times exercised an effective veto. This, too, can be expected to continue. In 1987 the USA held 18.47 per cent of the total votes in IDA; next came Japan with 8.81 per cent; West Germany was third with 7.09 per cent; Britain and France were fourth and fifth with, respectively, 6.33 per cent and 3.82 per cent.[79] At the other end of the scale, Afghanistan had about a quarter of one per cent of the total votes in IDA in the same year, Cape Verde had one-hundredth of one per cent and Somalia had a fifth of one per cent.[80]

THE IBRD

The 'big five' in IDA are also the big five in the IBRD. Here the USA had 19.63 per cent of total votes in 1987, Japan had 5.58 per cent, West Germany had

5.52 per cent and Britain and France had 5.32 per cent each.[81] In the same year Bangladesh had about a third of one per cent, Chad one-hundredth of one per cent, and Paraguay about a tenth of one per cent.[82]

Like IDA, the IBRD is active in the thirty-five poorest countries in the world: those with annual per-capita incomes below $400. Out of total IBRD loan commitments of $14.188 billion in 1987 about 25 per cent – $3.253 billion – were in favour of this group.[83] Unlike IDA, however, IBRD loans are not made on terms that are sufficiently concessional to allow them to be classified as Official Development Assistance.

Rather than being funded out of the multilateral aid budgets of member states, therefore, IBRD has to raise the bulk of its finances on international capital markets – indeed, it is the world's largest non-sovereign borrower. It pays commercial rates of interest but, because of the volume of its business and because of its excellent 'triple-A' credit rating, it manages to do very good deals for itself: 7.73 per cent on average in 1987. It then takes the funds that it has borrowed and relends them to its developing-country clients at a higher rate of interest: 8.78 per cent in 1987.[84]

For the poorest nations – which are generally regarded as a 'bad risk' by bankers – the IBRD is a source of finance which would simply never be forthcoming from commercial sources. On the other hand, for middle-income developing countries (Brazil or Indonesia, for example) – which take up the bulk of its loans – the terms that it offers are generally significantly better than those they themselves could obtain on the open market. Typically, in addition to a relatively advantageous interest rate of around 9 per cent based on its own cost of borrowing, the IBRD allows five-year grace periods before repayments begin, and fixes maturities of up to twenty years.[85] Although this may not be 'aid' in the strict sense of the word, it is certainly development finance of an entirely different order from that provided by commercial banks. It is, furthermore, frequently mixed with aid credits from IDA, from other multilateral agencies, and from bilateral donors in the financing of specific projects.

The IBRD *never* allows its clients – the governments of developing countries – to reschedule their debts. There is no flexibility on this point at all. Interest and principal have to be paid exactly on time and precisely as specified in the loan agreement, or the borrower is declared in default.[86]

It is a matter of record, however, that there has not yet been a default on any IBRD loan.[87] Debtors, anxious not to cross swords with so powerful an institution – and keen also to maintain their access to its credits in the future – go to great lengths to ensure that all their commitments are met.

The result – although other lenders to the Third World today find themselves embroiled in a non-stop round of rescheduling, rolling over and 'forgiving' of debt – is that the IBRD is able to stand aloof and to continue blithely with business as usual. It has in fact recorded a net income in every single financial year since 1948.[88] In 1987 it took in $1.1 billion more in repayments of interest and principal on old loans than it paid out in new loans to the developing countries.[89]

What we have here, then, is an institution that functions in an 'aid-like' manner and that lends to some of the poorest and riskiest countries on earth. But it is *also* an institution that consistently makes a profit and that is regarded as highly credit-worthy by money managers on Wall Street and in the City of London.

How does the IBRD get away with being all these different and contradictory things at once? The answer, primarily, is because it is protected from the pressures and turbulence of its position by the enormous strength of its capital base. This is divided into two parts: 'paid-in' capital and 'callable' capital.

The former, as the name suggests, is the sum of money that member governments have actually handed over to the Bank. It is a relatively small amount, just $7.2 billion in total – barely half of one year's lending.[90] The latter, however, is vast – $77.9 billion[91] – and represents a resource that can be *called upon* in the event that something goes seriously wrong. Paid-in capital is thus money in hand which the Bank can use; callable capital is an intangible asset, best thought of as a guarantee to the Bank's creditors, that exists only as a *promise*.

The scale of this promise can be illustrated with reference to the five major shareholders in the IBRD. In 1987, for example, the United States had an obligation 'subject to call' of $15.866 billion; in the same year – the forty-first that the Bank had been in business – US paid-in capital reached a cumulative total of just $1.537 billion. The figures for Japan were $4.495 billion and $430 million respectively. For West Germany they were $4.473 billion and $428 million. For Britain they were $4.269 billion and $429 million. France in that year had $4.288 billion 'subject to call' but had paid in a cumulative total of only $410 million.[92]

The Bank's more prosperous members are thus like rich uncles who enable their nephew to undertake some rather risky business ventures by giving him a little seed money to invest and by acting as guarantors for any borrowing he does. What the rich uncles get – in return mainly for paper promises – is kudos and also the very real political and economic leverage that results from their effective control of an influential multilateral development institution.

So far so good. But are there any circumstances under which these paper promises – the financial guarantees that the Bank's callable capital represents – might actually have to be honoured?

In the context of burgeoning Third World debt, now in excess of $1,000 billion, it is *just* conceivable that several of the IBRD's major loans (say, in Brazil, India, Indonesia and Mexico) might cease to perform at the same time. Overnight this would cause a drastic reduction in the Bank's income from payments of interest and principal and might, in an extreme case, render it unable to service its own liabilities to the money markets. It would then effectively be in receivership and it would have to call in its callable capital in order to pay off its creditors.

At this point a reminder is in order: ultimately it is the tax-payers of the World Bank's wealthy member states who are the source of almost all its callable capital. If the IBRD were to fold, then it would be these tax-payers who would have to bear the financial consequences. Because of this there is no way that the institution can be regarded as a free-floating independent entity. On the contrary, it must be accountable for its behaviour – and it must be accountable to *us*.

This question of accountability in fact transcends the issue of financial liabilities: the World Bank is strong because of our collective financial strength, powerful because we – the people of the wealthy nations – are powerful. The Bank acts in *our* name in the developing countries and, as we shall see later, there is much that it does there which is dubious, much that harms the poor and the vulnerable, much that scars and wrecks the environment, much that is arrogant and wrong.

We have a right to a detailed accounting for all of this. At present, however – and this is a theme that I shall return to at several points in this book – we do not get it. On the contrary, those who attempt to learn more about the Bank than is revealed in its glossy public-relations handouts find that they must first crack an arcane code of secrecy and obfuscation that would be more appropriate in a military intelligence service than in a development institution.

PROJECT LENDING

World Bank lending – whether it comes from the IBRD on near-commercial terms, or from the IDA on extremely concessional terms – has traditionally been made to support specific projects in the developing countries. Although important changes are now under way, this orientation remains dominant. In 1987, for example, when the combined lending of the IBRD and the IDA totalled $17.674 billion, 21 per cent ($3.435 billion) went to the energy sector: most of this was finance for giant hydroelectric dams and for the construction of power-stations, but some also went to oil, gas and coal-mining projects. In the same year agricultural and rural development schemes got $2.930 billion (16.6 per cent of the total). Projects in the transportation sector – notably roads – got $1.745 billion (9.9 per cent); urban development schemes got $1.469 billion (8.3 per cent); water supply and sewerage projects got $969 million (5.5 per cent); telecommunications got $682.3 million (3.9 per cent); and industry got $418 million (2.4 per cent of the total). Other sectors in which projects received assistance – albeit on a generally smaller scale – included education, population, health and nutrition.[93]

The shares of the different sectors are not necessarily constant from year to year. In both 1985 and 1986, for instance, agricultural and rural development schemes got a much larger percentage of the total than they did in 1987, but telecommunications projects got a significantly smaller percentage – 0.8 per cent in 1985 and just 0.3 per cent in 1986, as against 3.9 per cent in 1987. The share of energy projects, on the other hand, did not vary so much over the three-year period (20 per cent in 1985 and 18.5 per cent in 1986 as against 21 per cent in 1987).[94]

About two out of every five Bank-assisted projects are the subject of 'co-financing' (that is to say other bilateral and multilateral aid agencies also put money into them). Even where there are no international co-financers, however, it is rare for the Bank to contribute much more than a third of the total sum required: most of the rest has to come from the government of the recipient country. Used almost exclusively to meet foreign-exchange costs, the Bank's funds are, furthermore, only released against specific purchases of equipment or to cover other direct expenses of implementation as and when they are incurred. The borrower does not get all the money at once (or anything like at once); on the contrary, project loans can take up to ten years to disburse.[95]

SECTORAL AND STRUCTURAL ADJUSTMENT

Quicker disbursing – although still project-orientated – are the Bank's 'sector adjustment loans'. In these only part of the money is used to meet the direct costs of specific projects while the rest goes to support policy changes in the relevant sector. For example, the government of Pakistan obtained a loan of $178 million from the Bank in 1985. Some of the money was for projects in the energy sector; the rest was disbursed against promises from the government: (*a*) to increase the price of natural gas in order to provide a greater incentive to private entrepreneurs to take part in exploration and development; (*b*) to reduce subsidies for national electricity prices so that, in future, these would more accurately reflect the costs of production; and (*c*) to generate electricity for the Karachi area using imported rather than locally produced coal.[96]

Such explicit, sector-wide policy-changes are the distinctive feature of sector adjustment loans. What they represent is a desire by the Bank not only to be an important source of finance but also to play a central rôle in the decision-making processes in developing countries.

It is in another type of loan, however – the 'structural adjustment loan' (SAL for short) – that this desire achieves its purest expression. The characteristic feature of such loans is that they are completely disconnected from projects and are disbursed, usually very quickly, in return for major economic policy changes at the national level. Such changes are brought about 'with considerable analytical support from the Bank'[97] and are said to be the result of 'policy dialogue'.

Third World governments that agree to go this route are rewarded by being allowed to spend the money that they receive on just about anything they like.

For example, the Bank recently put up an $80 million SAL in support of an 'economic recovery programme' in Costa Rica. The stated aim of this programme is to promote faster growth, especially through the expansion of exports in markets outside Central America. Like the sector loan to Pakistan, the cash for Costa Rica is tied to economic policy changes, but this time the changes are at the macro level, rather than at the level of a single sector such as energy. Particular conditions attached to the loan cover such matters as tariffs (which are to be lowered) and other forms of protection (which are also to be reduced), exchange-rate management (including devaluation), the government's budgetary policies, and the scale of public-sector involvement in the economy. In common with all other SALs, the money is not disbursed against specific purchases but can be used very freely for a wide variety of purposes including importing goods from abroad, paying off old foreign debts or – if the inclination is there – lining the private pockets of corrupt government Ministers.[98]

Whether applied to a single sector or to an entire economy, adjustment loans are therefore about policy. A generous observer might see them as a way of encouraging governments to accept good advice. Others have suggested that they are more like bribes used by the technocrats at the World Bank to persuade powerful officials in poor countries to hand over important aspects of national sovereignty – to exchange, in short, national birthrights for a mess of pottage. Others still, doubtful of the Bank's ability to manage developing economies at all, suggest that SALs are really a case of the blind leading the blind.[99]

Controversial though they may be, however, there is no doubt that structural adjustment loans are the coming thing. The Bank, for a start, is steadily increasing the share of SALs in its overall portfolio. In 1986 adjustment lending was just 19 per cent of the total; by 1987, at more than $4 billion, it was 23 per cent of the total.[100] President Barber Conable is committed to making even more loans of this kind during the 1990s and says unequivocally: 'Structural adjustment is absolutely fundamental to the Bank's assistance strategy . . . there is no alternative.'[101]

FOLLOW THE LEADER

One of the reasons that I have considered the Bank at such length in this chapter is that it is the pace-setter of Development Incorporated. It is not just, as noted earlier, that a growing number of regional development banks have been specifically modelled on it – although this is indeed the case. Much more important is the fact that *all* official aid agencies, whether bilateral or multilateral, co-operate very closely with it, imitate its policies and its sectoral priorities and, to a large extent, share what might be called its 'philosophy of development'.

Thus at a time when the Bank is putting more and more emphasis on policy dialogue with developing countries it is almost a matter of course that Christopher Patten, the UK's Overseas Development Minister, should speak enthusiastically of British 'support for structural adjustment' and should affirm: 'We will devote a greater share of our aid budget to policy reform.'[102]

Describing its programme in the late 1980s, USAID beats exactly the same drum as Britain when it tells us: 'Through policy dialogue, the United States communicates with governments to eliminate inappropriate subsidies, price and wage controls, trade restrictions, overvalued exchange rates and interest rate ceilings that curtail economic performance.'[103]

And, of course, much the same sorts of thing are being said by aid officials in France, Germany, Italy, Japan and elsewhere: to a greater or lesser extent all the bilateral agencies in the Western bloc have followed the World Bank's lead and are now making substantial chunks of their aid conditional on structural adjustment and policy reforms in the recipient countries.

THE IMF

Interestingly enough, although the Bank is undoubtedly the main force for proselytising the structural adjustment 'message' within the aid industry, the concept itself is actually the brainchild of the International Monetary Fund – which has been obliging countries to adjust in one way or another since the 1940s. Like invisible rays, ideas on economic development flow back and forth across Washington's 19th Street between the headquarters buildings of the Bank and the Fund; it is, therefore, not at all surprising that the former acquired its enthusiasm for structural adjustment from watching the latter at work.

IMF–World Bank co-operation indeed extends far beyond getting together to organise the bacchanal that celebrates the joint annual meeting of their Boards of Governors. However, the fact that they both buy their champagne from the same stores is by no means unimportant as an indicator of the kinds of value they share. Since they also entertain their guests in the same five-star hotels, rent their limousines from the same dealers, and love the same kinds of gourmet food, it is fairly clear that the two institutions have a great deal in common. They both also have the same kinds of management structure. Votes at the IMF – exactly as at the Bank – are linked to the degree of financial contribution that each member state has made. Again, the lion's share is taken by the five leading industrialised countries: the USA (19.14 per cent); Great Britain (6.63 per cent); West Germany (5.79 per cent); France (4.81 per cent); and Japan (4.53 per cent).[104]

The IMF is not now – and never has been – an aid agency. It is, however, so heavily involved in the provision of finance to the Third World that it has become an integral – indeed, a central – part of Development Incorporated. Its mission is to supply member states with money to help them to overcome short-term balance-of-payments difficulties, but such money is only made available after the recipients have agreed to policy reforms in their economies – to structural adjustment, in short. Close supervision of the implementation of these often sweeping reforms is an integral part of the deal; developing countries, however, have a strong incentive to accept such supervision since it makes them more 'credit-worthy' in the eyes of other potential lenders: it has been estimated that every dollar provided to the Third World by the IMF 'unlocks' a further four to seven dollars of new loans and refinancing from commercial banks and rich-country governments.[105]

It also unlocks the very large amounts of development money at the disposal of the World Bank. Indeed, the crucial connection between the two institutions is that membership of the Bank (and thus eligibility for IBRD and IDA loans) is conditional upon membership of the IMF. This has been described by one observer as a classic carrot-and-stick device: 'Without IMF membership no admission to the World Bank, without conformity to IMF rules no development aid from the World Bank.'[106]

A Cosy Conspiracy?

A great deal of mutual back-scratching goes on. The Fund and the Bank state that they 'share the common objective of assisting members in their efforts to improve economic conditions in their countries . . . The areas of economic policy dealt with by the two institutions are complementary and inter-related, as is the financial assistance each can provide.'[107] To this end, Bank staff participated in Fund missions to seventeen countries in 1985–6 and Fund staff participated in Bank missions to eighteen countries; parallel or overlapping Fund and Bank missions took place to forty-four countries – in some cases more than once to the same country. In 1986–7 Fund staff participated in seventeen Bank missions and Bank staff participated in fifteen Fund missions. 'In addition,' according to the IMF's 1987 annual report, 'there were numerous instances of parallel or overlapping Fund and Bank missions in which the staffs of the two institutions collaborated closely in the field.'[108]

The purpose of all this teamwork is extremely specific: when IMF and Bank staff travel southward together they do so in order to spread the word of structural adjustment – to persuade governments to submit to policy reform.

The unanimity of the two institutions on this issue is such that, on the rare occasions when they are rejected, they close ranks against the offending country. In 1987, for example, Zambia broke off its dealings with the IMF. Immediately thereafter disbursements of moneys under World Bank loans stopped. Neither did the punishments end here: once it was clear that the break with the Fund was irrevocable, Britain's Overseas Development Administration also withdrew a substantial loan that it had agreed to extend only a few months earlier. 'In general,' as one Zambian economist observes, 'other donors are only willing to co-operate with Zambia when an agreement has been reached with the IMF.'[109]

Under such circumstances it is difficult to avoid the conclusion that some sort of conspiracy is afoot – a conspiracy in which rich countries and their institutions unite to force Third World nations to adjust. This view, however, is explicitly denied by Christopher Patten, Britain's young and energetic Overseas Development Minister. 'It is,' he says, 'ludicrous to see structural adjustment as being imposed on unwilling recipients by bloated Western capitalists.'[110]

And in fact he is right.

The recipients in question are the *governments* of developing countries and most of them – with the odd exception like Zambia in 1987 – are not in the least bit 'unwilling'. On the contrary, corrupt Ministers of Finance and dictatorial Presidents from Asia, Africa and Latin America are tripping over their own expensive footwear in their unseemly haste to 'get adjusted'.

For such people money has probably never been easier to obtain than it is today: with no complicated projects to administer and no messy accounts to keep, the venal, the cruel and the ugly are laughing literally all the way to the bank. For them structural adjustment is like a dream come true. No sacrifices are demanded of them personally. All they have to do – amazing but true – is *screw the poor*, and they've already had plenty of practice at that.

THE CASE FOR ADJUSTMENT

As we shall see later, the consequences of the 'policy dialogues' undertaken during the 1980s between the men in suits from Washington and the men in uniforms from Santiago or Kinshasa – or wherever – have been utterly disastrous for the worst-off and most vulnerable groups in the Third World. This has been so because of the nature of the structural adjustment and economic 'stabilisation' measures devised by the Bank and the Fund.

To understand exactly why these measures should hurt the poor, however, it is first of all necessary to be aware of what it is that developing countries are being asked to adjust *to*.

Paramount is the profoundly negative effect of the 'second oil shock' – the hike in oil prices that occurred in 1979. Overnight, throughout the Third World, import bills soared while export earnings stayed where they were – and in many cases (particularly in Africa) continued on a long slow trend of decline. For the group of poorest countries the consequences were easy to see: between 1979 and 1981 their combined trade deficits rose from $45 billion to $90 billion.[111] Even in middle-income developing countries the economic costs were high: between 1979 and 1981, for example, the oil import bill of the Philippines increased from $1 billion to almost $2.5 billion.[112] Obviously – as the Bank and the Fund rightly point out – financial turbulence on such a massive scale does call for rapid adjustment.

In arguing their case for policy reforms, the two institutions also draw attention to the important issue of Third World debt – which now exceeds a *trillion* dollars. As we shall see in Part Four, the grandiose development projects for which much of the money was borrowed in the first place have often turned out to be boondoggles and white elephants, castles in the sky and cathedrals in the desert that don't even pay their own way, never mind make a profit. In addition, many loans were contracted on variable rather than fixed terms – a disastrous situation for the borrowers since the money markets have been characterised by historically high interest rates in recent years. Poor countries, as a result, have been forced to allocate ever more of the revenues they earn from exports to servicing their old debts. Repayments of interest and principal, for instance, now cost Brazil four-fifths of its entire annual export earnings – a sum of money equivalent to the minimum annual salary of sixteen million workers. The Latin American country handed over an amazing $55 billion to its creditors during the period 1982–7.[113]

The oil-price hike of 1979 and the mounting debt burden are not, of course, the only reasons for the policy reforms that developing countries have had to implement during the 1980s. They are, however, important factors in a wider and powerfully interconnected matrix of pressures to which the Third World is exposed, and they help to explain why the IMF and the World Bank, together with the bilateral agencies, support structural adjustment. Nations that consistently import more than they export, and that spend more than they earn, *are* living in a sort of economic Cloud-cuckoo-land and *should* be obliged to do something about it. At the very least they should not expect to go on getting aid if they are not prepared to put their own houses in order. If they did, then they would be as unadmirable as the spendthrift who expects friends and relatives to stump up the necessary cash whenever he gets into financial difficulty.

This, of course, is a gross oversimplification: not all Third World countries – and very few Third World *people* – are 'spendthrifts'. Neither do I want to give the impression that the developing nations are entirely to blame for their own predicament – although this seems to be very much the view of the Fund and the Bank. On the contrary, the factors at work are largely external in nature, and poor countries have little or no control over them: the price of oil and rising interest rates are not their fault; they cannot be held responsible for the deteriorating terms of trade that, over the last twenty years, have radically reduced the value of the commodities they export; they are not culpable for protectionism in rich countries that makes market access difficult; finally, neither they – nor anyone else alive today – can logically be condemned for a history in which Northern empires prospered at the expense of the South.

All these things are true, but it is also true that there is no mileage in blaming others, or the weather, or the past – or any other external entity or influence – for one's own problems. Third World leaders who are prone to the 'victim complex' and who give it vociferous expression in various fora are, quite literally, wasting their breath. Calls for a 'new international economic order' and other such formulas are just so much hot air: no amount of UN conferencing or pious speeches is going to conjure these notions out of the ether and give them corporeal form.

Developing countries exist, here and now, amidst the very stark and tangible realities of the late twentieth century. The most important of those realities by far is that they *must* accept the existing world order as a given – if only because they are virtually powerless to change anything outside their own borders. For those countries that are spending more than they earn, and that have nothing special to bargain with – for example, a vital strategic location – structural adjustment is a simple, inescapable, unavoidable pragmatic necessity.

To this extent the institutions of Development Incorporated are not wrong to make the finance that they have on offer conditional on major policy reforms in the recipient countries. What is unfortunate, however, is the *nature* of the reforms that are called for.

THE POOR MAN'S BURDEN

In order to achieve the admirably clear and simple goal of increasing a country's revenues and reducing its expenditures, structural adjustment will typically involve all, or most, of the following 'austerity' measures: devaluation of the local currency (because, in theory, this will discourage imports – by making them more expensive – and provide a stimulus to exports); draconian cuts in government expenditure, particularly spending on education and health care; radical reduction or complete elimination of food and other consumption subsidies; measures like reductions in wages and restrictions in the availability of credit, which are also designed to reduce the overall level of consumption within 'adjusting' societies; across-the-board abolition of price controls, coupled with privatisation of public utilities and immediate price increases for the services they provide (like water, electricity, etc.); and, finally, higher taxes and higher interest rates.[114]

With astonishingly few variations to allow for differing local circumstances, this package of measures is applied *in every single country* that takes the IMF's or the World Bank's shilling.[115] It does not require uncanny prescience to predict the consequences for the worst-off and most vulnerable groups in the Third World: of course cuts in budgets for primary health care hurt the poor; of course cuts in wages hurt the poor; and of course higher prices for basic services hurt the poor.

This logic is borne out by the facts:

- During 1977–85 Peru allowed its development to be guided largely by the IMF and undertook two major structural adjustment programmes. In this period the average per-capita income of Peruvians fell by 20 per cent; inflation soared from 30 per cent to 160 per cent; unemployment and underemployment both increased dramatically; and wages in the formal sector of the economy dropped like stones: at the end of 1985 a worker's pay packet was worth only 64 per cent of what it had been in 1979 and only 44 per cent of what it had been in 1973. Meanwhile total government expenditure on 'social' sectors like education and health care dropped from 26 to 18 per cent of the national budget, food and fuel subsidies vital for poor families were completely eliminated, average food availability per capita declined by 26 per cent and child malnutrition increased substantially – from 42 to 68 per cent of the child population.[116]

- In 1984 the government of the Philippines, then – and in 1985 as well – still led by the tyrannical President Ferdinand Marcos, reached an agreement with the IMF. In exchange for the Fund's balance-of-payments support, the government undertook to institute sweeping reforms in the areas of tariffs, public investment and energy, to restrict government 'social' expenditure, to increase taxes and to impose controls on credit creation. As a result, within just one year, GNP per capita had regressed a full decade to its 1975 level. Real earnings fell substantially for every category of worker and in every industry – by 46 per cent on average for all urban wage-earners from 1982 to 1985 and by 48 per cent amongst self-employed workers; in the rural areas the fall was 31 per cent for wage-earners and 41 per cent for self-employed workers. By the third quarter of 1985, real wages in urban areas had fallen to one quarter of World Bank estimates of a 'poverty threshold' for a six-person household, while rural wages had fallen even lower – to just 22 per cent of the minimum. Government expenditure per capita on education fell to 30 per cent below the 1979 level. Primary health care networks serving the poor were also badly hit – by the end of 1985 total government expenditure on primary health care was five times less than it was on subsidies for just four ultra-modern private hospitals catering to upper-income groups.[117]

- Structural adjustment in Sri Lanka – where food subsidies have been sharply curtailed – has meant that the poorest 30 per cent of the population have suffered an uninterrupted decline in their calorie consumption during the 1980s while the top 50 per cent have improved their intake. Expenditure on education and health care per capita has fallen significantly.[118]

- In Chile, adjustment policies have caused massive increases in unemployment and also an oddly skewed inflation that seems to have hit goods purchased by the poor much harder than goods purchased by the rich. Malnutrition amongst school-age children has increased in the city of Santiago, as have diseases of poverty like tuberculosis, typhoid and hepatitis.[119]

- In Jamaica, an agreement signed with the IMF in 1984 led to the removal of government subsidies that had previously kept food costs down for poor and vulnerable groups, and education and health expenditure per capita were also slashed. The proportion of children showing signs of malnutrition rose and real family incomes fell steeply.[120]

- In Brazil structural adjustment sponsored by the IMF and the World Bank has led to greatly reduced social spending by the government during the 1980s – notably on basic health care and on education. There have, as a result, been sharp increases in the infant mortality rate and in failure and drop-out rates in schools. Child abandonment and delinquency have also increased.[121]

- On average, every year from 1980 to 1985, there were forty-seven countries in the Third World pursuing IMF-sponsored structural adjustment programmes (and the flow of resources from the Fund during this period totalled $30.3 billion). There were also twenty-one developing countries with structural or sector adjustment loans from the World Bank, and a number of other countries were adjusting in various ways at the behest of powerful bilateral-aid donors. During this same period it was far from coincidental that three-quarters of all the countries in Latin America and in Africa experienced marked *declines* in per-capita income.[122] The children of poor families were worst hit, with deteriorations in child welfare registered throughout the developing world. Eight countries in Latin America, sixteen in sub-Saharan Africa, three in North Africa and the Middle East, and four in South and East Asia experienced particularly severe problems; in almost all cases these were attributable directly to the privations caused by structural adjustment.[123]

If the Third World governments that actually implement IMF and World Bank 'policy reforms' sought to serve rather than dominate their own people, if they were genuinely devoted to the public good rather than to their private wealth and power, then it might not be necessary for structural adjustment to cause such pain.

In a country like Pakistan, for example, where 34.8 per cent of the national budget is spent on the military and just 1 per cent on health care,[124] it is clear that the burden of expenditure cuts does not *have* to be borne by the poor: the government has a choice regarding what to cut, what to keep.

The same is true in Sri Lanka where, in one recent year, the sum of 1.7 billion rupees was allocated to food subsidies for the poor against an estimated need of just under 3 billion rupees. It was argued that lack of resources did not permit a rise in the allocation to the required level. This admirable commitment to austerity, however, did not prevent the government from giving a subsidy of 1 billion rupees to the national airline.[125]

Likewise, in a country like Zaïre – which has been 'adjusting' with the IMF and the World Bank for years – is it really essential to dismiss 7,000 teachers from the school system for 'budgetary reasons'[126] when President Mobutu Sese Seko owns fifty-one Mercedes-Benz motor cars, eleven châteaux in Belgium and France and a beachside villa on the Costa del Sol?[127]

Outrages and anomalies like these, as we shall see elsewhere in this book, characterise the behaviour of a great many governments in the Third World – governments that are only strengthened and empowered by the funds made available to them through structural adjustment lending. Very few of these régimes have a genuine popular mandate, and virtually none has more than a passing concern for the poor in its own country. Some abuse human rights in the most direct and repulsive manner, others are profligate wastrels and scoundrels, most are infected by the virus of corruption.

The agencies know this – and ignore it: the conditions that governments must meet prior to receiving structural adjustment loans have, for example, *never* included improved human rights, increased freedom of speech, reduced military spending, controls on graft, or any other similar reforms.

The agencies are also well aware of the damage that adjustment can do, particularly amongst the poorest of the poor[128] – but they ignore this, too. Token gestures of mitigation may be made from time to time in the interests of public relations but the truth is that the machine continues to roll remorselessly on. The Fund and the Bank, Christopher Patten with his promise that Britain's Overseas Development Administration will 'help aid recipients make the painful adjustments which are necessary',[129] the US Agency for International Development with its commitment to policy dialogue, and just about every-other Western aid agency and development-finance institution of any significant size, are today all riding on the same bandwagon.

UNSUCCESSFUL, EVEN IN ITS OWN TERMS

If this widespread drive for adjustment resulted in concrete and measurable economic achievements, then the harm done to the poor might be acceptable – at least to those who believe that ends justify means. In reality, however, success stories of any kind are hard to locate.

The agencies themselves point to the often significantly improved export performance of adjusting countries. Even here, however, every silver lining has a cloud: obviously if twenty countries all producing similar agricultural commodities all increase their exports at the same time, then world markets for these commodities will become glutted and prices will fall – thus ultimately reducing rather than increasing export *revenues*. With more and more countries undertaking adjustment programmes, this already important issue is likely to loom ever larger in the future. In consequence, the World Bank is now seriously suggesting that it should take on the rôle of a colonial power dictating exactly what should be produced where within its empire: in a recent policy study, for instance, it advocated that 'SAL programmes across countries should be made mutually consistent so that markets for particular commodities are not accidentally saturated by too many expanded supply sources'.[130]

Increased exports are, furthermore, only one amongst several key objectives of structural adjustment. Reduced budget deficits are regarded as being of at least equal importance. It is therefore disturbing to learn from one confidential internal study of World Bank SALs since 1980 that only *two* recipient countries have in fact managed to reduce their budget deficits substantially.[131]

Another central purpose of structural adjustment programmes is to achieve greater private-sector involvement in national economies. As the World Bank itself puts it: 'By removing economic activity from the clumsy and inefficient administration of government and returning it to the market-place, the elimination of distortions and rigidities will be more readily achieved.'[132] Ironically, however, SALs have often had the opposite effect. During four years of World Bank-sponsored structural adjustment in Turkey, for example, the share of private investment in total investment declined from 48.8 per cent to 40.9 per cent.[133] Elsewhere, according to confidential internal documents, Ivory Coast's SAL was used to 'finance the arrears of several state agricultural enterprises' – in other words to subsidise inefficient government bureaucracies; Kenya's SAL 'did not address the question of possible divestiture of the government's share in [parastatal] enterprises'; Senegal's SAL paid 'for the development expenditures of parastatals, mainly in the agricultural sector'; and it was the civil service that got most of the money from Thailand's SAL.[134] Similarly in Zambia, before it broke with the IMF, one Fund official made this comment on earlier structural adjustment efforts in that African country: 'It is fair to say that what we have done is to allow Zambia to maintain a standard of living for its civil service [whose payroll amounts to 20 per cent of the country's Gross Domestic Product] which is totally out of sync with the rest of the economy.'[135]

Authoritative reports on consistent failures and errors like these, coupled with readily available data on the established tendency of SALs to harm the interests of the poorest and most vulnerable members of society, have had little effect on the thinking or behaviour of the World Bank and the IMF. On the contrary, as we have seen, the rôle of structural adjustment is steadily increasing within the development effort as a whole.

That this should continue to be the case despite mounting evidence of the dangers and human costs is at least partly attributable to the arrogance, hubris and insensitivity of senior policy-makers at the Bank and the Fund – endearing characteristics that one sees charmingly on display at the joint annual meetings of their Boards of Governors.

Linked to this is the fact that when officials of the two institutions go to the Third World it is not paupers that they talk to – or socialise with – but, rather, Ministers, Presidents and senior civil servants. Peasants and slum dwellers, the landless and the street kids are seen only dimly by the visiting bureaucrats, if they are seen at all. It is thus hardly surprising that the concerns and wellbeing of the poor, together with their energies, their enterprise and their potential, get ignored in the 'adjustment process'. Such an outcome is inevitable in a system that allows policy reforms to be concocted by well-heeled strangers in collusion with the local élite: neither of these two groups has any direct experience of poverty.

TRIUMPH OF THE INTERMEDIARIES

This is a problem that extends beyond individual personalities and that afflicts the development industry as a whole. It is a problem of alienation – of a world in which go-betweens have been given a virtually unrestricted mandate to make deals, shape events, and decide the future of millions.

In the simplest possible terms, the problem looks like this: we, the tax-payers of the wealthy nations, have arranged for middle-men to act in our name to help the poor in the developing countries. The middle-men in question are the staff of the various institutions reviewed in this chapter – notably the bilateral and multilateral aid agencies, the UN technical-assistance organis-ations, and the various development banks and funds. Nobody really watches or controls any of these institutions: if they are accountable at all, then they are accountable only to other institutions of the same type. Their excessive secrecy, their 'confidentiality', their 'classified' and 'restricted-access' docu-ments, and their closed-session meetings, all conspire to prevent any kind of public oversight of their doings.

Even UNESCO, dedicated by its charter to promote 'human rights and fundamental freedoms' (including freedom of speech), requires staff 'not to communicate to any person any information known to them by reason of their official position' – an obligation that does not cease when they retire or resign.[136] Exactly the same restriction applies in all other UN agencies which, nevertheless, look quite transparent beside the World Bank, an institution that has perfected the art of bureaucratic impenetrability. Here even the Governors are forbidden access to some staff evaluations of particularly controversial projects and programmes. Regarded as 'internal papers', these documents are 'not available to governments or to the general public'.[137] Likewise documents prepared for the Board of Directors to enable decisions to be taken on whether or not to approve loans are 'strictly confidential' and 'not officially available beyond restricted distribution'.[138] Ordinary tax-payers from Bank member states are permitted no access at all to any information of any kind on the institution other than the anodyne material that it itself chooses to publish.

At the IMF a very wide range of data is secret, with special safeguards and restrictions covering staff reports on national economies, consultation reports, and papers presenting a member state's request for the use of Fund resources: 'All such reports are confidential and may not be released, *even by the member concerned*.'[139]

Amongst the bilateral agencies, although some, like USAID, are relatively 'open', others are closed tight. Britain's Overseas Development Administration, for example, conceals the detailed information that it compiles on most of its projects and programmes behind the suffocating curtain of the Official Secrets Act. British tax-payers wishing to do nothing more sinister than visit the library must be escorted, must remain under supervision, and are only allowed to look at edited extracts of project documents (the larger parts are 'classified'). This hardly seems appropriate in the publicly funded aid administration of a major Western democracy.

In the developing countries, too, middle-men are to be found who behave as though they are accountable to no one. Here they 'represent' the poor and are not aid officials but, rather, Ministers and Presidents. Unfortunately many of them are little more than brutal, simpering thugs and most have gained power not through the ballot box but via the barrel of a gun. In 1988 some twenty-nine developing countries in Africa, ten in South America, six in the Middle East, three in South Asia and ten more in the Far East were ruled by the military – with most of the rest labouring under one or other form of civilian tyranny.[140]

With international civil servants on the one hand, and gangsters and psychotics on the other, we thus have a situation in which aid agencies talk to governments and governments talk to aid agencies; governments also talk to other governments, and the aid agencies talk amongst themselves. If this is 'development', then it is nothing more than a transaction between bureaucrats and autocrats – a deal that gets done, in the name of others, by intermediaries and brokers. The real principals in the affair – the tax-payers in the wealthy countries, and the poor in the South – are treated as though they are somehow incidental to the main event.

This comprehensive alienation on a truly global scale has become a *fait* so *accompli* that no one now seriously questions the structure or the institutions, the motives or the behaviour of the development industry. In some vague and woolly way it is just 'there'.

BEGINNINGS

It has not, however, been 'there' for very long; indeed, it is entirely a creation of our own life and times. Fittingly, given all the vacuous palaver that it has generated since, it began with two huge conferences – the founding conference of the United Nations which took place in San Francisco in June 1945 and, before that, the International Monetary Conference held at Bretton Woods, New Hampshire, 1–22 July 1944.

Of the two, Bretton Woods was by far the more significant. The primary task of the meeting was to lay the foundations for an open and stable monetary system for the post-war world. But a secondary purpose was to take steps towards the realisation of the 'four freedoms' that President Roosevelt had defined as the longer-term objectives of the Western allies, including 'freedom from want . . . everywhere in the world'.[141] The upshot was the creation of both the World Bank and the International Monetary Fund.

Neither institution was initially very active in helping to free the developing countries from want.

The Fund was much more concerned with industrialised economies – and remained so for years. The Bank, for its part, focused its early lending on projects aimed at the reconstruction of post-war Europe: France, the Netherlands, Denmark and Luxembourg were the first four recipients of IBRD loans. In 1948, however, Chile joined the list and, in 1949, Mexico and Brazil followed suit. Thereafter, lending increasingly shifted towards the South, bearing out a remark made in 1949 by the World Bank's second President, John J. McCloy: 'The reconstruction phase of the Bank's activity is largely over and the development phase is under way.'[142]

At about the same time, a significant change of emphasis was also beginning to take place in the other great multilateral body set up at the end of the Second World War – the United Nations. Following the signing of the UN Charter in San Francisco on 26 June 1945, the organisation installed itself in its permanent headquarters in New York. Its immediate preoccupations were with consolidating the peace and contending with the huge human disruptions that the war had caused in Europe. As a result probably its most active department in the early days was the UN Relief and Rehabilitation Administration, which catered for refugees. When UNRRA was eventually wound up in 1947–8 most of its staff were transferred to other specialised agencies that were then emerging within the United Nations system.[143]

From then on, the concerns of the UN – like those of the World Bank – increasingly shifted away from Europe and began to focus instead upon the poor South. A key date was 4 December 1948 when the General Assembly drew specific attention to the lack of expert personnel and technical resources in what it called 'underdeveloped areas'.[144] Under Resolution 200, it subsequently authorised funds to enable the Secretary General to mobilise 'international teams of experts through the United Nations to advise governments on economic development; to assist in training technicians in the developing countries; and to assist governments in obtaining technical personnel, equipment and supplies in organising their development efforts'.[145]

Neither was the new focus limited to the multilateral agencies. In the USA President Harry Truman's Point Four Plan, announced in 1949, called for a 'worldwide effort for the achievement of peace, plenty and freedom'. This call was predicated on the President's view that:

> More than half the people of the world are living in conditions approaching misery . . . their economic life is primitive and stagnant. Their poverty is a handicap and a threat both to them and to more prosperous areas . . . I believe we should make available to peace-loving peoples the benefits of our store of technical knowledge in order to help them realise their aspirations for a better life. And, in co-operation with other nations, we should foster capital investment in areas needing development.[146]

In a very real sense, 'foreign aid' had arrived; furthermore, the UN, the World Bank and Harry Truman all seemed to agree about what it should be used for: 'development'. They also agreed that there was a specific group of countries that should get it.

One consequence of this was to impose a fictitious unity upon nations that were widely separated in every sense – geographically, culturally, economically and politically. The idea that they had something fundamental in common derived directly from the fact that they all came to be seen as eminently 'aidable'. As the respected British economist Lord Bauer puts it:

> The Third World and its antecedents and synonyms, such as the underdeveloped world, the less developed world, and the developing world (all still used) and now also the South, are for all practical purposes the collection of countries whose governments, with the odd exception, demand and receive official aid from the West. The concept of the Third World or the South and the policy of official aid are inseparable. They are two sides of the same coin. The Third World is the creation of foreign aid: without foreign aid there is no Third World.[147]

MOTIVE FORCES

While it would be convenient to believe that the decision to launch large-scale aid programmes was the product of clear and uniform thinking on the part of the industrialised nations in the post-war era, the truth is otherwise. From the outset a number of quite different motivations were at work – and at work side by side. The result, today, is that the collective psychology of aid-giving is schizophrenic, shot through with contradictory urges and rationalisations, some of which are benign, some sinister and others just plain neurotic.

To take the case of the United States first, there was, from the very beginning, a strong lobby advocating aid as a moral and humanitarian virtue; Truman was probably the most powerful progenitor of this line of thought.

Another was Herbert Hoover who – at Truman's request – made a 50,000-mile tour of thirty-eight countries just after the war to assess global food supplies and to see how surpluses from North America might be deployed. On his return he addressed the American people in the following stirring tones:

> Of the Four Horsemen of the Apocalypse, the one named War has gone. But Famine, Pestilence and Death are still charging over the world. Hunger is a silent visitor who comes like a shadow. He sits beside every anxious mother three times a day. He brings not alone suffering and sorrow, but fear and terror. He carries disorder and paralysis of government. He is more destructive than armies; not only in human life, but in morale. All of the values of right living melt before his invasion and every gain of civilisation crumbles. But we can save these people from the worst – if we will.[148]

Not long after Hoover had made this high-minded appeal, other influential Americans were finding other reasons to save the poor from the worst. Not only was it morally right to do so, they pointed out, but also it could be good for business. In the 1950s the then President of the World Bank, Mr Eugene Black, travelled around the USA drumming up support for increased aid. His message was a simple one:

> Our foreign aid programmes constitute a distinct benefit to American business. The three major benefits are: (1) foreign aid provides a substantial and immediate market for United States goods and services; (2) foreign aid stimulates the development of new overseas markets for United States' companies; (3) foreign aid orients national economies towards a free enterprise system in which United States firms can prosper.[149]

Similarly, in 1964, Senator McGovern had this to say: 'The people we assist today will become our customers tomorrow . . . An enormous market for American produce of all kinds will come into being if India can achieve half the productivity of Canada.'[150]

And not only India, of course. Between 1945 and 1950, Pakistan, Ceylon, Burma, the Philippines, Indonesia, Jordan, Syria and the Lebanon had also became independent nations open to US commercial penetration. In 1954 Cambodia, Laos and a divided Vietnam became self-governing, and in 1957 Malaya won its independence from Britain. In Africa, Libya became independent during the 1950s, the former Italian colony of Eritrea joined with Ethiopia and, in 1960, the former British and Italian Somalilands united to form the Somali Republic. At about the same time Sudan, Morocco, Tunisia and Egypt were removed from imperial control. The Gold Coast was transformed into independent Ghana. Togoland, the Cameroons and Guinea soon followed to independence. In the Caribbean, Puerto Rico and the Netherlands Antilles achieved new styles of self-government, and the Federation of the British West Indies approached independence within the Commonwealth.

The majority of these newly independent nations, and many others soon to join them, were deeply impoverished. Truman and Hoover had already defined this as an outrage to morality. Black and McGovern had drawn attention to the benefits for American entrepreneurs that aid could bring. Now the Cold War provided a new incentive. In the view of Washington policy-makers there was a grave danger that – left to their own devices – the emergent states might fall under communist domination. This danger had to be averted at all costs; aid quickly came to be seen as the means to achieving this political end.

Thus, Senator Hubert Humphrey in 1957: 'I have heard that people may become dependent on us for food. To me that is good news – because before people can do anything they have got to eat. And if you are looking for a way to get people to lean on you and be dependent on you, in terms of their co-operation with you, it seems to me that food dependence would be terrific.'[151] Likewise, President Kennedy in 1961: 'Foreign aid is a method by which the United States maintains a position of influence and control around the world and sustains a good many countries which would definitely collapse or pass into the communist bloc.'[152] Seven years later President Nixon added: 'Let us remember that the main purpose of aid is not to help other nations but to help ourselves.'[153]

To the mishmash of American motives for giving aid, the wealthy industrial-ised nations of Europe soon added another important element: guilt. Unlike the United States, they had been deeply involved in the countries of the South for many years and, in some cases, for centuries. As the winds of change began to blow and as the process of decolonisation quickened in the 1950s and 1960s, they increasingly found themselves blamed for the poverty of their former possessions. Kwame Nkrumah, the first President of Ghana, was an eloquent spokesman for this point of view. The colonial powers, he thundered,

> were all rapacious; they all subserved the needs of the subject lands to their own demands; they all circumscribed human rights and liberties; they all repressed and despoiled, degraded and oppressed. They took our lands, our lives, our resources and our dignity. Without exception, they left us nothing but our resentment . . . It was when they had gone and we were faced with the stark realities – as in Ghana on the morrow of our independence – that the destitution of the land after long years of colonial rule was brought sharply home to us.[154]

Such accusations found a receptive audience in countries like France, Britain and Italy, which had been the dominant colonial powers, and it is no coincidence that most of them greatly increased – and formalised – their bilateral aid during this period. It was in 1962 that the Development Assistance Committee of the OECD was formed; around the same time France set up its Ministry of Development Co-operation and Britain its Ministry of Overseas Development (now Overseas Development Administration).

Meanwhile the *mea culpas* and the self-flagellations of the erstwhile imperial-ists grew strident. In Britain in 1969, for example, Cyril Connolly wrote: 'It is a wonder that the white man is not more thoroughly detested than he is . . . In our dealings with every single country, greed, masked by hypocrisy, led to unscrupulous coercion of native inhabitants . . . Cruelty, greed and arrogance . . . characterised what can be summed up in one word, exploitation.'[155] Likewise a pamphlet published by Cambridge University students in the early 1970s proclaimed: 'We took the rubber from Malaya, the tea from India, raw materials from all over the world and gave almost nothing in return.'[156]

It was in such a fashion, through guilt, that Europeans at a particular moment in their history came to see foreign aid as a vehicle of restitution, of righting past wrongs, of buying pardon. No doubt, in a perverse and masochistic sort of way, this was immensely satisfying to all concerned. The net result, however, when thrown together with the stew of American intentions, was that the international aid process became a seething pot-pourri of humanitarianism, commercial self-interest, strategic calculation and bad conscience – a perfect recipe for all the contradictions, confusion and pathological disorders with which aid-giving is afflicted to this day.

BUREAUCRATIC SURVIVALISM

Over the years the problem has been made infinitely worse by the conduct of the aid bureaucracies themselves. They have sycophantically nourished and indulged the abiding motivational psychoses of the donor governments and they have added their own touches of irrationality, indecision, compulsive behaviour, greed, caprice, muddle and disorientation.

The most important element in this is that all the institutions of Development Incorporated, whether bilateral or multilateral, seem to have at least one thing in common: an uncanny ability to sense the prevailing mood in the donor countries and to adapt themselves to it. This is a genuine family characteristic, a genetic trait that programmes each and every one of them for survival: if humanitarianism is in the air, then they will make humanitarian statements; if environmental movements seem to be gaining political support, then the agencies will inject some ecology into their rhetoric; they will also – as and when required – make the necessary noises to assuage national guilt complexes, to pander to security neuroses, and even to emphasise the profit motive if that seems expedient. Meanwhile, if welfare-statism is on the ascendant in the donor countries, the aid agencies will highlight their own rôle in the international redistribution of wealth and, like as not, will seem to see central planning as an important factor in the development process. If conservative values are enjoying a resurgence on the other hand, then notions like 'structural adjustment' will be promulgated, the virtues of private enterprise will be extolled and 'market forces' will be assigned a god-like omnipotence.

The variations and possibilities are virtually infinite. As a result, since the Second World War, the aid industry has, at one time or another, appeared to believe *all* of the following things:

- That progress in the poor countries will only be achieved through rapid, high-tech industrialisation administered by central-planning boards under the aegis of the state; after a few years the benefits will 'trickle down' to the poor;

- Ditto, except that state control and central planning are inefficient and that private entrepreneurs must be given a free hand in the industrialisation process;

- That the industrialisation drive has been premature and that progress in poor countries can in fact only be achieved by boosting agriculture – since this is the real economic base of the majority of people in the majority of developing countries;

- That agriculture is best boosted by supporting large-scale farms;

- That agriculture is best boosted by supporting small farmers;

- That wealth will *not* trickle down to the poor and that, therefore, development must be 'bottom-up' in design rather than vice versa;

- That the main focus of development should be on meeting the 'basic needs' of poor and vulnerable groups through the provision of primary health care, village-level education systems, food subsidies, etc.;

- That it may, unfortunately, be necessary to *neglect* the basic needs of poor and vulnerable groups in order to achieve 'structural adjustment' to a hostile international economic environment;

- That it is possible to have 'adjustment with a human face' that achieves austerity goals but that *also* builds in protections for the poorest;

- That it is impossible to have adjustment and growth at the same time;

- That it *is* after all possible to have adjustment and growth at the same time.

The various beliefs and ideas contained in these statements – plus a great many others – have not succeeded one another in any kind of smooth chronological order. Sometimes two or three notions of what development is really all about have co-existed for a year or so – with, for example, USAID advocating a 'trickle down' approach while the ILO emphasises 'bottom-up' projects. Sometimes – as with the basic-needs philosophy which enjoyed its heyday in the late 1970s – agencies have disagreed on implementation although not on the principle: UNICEF and WHO, for instance, have frequently argued over primary health care methodologies.

These little inconsistencies, however, have occurred within broadly identifiable – and constantly changing – currents of thought and action. Indeed, the truth is that notions on how aid should be used to promote development have, since the 1940s, been at least as subject to the whims of fashion as the length of men's hair or the hemlines of women's skirts. In order to comply with the latest fad – however ephemeral – no institutional contortion act has proved to be too difficult for Development Incorporated to perform, no principle has turned out to be so rigid that it could not be bent, no manifesto has been prepared with such rigour that it could not later be rewritten, and no pledge has been felt to be of such a fundamental nature that it could not subsequently be broken.

If we were dealing here simply with academic theories, then none of this would matter very much. The problem is that every shift in mainstream thought about what development is supposed to be sooner or later finds pragmatic expression in projects 'in the field', and the shape of such projects is obviously crucially influenced by the policies of the donor agencies. The fact that these policies change radically – sometimes over quite short time-periods – means inevitably that there is a lack of coherence in the development drive: rather than being a concerted and determined effort to achieve clear and agreed objectives, what we actually end up with is something that stops and starts, lurches forward and then doubles back, kangaroo-hops in a particular direction one year and then veers off drunkenly in quite another the next.

Development is thus a very long way from being an exact science: no practitioner can honestly put his hand on his heart and swear that he knows that any particular approach will work – that, for example, 'adjustment with a human face' is going to be *better* than just plain old adjustment, or that a gung-ho effort to meet the basic needs of the poor is going to be a worthwhile improvement on large-scale industrialisation. Every new strategy is as tentative as the one that went before it; indeed, the very fact that development strategies *do* keep changing is a tacit admission of the failure (or anyway lack of success) of earlier efforts.

The real failure, however, is symbolised by the continued existence of the aid agencies themselves: if they were doing a proper job of promoting development in the Third World, then, presumably, they should have put themselves out of business by now. Over almost fifty years they should have dealt systematically with the problems that they were established to solve, closed up shop and stopped spending tax-payers' money.

They have done no such thing, however. On the contrary, they have managed to stay firmly on the scene despite the rapid changes that have taken place in the post-war world. Neither have they simply, doggedly persisted: the majority have grown from year to year with ever bigger budgets, ever more projects to administer and ever more staff on their ever-expanding payrolls.

Employed to serve the poor, these staff rank ironically amongst the best-paid professionals on earth. Their mission is to work for the deprived – and yet they themselves enjoy an astonishingly rich and diverse range of perks and privileges. They never cease to advocate the cause of the weak and the lowly; paradoxically, however, many amongst those who speak most movingly at the glittering international gatherings have acquired great personal power and prestige and are hopelessly addicted to the trappings of status and authority.

Patricians at public expense, they thus have the strongest possible vested interest in preserving a status quo in which aid continues to flow through their fingers.

The next chapter takes a detailed look at one branch of this aristocracy of mercy.

PART THREE

THE ARISTOCRACY
OF MERCY

. . . everywhere
The ceremony of innocence is drowned;
The best lack all conviction, while the worst
Are full of passionate intensity.

W. B. Yeats, *The Second Coming*

WHY DO PEOPLE work in development?

Most that I have talked to during the preparation of this book cite a variety of reasons. In the case of Europeans and Americans, the 'desire to help' was mentioned fairly frequently: 'It's nice if you can work and help other people at the same time,' said one fairly typical aid official. However this was rarely the only – or even the principal – motivation.

There were a number of people who were clearly 'in it for the money' – a consultant, for example, who boasted that he had mastered the UN's system for allocating contracts.

> It's all done by computer [he told me]. They have this list of names of likely consultants for each kind of job. You have to make sure that your name is on that list and you have to make sure that the experience and qualifications in your CV slot into the various categories that the computer has been programmed to like . . . I've never been without a contract for more than a few weeks in the last ten years and I reckon I can keep going that way well into the twenty-first century.

Did he care where he was sent, or on what sort of projects he was employed? 'Not a bit. This is just a business for me . . . you have to know how to work the system, that's all.'

Pragmatic attitudes also prevailed amongst Africans and Asians who had landed work in the aid business. In most cases, they told me candidly, a job in the UN or in one of the development banks paid them at least ten times as much – and sometimes a hundred times as much – as they could possibly hope to earn in government service in their home countries. 'A completely different lifestyle,' one New York-based Pakistani admitted in his luxury apartment above the Hudson River. 'I won't try to pretend that I took this job out of idealism . . . the money was very important to me.' On his living-room wall was a framed certificate from Pan Am's Clipper Club confirming that he had flown more than 100,000 miles in the last year. 'It pays to buy your tickets for official travel from the same airline whenever you can,' he confided. 'They have these promotions that give you free flights when you've clocked up enough miles . . . I'm planning a round-the-world holiday.'

Even for Europeans and Americans, salaries in the aid business are generally much higher than they might expect to earn in other lines of work. The fringe benefits of overseas postings also represent considerable inducements to join the development set: 'You get a free furnished house and all the related costs are paid as well – water, electricity, etc. In one country they gave us our own generator so that we wouldn't have to do without light when there were power cuts.'

A popular perk provided to almost all fieldworkers is a lavish freight allowance 'to enable you to ship household goods out from home to the developing country you are going to work in and then to ship them back again at the end of your tour of duty'. One AID employee told me: 'You get a list of packers and movers from the agency and you're allowed 250 pounds of air freight and 1,500 pounds of sea freight per person, plus an additional allowance of 2,500 pounds for consumables – mainly paper products and food. Your furniture's already there, of course, and they also ship a car for you free of charge.'

Another AID official who had just returned from an overseas assignment showed me his cellar with some pride: it contained thousands of rolls of toilet paper stacked as high as the ceiling and occupying about half the floor space. 'It'll be years before we have to buy another roll,' he said. 'These were paid for by AID, shipped out to our house in Africa by AID and then shipped back here again at the end of the job.' His Washington home was lavishly furnished with batiks, rattan chairs, carvings and other 'ethnic' items from his various foreign tours of duty – 'all shipped home free'.

Development workers that I talked to in some of the worst hell-holes in the Third World admitted that their reasons for being there were often more financial than idealistic: 'I hate this country,' said one, 'but that's why I'm here.' Pressed on this point, she told me:

> The main reason that people accept a job in a place like this is so they can stash away money – and I'm stashing away a small fortune. Because it's classified as a hardship post, I'm automatically on 25 per cent above the basic salary for my grade. In addition it's a Muslim country, which means we work on Sundays – and that gets me another 25 per cent. My housing's paid, food is cheap and there's really nothing much else to spend money on, so I'm building up a nest-egg.

Initially to my surprise, I found that a disproportionately large number of elderly (and in some cases almost geriatric) officials were employed in hardship posts. Their reasons for being there were simple: 'My pension is calculated on the annual salary that I earn in my last three years,' explained one. 'By working here I get 25 per cent more than I would in other, more comfortable duty stations. If I can stick it out I'll get a correspondingly bigger pension.'

Some of the people I interviewed were virtually unemployable outside the aid business. A British geologist, for instance, had never succeeded in getting a full-time job in the UK in which he could use his training but had managed to

land several lucrative contracts overseas with United Natio
'There's not much demand for my kind of skills in Britain any
me. 'I've tried, but I just can't get work. That means I have a sn
either I'm at home and on social security or I'm abroad earning a good
from the UN . . . Which would you opt for?'

It is the staff of the voluntary agencies like Oxfam or Save the Children Fund
who most frequently cite altruistic and humanitarian concerns as being their
main or only reasons for going to the Third World; this is perhaps why they are
prepared to put up with by far the lowest salaries and by far the worst working
conditions in the development industry. 'I was just so infuriated that people
should be starving in Africa,' said one, 'and I thought that I could help.' Others
were more overtly political, or idealistic: 'It's wrong that some people should
have so much and others should have so little . . . I know it sounds naïve, but
I want to do my bit to end injustice.'

Such romanticism, however – and perhaps predictably – seems to be less and
less of a factor the older the subject is. Amongst fieldworkers in the voluntary
sector I have found repeatedly that a timidity begins to creep into their
behaviour around the age of thirty, that the early 'fire' dies down and that the
individual becomes more reflective, adopts a certain gravity of posture, and
seems to weigh his or her remarks carefully before uttering them.

What is happening here is that these people are beginning to consider their
own careers. Quite understandably they want to have children, or to own a
house (or both), and would definitely like to earn a little more money and have
some kind of secure future. If they have spent the first five, or seven, or ten
years of their working lives supervising irrigation projects or carrying out
nutritional surveys in the Third World, however, then the unfortunate reality
is that their options as 'civilians' back home are very limited – and virtually
non-existent if they have an ambition to continue 'helping the poor'. They
begin, as a result, to look at the possibility of a job in one or other of the various
official aid organisations.

For the upwardly mobile Peace Corps volunteer, for instance, a position
with the Agency for International Development looks like a logical 'career
move' offering higher status and a far better salary: as a result, today, more
than 500 full-time AID staffers were formerly in the Corps.[1] Similarly, in
Britain, a job with the Overseas Development Administration holds many
attractions for an Oxfam or a Christian Aid worker, or for a returned VSO.
Again, an effective promotion is involved with no immediate penalty to pay in
terms of your basic idealism – you get more money, you get much more
security *and* you still get the great feeling that comes from doing something
'worthwhile' for mankind.

It is the United Nations, however, rather than any of the bilateral aid
bureaucracies, that offers the best prospect of a lasting compromise between
altruism and self-interest. Whether you get a job in the Food and Agriculture
Organisation, in UNDP, in UNICEF or in any of the other agencies of the
system, you will be entering a career that pays you a colossal salary to go on

doing 'humanitarian' and 'socially valuable' work and that, furthermore, does so against a backdrop of liberal and progressive ideas with which you can feel comfortable.

Although smaller in resources, than, say, the World Bank or even USAID, there is no doubt that the United Nations system successfully presents itself as the moral centre of the development business. Guided by the lofty and principled terms of its Charter, it has become involved in an astonishingly wide range of 'good works'. Its numerous specialised agencies and other organs have established their principal offices in cities like New York, Geneva, Rome, Vienna and Paris; these in turn are provided with 'field support' in the developing countries by a total of 620 duty stations;[2] as a result acronyms like UNHCR, UNDP, FAO, WHO, UNICEF, WFP, UNFPA and UNEP have become household names in many remote and impoverished places – a sort of alphabet soup for the disadvantaged to drink from. Officials claim that over 90 per cent of the UN's activities are now focused on the promotion of economic and social development in the poor South: some 5,000 separate projects benefit from expertise and funding provided by UNDP; millions of refugees in thousands of camps get aid and protection from UNHCR; supplies and equipment are provided to some 300,000 health and day-care centres and schools by UNICEF.[3]

The great majority of idealistic charity workers and volunteers that I have encountered in the Third World thus nourish a none-too-secret ambition to 'graduate' to the United Nations – which they tend to see as doing in a bigger and more prestigious way the same kinds of thing that they themselves have been doing all along. Furthermore, their working lives in Africa, Asia or wherever have brought them into daily contact with UN staff – with whom they frequently co-operate on the same projects – and they have been able to learn how very high the standard of living can be in the international civil service. This close contact with the 'other half' inevitably has an impact on their own thinking and ambitions. As one Oxfam nutritionist told me:

> I've discovered that people with exactly the same qualifications and experience as me who are lucky enough to be employed by UNICEF or WHO instead of by Oxfam are earning three or four times as much as I am. Well, I want what they have . . . I want the villa and the car and the two servants. I want to be able to save some money at the end of every month. I don't think that's unreasonable, do you? I've been working in the field for five years now – a bloody hard slog and nothing to show for it. I think I deserve something better.

There was a time in my own life when I wanted to work for the UN. My motives, then, were the classic mixture of goodwill and personal calculation: the feeling that, within the world body, I could fully satisfy my own idealism and also reduce my overdraft at the bank, that I could benefit both myself and others at the same time, that – in short – I could have my cake and eat it, too. I went as far as requesting an application form. In the end, however, I did not fill it in.

The background to this lay in the 1970s, when I was one of the editors of *New Internationalist* magazine and had a great deal of contact with UNICEF and with the United Nations Fund for Population Activities (UNFPA). The *NI* had won lucrative contracts to undertake publicity work for both these agencies – notably the writing and production of press kits on children's and population issues which we mailed out to the international media and which generated very wide and positive coverage. I worked on these contracts for a couple of years and thoroughly enjoyed myself. For quite a while afterwards I continued to regard the UN system as a sort of Utopia and I saw UNICEF in particular, with its crusading message, as a beacon of decency and reasonableness in an unjust and cruel world.

Both UNICEF and UNFPA have their headquarters in New York, so that was where I was called for the rather frequent 'consultations' required by the clients. In what I much later came to realise was true United Nations style I used to jet back and forth across the Atlantic Ocean as though air tickets were no more valuable than bus tickets or a subway pass.

One minute I would be in the *NI*'s poky offices in rural Oxfordshire, the next a call would come in from New York querying a paragraph or a sentence and off I would go to Heathrow airport, to the (increasingly familiar) cabin of the 747, and thence to Kennedy and to the Big Apple itself. I would check into the Tudor Hotel on East 42nd Street ('Have a good day, sir'), sleep off my jet-lag and, the next morning, take a stroll over to United Nations Plaza to look at the massed flags waving outside the General Assembly before going on to complete the pleasurable little job that I had been called to this wonderful place to attend to.

I acquired an American Express card during this amazing period ('never leave home without it') and, for the first time in my life, began to regard international travel as a normal, everyday sort of thing rather than as a privilege and a luxury. I became familiar with dozens of bars and restaurants in New York, had my favourite places for 'brunch' and made many new and interesting friends. What was most stimulating of all, I think, was the uplifting atmosphere of idealism that seemed to prevail within both UNICEF and UNFPA – the feeling that all the problems of the world were somehow solvable and that we were the ones who were going to solve them.

Most distinctly of all, I remember walking out from the Tudor Hotel one bright winter morning and pausing to read the quotation from Isaiah that is carved into a wall opposite UN headquarters: 'They shall beat their swords into plowshares and their spears into pruning hooks: nation shall not lift up sword against nation; neither shall they learn war any more.'

At the time that simple message moved me to tears. It was only years later that I came to realise what spurious cant it in fact is for the majority of the UN's 50,000 employees,[4] how cynical many of them have become, and the great extent to which most merely go through the motions of working for a better world. The atmosphere of idealism that had once so uplifted me is, I now understand, just a veneer or – worse than that – a mere stage set, a one-dimensional façade that shouldn't fool anybody. Behind it there is almost nothing at all.

Whatever noble mission the United Nations may once have had has, I am now convinced, long since been forgotten in the rapid proliferation of its self-perpetuating bureaucracies – in the seemingly endless process by which empires have been created within the system by ambitious and greedy men and then staffed by time-servers and sycophants. Rather than encouraging humility and dedication, the world body's structure seems actively to reward self-seeking behaviour and to provide staff with many opportunities to abuse the grave responsibilities with which they have been entrusted.

ROTTEN FROM THE TOP DOWN?

Evidence of this rot can be found at all levels but is most blatant at the very top with the Directors General (sometimes also called Executive Directors) of the bigger agencies. Amongst the few 'elected' officials in the United Nations system, these men (and they are all men) are voted into their jobs by delegates of member states, normally at intervals of five or six years. Once installed they acquire massive discretionary power over development programmes that affect the lives of millions of poor people – a power that is symbolised by the range of perquisites that come with high office: the black chauffeur-driven limousine with motor-cycle outriders, the retinue of fawning retainers, automatic access to VIP lounges at airports, the attentive ear of elder statesmen around the world.

In terms of the protocol that surrounds them, the budgets that they have at their disposal, and their ability to exert direct influence over the lives of others, agency chiefs seem to have more in common with Presidents, or perhaps even with royalty, than they do with other members of the human race. Of one it has been said:

> His style was that of a little Napoleon. As his car drove up to the front entrance the porters would stand deferentially with the glass doors open; another porter would be scurrying across the length of the main hall to the special lift so that its doors would be open by the time the DG reached it. If he was feeling angry he was liable to stride quickly through, his eyes baleful and tail lashing; if he felt easy he could show such casual charm to a porter, a passing typist or anyone else he happened to run into, that they passed the day basking in the glow.[5]

Those who have made it to the top in the development business seem invariably to want to stay there. In 1988 the heads of the World Health Organisation and the International Labour Office had both held office for almost two decades. The year before, a titanic struggle had taken place at the United Nations Educational, Scientific and Cultural Organisation and at the Food and Agriculture Organisation as the long-serving bosses of these two institutions fought tooth and nail to keep their jobs in the face of strong Western opposition to either of them getting a third term. The upshot, in November 1987, was that Ahmadou Mahtar M'Bow, the Senegalese Director General of UNESCO, was replaced by Federico Mayor of Spain. FAO's Director General, Edouard Saouma, on the other hand, *was* reappointed and could look forward to six more years of unchallenged supremacy at the helm of the UN's largest specialised agency. Here, in the words of one observer: 'He can, and often does, decide over life and death in the middle of famine.'[6]

Mr Saouma's record in the fulfilment of this awesome responsibility is not an unblemished one. That, in itself, is hardly surprising, since everyone makes mistakes. However, some extremely grave charges have been levelled against him and it is difficult to turn a blind eye to all of these. For example, it is alleged that in 1984, at the height of the Ethiopian famine, Saouma held back food aid for twenty days at a time when emergency consignments were urgently required. According to testimony from other FAO officials and from the former Ethiopian Relief and Rehabilitation Commissioner Dawit Wolde-Giorgis, this delay occurred simply because Saouma disliked Tessema Negash, then Ethiopia's Assistant Delegate to FAO, and wanted him removed from office: only when Negash was recalled to Addis Ababa was the food released. In Dawit's own words:

> I went [to FAO headquarters in Rome] and tried to brief [Saouma] on what was going on in Ethiopia . . . He interrupted the discussion and told me that our representative was not a very likeable person . . . that it would be very difficult for him to really co-operate with the Ethiopian government as long as we had Tessema Negash as our FAO representative . . . There I was trying to brief a senior UN official about the impending disaster and the number of people dying every day and I was confronted with personal problems . . . that was sickening.[7]

When I approached Saouma in 1989 for an interview to clarify this and other matters, he declared himself unable to receive me because of his 'many commitments'. I was, however, sent a duplicated press handout in which the accusations concerning Ethiopia were strenuously denied. I would have been more convinced if I had been given the opportunity to question Saouma face to face.

Be this as it may, more general criticisms of FAO's Director General were also in the air at the time of his re-election. These criticisms – all of which Saouma rejected as untrue – concerned his management style, particularly disliked by the US government. According to a State Department telegram sent out to all embassies in October 1987: 'Edouard Saouma's . . . highly personalised leadership . . . at FAO . . . has sapped the initiative of the Secretariat and its willingness to make decisions. Continuation of that sort of leadership would be likely to diminish the organisation's effectiveness.'[8] In a less restrained vein, one senior Canadian official accused the FAO chief of practising 'terror tactics',[9] while the former Canadian Minister of Agriculture,

Eugene Whelan, remarked that 'any similarity between what we know in a democratic country and running the FAO is purely coincidental'.[10] Britain refrained from direct censure but on several occasions made plain its view that heads of UN agencies 'should not serve more than two terms'.[11]

Interestingly enough, despite the fact that he was seeking re-election for a third term, Saouma went on record during his campaign to state that he, too, was 'for the principle' that UN chiefs should serve only two terms in office. He argued that he was making an exception to this important rule in his own case only because he felt that FAO needed an experienced hand at the helm during a period when the Organisation was experiencing a liquidity crisis.[12]

When Saouma first took office in November 1975, FAO's statutes expressly stipulated that the Director General should serve only one term of just four years. From the outset, the new incumbent lobbied busily with representatives of member states to allow multiple six-year terms of office and, in 1977, FAO's annual conference adopted a resolution to this effect. This achieved, according to one former FAO official: 'Saouma, equipped with all the prerogatives and opportunities open to him as Director General', began 'campaigning for re-election – a state of affairs that was to have been ruled out by the provision that serving a further term was not allowed'.[13]

Having benefited from a change in the rules that enabled him to compete a second time, Mr Saouma was also in due course rewarded by the United Nations system for starting his campaign early: when he came up for re-election in November 1981 he was adopted as the sole candidate and was returned to office by a majority of 138 votes to one.[14]

Thereafter he focused his energies for several years on extending his control over the Organisation and its vast resources. In the process FAO became increasingly secretive and unwilling to provide information on its projects and programmes or even on the exact size and disposition of its staff.[15] At the same time, however, Saouma sought ever larger and more lavish budgets – which showed a rate of growth of 63 per cent between 1980 and 1984, triple that of other UN development agencies during this period.[16] By mid-decade the organisation was spending in excess of $1.5 million *every day* – to little effect in the opinion of many; more than two-thirds of its staff were to be found at their desks in Rome rather than working on agricultural projects in the developing countries.[17] Commenting on this state of affairs, one exasperated Western delegate hinted that a withdrawal of financial support from FAO would be likely if Saouma were to get a third term in office: 'At least six of us will decide that enough is enough. It's not that we want control, but we are responsible to our tax-payers and our tax-payers are entitled to an organisation which actually helps people grow food.'[18]

Western opposition like this, which had been non-existent in 1981, saw to it that Saouma was not allowed to fight the 1987 election uncontested. Initially two alternative candidates were put up: Señor Gonzalo Bula Hoyos of Colombia and Mr Moise Mensah of Benin. During a year of intense lobbying by all three, however, it gradually became clear that Saouma was going to win again. Bula Hoyos pulled out before the election took place and, in the final ballot, Moise Mensah attracted only fifty-nine votes to Saouma's ninety-four.[19]

The secret of Saouma's success was spelled out in no uncertain terms by Señor Bula Hoyos when he resigned his own candidacy: 'He always travels with his cheque book,' the disappointed Colombian complained, 'and he can buy favours and votes simply by asking governments "Which project do you want?"'[20]

Saouma categorically rejects such allegations. It is a fact, however, that FAO's electoral system allows the delegate from a poor aid-receiving country – Djibouti, for example, or Togo – as much weight as the vote of the delegate from a rich aid-giving country like the United States or Britain; it follows that the logical technique in such an election is to woo small nations which could use a bit of extra assistance.

Amongst the more formidable weapons in Saouma's re-election arsenal – according to his detractors – was one that he had designed and fashioned himself during his first term of office: FAO's Technical Co-operation Programme, now worth approximately $40 million a year, about half of which is spent on capital goods (a departure from FAO's normal technical-assistance practices). Attribution of projects under this programme is very much at the Director General's personal discretion: something, critics charge, that makes them ideal as rewards to faithful delegates. Saouma has classified the list of beneficiary countries as a 'top secret' internal document; it is, as a result, not available to journalists or the general public. Following his 1981 re-election, however, a number of leaks confirmed that TCP projects around that time did go to the more ardent supporters of his sole candidacy.[21] In the 1987 election, delegates from the member states of the Organisation of African Unity were the crucial group of voters because they were expected to ensure Saouma's ouster by backing Mr Mensah. They were swayed from doing so, however, possibly by the prospects of special largesse under the Technical Co-operation Programme. According to diplomats no more than a dozen of the fifty African nations in the end cast their vote for the African candidate.[22] FAO denies any suggestion that TCP funds are used to buy votes and points out that a panel of independent consultants judged the Programme to be 'both timely and relevant to the urgent needs of member countries'.[23]

Mr Saouma's third six-year term in office is worth a significant sum of money to him personally: $813,276 net, excluding fringe benefits.[24] Not even his most impassioned detractors suggest that his single-minded pursuit of re-election was motivated entirely – or even mainly – by an urge to keep his hands on the Director General's fat pay packet; it has been pointed out by more than one, however, that there is something troublingly anomalous about running a development agency and at the same time earning so much. This, as simply stated by Raymond Lloyd – who himself resigned from FAO in disgust after twenty years' service – is 'the paradox of working for the poor and under-privileged from a position of wealth and power'.[25]

It is a paradox that is undoubtedly heightened by the style of FAO's autocratic Director General. He insists on being called 'Your Excellency', and occupies an office that would do justice to an Oriental potentate. He also displays some of the vanity that often comes with high office: television cameramen who have filmed interviews with him say that he has a professional make-up artist attached to his staff whose job it is to powder, brush and groom him before he goes on the air.

More generally, the way that business is conducted at the agency's Rome headquarters seems to be an extension of the Director General's dominant personality. Visitors to the six-storey white marble ministerial palace near the ancient Colosseum only get past the private army of patrolling security guards if they can prove that they have appointments; once inside they are required to wear coloured tags indicating their destination. In the case of journalists an escort from the press room is provided – presumably to ensure that no 'snooping' takes place and that officials talked to give the right answers to questions. Several senior members of staff have been suspended for making 'unauthorised statements' to the press and Saouma maintains additional control over the flow of public information about FAO by denying his more outspoken critics any access to headquarters. Meanwhile the agency's information division disposes of more than $12 million a year[26] producing lavish brochures and reports extolling – in full colour – the virtues of FAO's services to the dispossessed and the disadvantaged.

One gets the sense from all this of an institution that has lost its way, departed from its original mandate, become confused about its place in the world – about what exactly it is doing, and why. Neither is FAO exceptional in this regard: throughout the United Nations system the goal of helping the world's poor to achieve a better life often ends up being relegated to second or third place – or completely forgotten. At all levels, staff show a tendency to become sidetracked, indeed obsessed, by issues of a personal nature: notably their pay and their privileges.

Cut Costs but not Fringe Benefits

One New York-based professional working for the UN, for example, was certainly not advocating greater concern about hunger in Africa or demanding that more be done to reduce mortality rates amongst the poor of Asia when he recently incited his colleagues to action with the words, 'Let us march today, my friends, let us show our anger.' His outrage was reserved for something much closer to home: a suggestion that parking charges in the garage beneath the UN's East River headquarters should be increased from $20 to $80 per month. New York residents not lucky enough to work for the international civil service face bills at private garages ranging from $220 to over $300 a month.[27]

Pressure on the United Nations to oblige its staff to pay something approaching an economic rate for their parking – and to relinquish other perks as well – is part of a broader campaign being mounted by critics of the organisation who include a growing caucus of American Congressmen and

Senators. Traditionally the source of 25 per cent of all UN funds, the United States government began in the mid-1980s to demand more accountability from the world body with regard to how it disposes of its budgets. This move was based on a strong feeling that the USA was being 'taxed without representation' in the General Assembly where – as in FAO – its vote on budgetary matters carried no more weight than that of any of the other 159 member nations.

In order to remedy this, the 1985 Kassebaum Amendment to the Foreign Relations Authorisation Act stipulates that the USA should pay no more than 20 per cent of the assessed annual budget of the United Nations or of any of its agencies that do not adopt weighted voting procedures on 'matters of budgetary consequence' – i.e. that persist in not allowing Americans a say in how the dollars they provide are spent.[28] One of the main reasons given for the introduction of the Amendment was the UN's decision to build a $73 million conference centre in Ethiopia at a time when the famine in that country was at its height. Senator Kassebaum summed up US objections when she said: 'The cost of the first phase of this building will be $73.5 million, of which the United States share will be 25 per cent . . . it will cost us $18.5 million to pay for that conference centre in Ethiopia so that they can stand on the twenty-ninth floor and watch the rest of the country starve to death.'[29]

Shortly after Kassebaum, Congress dealt the United Nations another body blow in the form of the Gramm-Rudman Act of December 1985. The intent of this Act was to balance the US budget through the imposition of progressive cuts in government spending over the five years up to 1991. As far as spending on the United Nations was concerned, this meant that the USA withheld a large part of its 1986 assessed contribution, eliminated altogether from the 1987 budget moneys being kept in abeyance in accordance with the Kassebaum Amendment, and cut back sharply on voluntary contributions as well.

The net result was that the UN was plunged into a financial crisis, which, far from improving, has since steadily deepened. At the end of 1987, US withholdings and arrears had risen to $342.8 million. The serious implications of this shortfall were, furthermore, much exacerbated by the fact that ninety-two other member states were also behind in their payments.[30] To some extent anticipating this predicament, the UN had already launched an economy drive led by Secretary General Javier Pérez de Cuéllar. Measures up for consideration included postponement of the notorious conference centre in Ethiopia (and another in Thailand), cut-backs on the number of publications issued, deferral of certain low-priority programmes and activities, and a temporary freeze on the hiring of new staff.[31]

Even such short-term and cosmetic economies as these were, however, bitterly disputed by international civil servants keen to preserve their privileges. One of the more ridiculous bits of in-fighting was provoked by the Secretary General's decision to halt the supply of carafes of iced water to the thirteen meeting rooms at UN headquarters in New York. Following a motion that the carafes should be restored, the issue was debated for several hours by the Committee on Administrative and Budgetary Questions. Explaining the tough economy Controller Richard Foran said it was easy to underestimate the cost of filling pitchers of water in thirteen conference rooms twice a day. There were 159 delegates per room and no fewer than five porters had to 'rush around' and change the glasses between meetings. The total saving that the Secretary General hoped to achieve by cutting out this service was thus in the region of $100,000 a year. The first delegate to speak noted (probably quite correctly) that if the committee voted to restore the pitchers of water at a time of widespread cut-backs in aid to impoverished countries the symbolism would be 'unfortunate'. Another, however, felt it was inequitable that the Committee Chairman, the Controller and others on the podium still had pitchers of water. As the meeting dragged on into the evening a third speaker pointed out that overtime for translators and guards for the meeting itself might end up costing as much as the discontinued water service. When no decision was reached, the Committee voted to put the whole matter up for consideration by the General Assembly.[32]

Other cost-cutting measures were also hotly debated at committee level and by the Assembly. East Europeans, for example, opposed de Cuéllar's proposed moratorium on recruitment of new staff on the grounds that their own nationals were already under-represented in the UN.[33] When asked what they would do if their budget were cut by 10 per cent, members of the Committee on Palestine refused to discuss the idea, while another committee would not under any circumstances contemplate its high-level members giving up the privilege of first-class air travel.[34] Likewise Africans refused to cut appropriations for the UN Council for Namibia and Latin Americans opposed cuts involving the rights of migrant workers.[35]

'I am like a doctor,' a weary de Cuéllar said at one point. 'I have written a prescription to help the patient. If the patient doesn't want all the pills I've recommended that's up to him. But I must warn that next time I will have to come as a surgeon with a knife.'[36]

Some of the fringe benefits enjoyed by United Nations personnel look like obvious candidates for surgery: in the year after the launching of de Cuéllar's economy drive the United Nations paid out more than $60,000 to hire a chauffeur-driven limousine for a senior employee[37] and $200,000 to cover the cost of constructing leisure facilities for use by staff – including a shooting range in New York.[38]

TRAVEL ON THE GRAVY TRAIN

Other perks, too, show no signs of disappearing, amongst them the opportunity that UN employment affords for frequent travel: to conferences, on 'missions' to assess projects in developing countries, and so on. Visiting foreign lands on official business undoubtedly represents a considerable psychological windfall in that it provides – at no cost to oneself – new experiences, variety and a break from office routines. It is also beyond dispute that many employees routinely save money whenever they undertake an overseas trip. Not only do they avoid paying their own subsistence costs at home for the period that they are away but also they are usually able to pocket some part of the generous per diems that they receive – often well in excess of $100 per day.[39]

Such behaviour would be easy to overlook were it not for the fact that staff travel constitutes a significant element in United Nations budgets. Some time ago, for example, the President and Executive Board of the United Nations Educational, Scientific and Cultural Organisation claimed and received reimbursements of $1,759,548 for their own travel and lodging costs for just one year; this contrasted with outlays of $49,000 on education for handicapped children in Africa, $7,200 for curriculum development in Pakistan and $1,000 for teacher training in Honduras.[40] At the Food and Agriculture Organisation the annual budget for travel by all staff exceeds $14 million.[41]

Official travel is thus a gravy train (or perhaps a jumbo jet) on which everyone wants to book a seat. Far from efforts being made to cut down on costs in this area the UN seems dedicated to search out every possible opportunity to spend more. As Tommy Koh, a former Singaporean Ambassador to the world body, observes: 'Members of the UN Council on Namibia go on junkets to preach the gospel of a free Namibia to those who are already converted to the cause; members of the Economic and Social Council hold their summer meetings in Geneva just because the weather is more pleasant in Geneva during the summer than it is in New York . . .'[42]

A list of a few of the UN's great plans and declarations (for the most part not acted upon) immortalises the names of some of the more exotic locations favoured by international civil servants: Arusha, Alma-Ata, Lima, Nairobi, New Delhi, Caracas, and Mar del Plata have all been the venues for meetings attended by hundreds – and sometimes by thousands – of delegates. The most privileged bureaucrats get more out of all this than just their per diems, a suntan and the pleasure of whittling away long hours with glamorous travel agents and glossy brochures. In one United Nations department a number of officials are *permanently* registered as being on duty travel and are paid accordingly.[43]

All in all the habit of sending its staff on ever more frequent overseas trips now costs the United Nations system almost $100 million a year[44] – this is more than the value of the annual exports of several developing countries. A measure of the important rôle that jet-set membership plays in the life of the world body is that serious proposals have been put forward to the effect that it should establish its own travel agency.[45] In the mean time the General Services Office of the Secretariat in New York continues to pay almost $1 million a year to twenty staff who are employed solely to make travel arrangements.[46] They are aided in this task by private agencies which find it financially worthwhile to have branch offices in most of the main United Nations buildings in New York and Geneva – indeed, in the latter city the business is so lucrative that one travel agent has opened offices in each of the several wings of a single UN building.[47]

There is considerable resistance to attempts to reduce the cost of travel by buying discounted or 'bucket shop' tickets. FAO argues against such an economy on the grounds that it 'would restrict full freedom of staff to travel on any airline of their choice'.[48] Likewise another United Nations body, the International Telecommunication Union, considers unacceptable 'any change in arrangements which might diminish existing standards of travel or require a change in staff regulations'.[49]

It must be admitted that these regulations are complex in the extreme. The official document that deals with them takes the form of an 'administrative instruction' entitled 'Standards of Accommodation, Travel Time and Rest Stopovers'.[50] This chunky memo sets out, amongst other pieces of bureaucratic arcana, the exact terms of reference of the 'nine-hour rule'. Apparently honoured by the senior UN officials to whom it applies as often in the breach as in the keeping,[51] this states that:

> Under-Secretaries General and Assistant Secretaries General and, where applicable, their eligible family members, shall be provided with first-class accommodation for travel on official business and on appointment, transfer or separation, when the duration of a particular flight exceeds nine hours; for flights under nine hours' duration, these staff members shall be provided accommodation by the class immediately below first class.[52]

The official pecking order is established in the next paragraph:

> Staff members below Assistant Secretary General and, where applicable, their eligible family members, shall be provided accommodation by the class immediately below first class for travel on official business and on appointment, transfer or separation when the duration of a particular flight exceeds nine hours; for flights under nine hours' duration, these staff members shall be provided with transportation at the least costly airfare structure regularly available.[53]

It is surprising how many destinations are more than nine hours' flight from UN headquarters in New York. A list of 178 frequently visited cities contains no fewer than 130 which permit the nine-hour rule to be applied:[54] according to their seniority, international civil servants may purchase first- or club-class tickets to all such destinations. Long-haul travel also brings another privilege: a generous entitlement to 'rest days' on full pay before starting work. Thus a UN staffer gets two days of paid leave on top of his existing six-week vacation allowance every time he flies from New York to, say, Singapore, Nairobi or Bangkok, and two more days when he flies back. The compensation for the pain of visiting Tahiti, however, is just one day each way while those unfortunate enough to be sent on a mission to Nassau in the nearby Bahamas get no extra paid leave at all.[55]

A CLASS APART

Travel perks are not the only things that identify members of the 'international set' as a class apart. The recent publication of the results of an inquiry by Senator Jesse Helms provided infuriating additional evidence about how the other half live to the 18,000 civil servants who work in New York City for the United States government. While they neither get – nor expect – any rent subsidy to help them keep up with the astronomical cost of accommodation in the Big Apple, the Helms inquiry revealed that other Americans – those attached to the United Nations – were faring much better. One Deputy Chief Delegate, for example, was receiving a subsidy of $10,661 *per month* towards the cost of his three-bedroom apartment in River Tower, a luxury high-rise situated at 420 East 54th Street, close to UN headquarters. The building, described by an estate agent as 'one of the fanciest' in New York, had the benefit of its own wine cellar, direct dialling to the concierge, valet and housekeeper, its own florist and vintner, several fine restaurants, and two levels of underground parking.[56]

Perhaps it is the freewheeling, get-rich-quick atmosphere inevitably created by over-generous perks and privileges like these that encourages some employees to attempt to line their pockets by dishonest means. There is, in addition, evidence to suggest that fraudulent behaviour is actually condoned – at least in the upper echelons of the UN bureaucracy. In 1986 eight members of staff were disciplined for falsely claiming more than $100,000 in education grants for their children. Seven were dismissed; the eighth, however, Mr Ramaswamy Mani of India – who insisted that he received the extra money inadvertently – stayed on. Following the personal intervention of the Secretary General on his behalf, the Disciplinary Committee's recommendation that he should be sacked was set aside and he was merely demoted. This brought charges of favouritism: Mr Mani was the chief assistant (and a close personal friend) of Jean Ripert, the Director General and number two man at the UN. 'Anyone above a certain level gets the attention of the Secretary General,' complained an official of the Staff Committee, 'but below there is no mercy.' Prior to his demotion Mr Mani commanded an annual salary in the region of $105,000; the $2,000 pay cut that he suffered for his misdemeanour was accurately described by one colleague as 'peanuts in financial terms'.[57]

To work for the United Nations in any kind of senior capacity is thus to join a privileged aristocracy that is effectively insulated from the exigencies of everyday life. At FAO in Rome there are 750 individuals whose pensionable remuneration ranges from $70,000 to $120,000 a year – these include eleven Assistant Directors General, thirty-one Senior Directors, 125 Directors, 362 Senior Officers and 221 First Officers.[58] The Rector of the United Nations University is paid three times as much as the Norwegian Prime Minister.[59] Many other UN officials, notably the growing number of personnel in the 'supergrade' bracket, earn more than any US public official except the President. One of these men, an Under-Secretary General, recently retired with a golden handshake of almost half a million dollars plus an annual pension of $50,000. Shortly thereafter the UN rehired him as a consultant at a fee of $125,000 a year.[60]

Little wonder, then, that the Joint Inspection Unit – an internal United Nations watchdog – has expressed reservations as to 'the justifiability of present levels of remuneration in the professional and higher categories'.[61] The JIU inspectors, however, admit that few other international civil servants share their doubts. Indeed: 'Staff representatives hold the view that remuneration is inadequate and wage an active campaign for higher salaries.'[62]

This is quite true. Many United Nations people genuinely believe that the pay and fringe benefits they receive are insufficient; accordingly they react with something approaching horror to any suggestion that they are over-compensated. Ed Freeman, the General Secretary of the Association of Professional Staff at FAO in Rome, is a case in point. In correspondence with me he hotly contradicted my view that the members of his association (motto: 'Service before Self') are overpaid freeloaders living off the fat of the land; on the contrary, he argued, they are required to make real personal sacrifices in order to work for the cause of world development.

To illustrate this, Freeman sent me a profile of 'Al Ristoro', a forty-four-year-old American who 'joined the Organisation a year ago as a P-3, Step 5' (in plain English, as a mid-level professional). Al's take-home pay in 1987 was just US$3,200 per month (4.5 million Italian lire). This amount was considerably below the average in the UN system at the time; nevertheless, Al reported that it had sounded OK to both himself and his wife 'before we came here'. Disillusionment quickly set in. The family had initially wanted to set up home in Old Rome but found they couldn't afford the rents there; eventually they took a house twenty kilometres out. 'Being half an hour's walk from the nearest public transport,' Al complained, 'I had to buy a car. That and the four million lire I had to pay in advance for rent and settling in just about took care of the 12 million lire installation allowance.'

Al's woes did not stop with having to spend his installation allowance on, well . . . installation. 'School fees', he protested, 'have cost me $7,000 over and above the education allowance for my three boys . . . Then there are medical bills. I think FAO has a terrific scheme, but I've had to pay more than $1,000 for what wasn't met . . .' Other immediate financial worries included winter clothes: 'Where we lived it was warm all the year round, so we don't own a single overcoat or anything heavy among the lot of us. My wife reckons it'll cost about $3,000 to fit us all out but I tell her we've just got to do it for a whole lot less.' All in all, the profile concluded, 'Al believes that he is going broke and won't be able to hack it to the end of his three-year contract.'[63]

There are other UN employees in Rome who share Al's predicament. To illustrate this point Mr Freeman sent me details of a letter received by the Association of Professional Staff from an officer of the World Food Programme (an FAO affiliate). This officer's great worry was the education of his children at a time when the US dollar was falling in value and private schools in Rome were putting up their fees: 'Unfortunately,' he lamented, 'the UN education grant remains at a maximum of US$4,500 per child per year (apparently with very little hope of an increase in the near future). This means that parental contributions have to make up for the entire increase in school fees . . .' That increase had been so severe that

> staff members in our situation could probably, and with considerable sacrifice, survive at most one more year in Rome. Many of our colleagues with children in the same school have already expressed their serious concern and I know of several cases where the cost of education has been a factor influencing their decision to take their children out of the school to continue their studies in their home countries or in Italian schools. These are not satisfactory alternatives . . .[64]

Of course one's sympathies go out to those forced to contemplate the horrific prospect of sending their offspring to an Italian school. Since members of the Association of Professional Staff are actually grappling with this nightmare today, it seems somehow in bad taste to remind them that more than 400 million children in the Third World cannot afford to go to any school at all[65] – are so poor, in fact, that they cannot even afford to eat: 280,000 of them *die* every week of malnutrition-linked conditions.[66]

In the context of this sustained global tragedy, however, the whingeing complaints of UN staffers about the erosion of their incomes or the latest threats to their 'acquired rights' do begin to look distinctly inappropriate, possibly even perverse. By any normal standards of measurement, the financial and other benefits they receive are very great.

This is so because their conditions of service are calculated according to the 'Noblemaire Principle'. Named after a French diplomat, Georges Noblemaire, who worked for the League of Nations during the 1920s, this states simply that salaries and entitlements in international organisations should be sufficient to attract as employees citizens of the country with the best-paid national civil service. United Nations pay rates are thus based today on a comparison with those of the federal civil service of the richest country on earth – the United States of America.

This comparison presently works out very much in the UN's favour. At all levels and grades, salaries and entitlements are significantly *better* than those in the US civil service. Thus, for example:

- United Nations staff members receive education grant benefits; US civil servants do not;[67]

- From their first day on the job UN staff members qualify for up to nine months' sick leave on full pay and a further nine months on half pay in any four-year period. By comparison a United States employee would have to work fourteen years with no sick leave whatsoever in order to accumulate nine months' sick leave at full pay;[68]

- Promotion 'steps' in the United Nations system are attained at a faster rate than in the United States civil service: in the United Nations it takes an averagely competent official just eight to ten years to reach the tenth step compared to eighteen years in the USA;[69]

- All professionals and above in the United Nations, together with their families, are entitled to fifteen days' home leave once every two years entirely at United Nations expense, plus extra days to cover the journey time to and from their home country. This entitlement is *additional* to the six weeks of ordinary leave that all United Nations staff receive each year. United States civil servants, by contrast, get just four weeks of annual leave;[70]

- United Nations professionals work, on average, 10.3 per cent fewer hours than their counterparts in the United States civil service; over the course of a year this adds up to a striking difference in input of 21.7 working days;[71]

- Regardless of the considerable cash value of such 'fringe benefits', take-home pay in the United Nations system is higher at every level than in the US civil service: the margin between the two presently averages around 24 per cent in favour of UN employees[72] and in some cases exceeds 30 per cent;[73]

- UN pensions are higher by up to 43 per cent than those in the United States civil service.[74]

Why exactly should pay and fringe benefits in the UN system be so much better than those in the world's best-paid national civil service? The answer given by Secretary General de Cuéllar is that it is 'crucial to maintain employment conditions that will allow the United Nations to attract and retain employees of the highest competence, efficiency and integrity'. He adds a warning: 'To seek to solve the organisation's financial difficulties at the expense of staff entitlements would be extremely short-sighted and counter-productive, and would have widespread adverse implications.'[75]

One agency head of department who I talked to made the same point rather more pithily. 'If you want to persuade top people to work in development,' he said, 'then you have to pay top dollar. If you pay peanuts you get monkeys.'

A PREMIUM ON MEDIOCRITY

On the face of things this looks like a strong argument. Some who know the United Nations extremely well, however, feel that despite paying top dollar the world body has still got too many monkeys working for it. According to one expert witness: 'There is nothing to indicate that systematic efforts are being made either to require a high level of staff qualifications or to train professional staff for the specific tasks they will be called upon to perform. On the contrary, the laxness that prevails in this matter would seem to put a premium on mediocrity.'[76]

These are not the words of some outsider with a grudge against the United Nations. Indeed, they are contained in an official document and were written by an internationally respected insider – Maurice Bertrand, a senior member of the UN's own Joint Inspection Unit. 'The average level of qualifications of staff in the professional grades,' he continues, 'bears no relation to their responsibilities . . . In the case of UNICEF the statistics show 30 per cent without any university qualifications, 32 per cent with a first degree, and only 38 per cent with a second or higher degree.' This state of affairs is 'comparable in most of the other agencies' and does not improve further up in the hierarchy: 'In the Director grades (D-1 and D-2) the percentage of staff members who have had no university education is roughly the same.'[77]

Bertrand's conclusion is damning:

> A sense of responsibility and managerial or analytical ability at the highest levels (Director, Assistant Secretary General, Under-Secretary General) are a matter of chance, depending on appointments which are often made without concern for qualifications or professional and administrative experience. The lack of a definition of the qualifications required for recruitment and promotion to higher grades, the indifference shown towards standards of work and competence, the absence of a system of in-service training, create a deplorable working environment in which the best staff members no longer find the motivation needed to dedicate themselves to their tasks.[78]

If the best lack all conviction it is also true – to borrow a line from Yeats – that the worst 'are full of passionate intensity'. The ardour of this latter group finds its natural expression in the growing number of staff unions and associations that exist within the UN, and in the increasing amount of time that the members of these devote to heated discussions about how to obtain for themselves still higher salaries and still better financial benefits.

At headquarters in New York, for example, the 120-member Staff Council – a legislative body of the Staff Union – holds one meeting every four to five days. The twenty committees that it has set up to study various issues each have ten members who also meet regularly. The Council claims that one of the main aims of this ceaseless activity is to study ways of improving staff efficiency. In a typical year, however, during which members of the Council discussed more than eighty subjects, adopted sixty-one resolutions and issued nearly fifty bulletins, the question of efficiency of staff was not raised once.[79] Pay and entitlements were, throughout, the main items on the agenda.

Other entities are engaged in similar deliberations. One is the Joint Advisory Committee which, together with its four subsidiary bodies and six working groups, has more than 100 members who attend several meetings a month. Another, the Staff–Management Co-ordination Committee, restricts itself to just two meetings a year; each of these, however, lasts for a full week and involves the participation of at least thirty-five senior staff and administrators.[80]

All such meetings are held during office hours and most are lengthy. Inevitably this means that the participants are taken away for considerable periods from their normal duties as international civil servants; the work of their colleagues who may need to confer with them is, of course, also disrupted because of this. To add insult to injury, none of these time-wasting distractions is paid for by the members of the associations concerned: salaries of officials and committee members, paper, typing, photocopies and even travel to outside meetings are all financed out of the regular budget of the United Nations.[81]

Another focus of staff members' energies which often diverts them from carrying out the duties and responsibilities for which they are paid is, ironically, the desire for promotion. This, in the assessment of Richard Hoggart, a former Assistant Director General of UNESCO, has

> the effect of a kind of illness which drives the more extreme cases to tranquillisers, bouts of frenetic marginal activity, or long hours of simply staring over their desks working things out inside their heads. The most important single urge is to 'make P-5' [top niche in the UN's 'professional' category]. A P-5 carries a number of diplomatic privileges, notably a CD plate for one's car. A good number of Secretariat members feel underneath, and so do their wives, that they will only be able to retire happily if they have that plate for their last few working years.[82]

Their chances of achieving this goal are surprisingly good: almost 60 per cent of professional posts in the United Nations are now at P-4 level or above. By contrast less than 25 per cent of professional posts in the United States federal civil service have a corresponding level of seniority.[83]

The reason for the 'more chiefs than Indians' syndrome in the UN is not by any means that the majority of staff are exceptionally talented or diligent. On the contrary, the engine of the whole process is mediocrity: it is now an established phenomenon that second-raters who have utterly failed to achieve promotion lobby to have their posts 'reclassified' – upwards, of course.[84] Thus in just one UN office – the New York Secretariat – no fewer than sixty-nine posts were upgraded during 1986–7. Amongst the lucky incumbents were three Directors who, at a stroke of a pen, became Assistant Secretaries General, twenty-six P-3s who became P-4s and twenty-four P-4s who became P-5s.[85] The institutionalisation of such activities throughout the international civil service has resulted in what the Austrian delegate to the UN's Advisory Committee on Administrative and Budgetary Questions has called 'a disquieting rate of grade creep manifested in a clear reduction in the proportion of junior posts and an increase in the proportion of senior posts'.[86]

Just as the system permits jobs to be artificially upgraded in order to mollycoddle otherwise unpromotable deadbeats, so also it allows those who should long since have been fired for incompetence to linger on. Speaking of UNESCO, Richard Hoggart says that no matter how poor a staff member's work may be it is virtually impossible to force him to leave. Use of the full apparatus of official and unofficial appeals – Staff Association, the official's Delegation, his Foreign Ministry, the UN Administrative Tribunal and so on – can drag the process out indefinitely. Furthermore:

> Even in the worst cases, 'equity', a moral commitment to someone who has served for, say, five years, requires that they be given at least a further three years' trial. The next time round equity demands that someone who has given eight years' service to the Organisation be not cast out . . . The only periods when such people show sustained energy and negotiating skill are when they are mounting their recurrent defences of their own positions.[87]

Thus, at every level of the multilateral agencies, maladjusted, inadequate, incompetent individuals are to be found clinging tenaciously to highly paid jobs, timidly and indifferently performing their functions and, in the process, betraying the world's poor in whose name they have been appointed.

One indication of how enfeebled the UN has become as a result of its increasingly bungling and weak-kneed staff is that it is now obliged to rely on substantial amounts of outside expertise in order to get its work done. Despite its already bloated payroll of 12,248 full-time employees, for example, the UN Secretariat in New York needs to spend an additional $11.1 million per biennium on 'consultants' – enough to finance approximately 175 work-years of professional assistance.[88] FAO's 10,500 staff are even less effective: the Rome-based agency requires so much 'external professional assistance' that it budgets an amazing $19 million per biennium for payments to consultants.[89] The annual *State of the World's Children Report*, UNICEF's flagship publication which goes out under the signature of its Executive Director, is in fact written and produced by an external consultant; the highly paid journalists and other professional communicators who staff UNICEF's own large information office in New York are apparently not up to the job.

Failings and inadequacies of this type amongst full-time personnel are highlighted in a recent authoritative internal report which states that 'management capacity, productivity and cost-effectiveness' have fallen behind at a time when the UN's payrolls have exhibited 'rapid growth'. Echoing Bertrand, the report adds that: 'The quality of work performed needs to be improved upon . . . The qualifications of staff, in particular in the higher categories, are inadequate and the working methods are not efficient. Today's structure is too complex, fragmented and top-heavy . . .'[90]

Indeed, it is so top-heavy that the UN's New York Secretariat has accumulated a total of fifty-seven Assistant Secretaries General and Under-Secretaries General. If the same management structure were adopted by, say, the US Department of Health, then that branch of the federal civil service would have to appoint 500 Assistant and Under-Secretaries; it presently manages to get along perfectly well with just a dozen.[91]

Personnel and associated costs today absorb a staggering *80 per cent* of all UN expenditures.[92] A body that claims it is struggling tirelessly for world development is thus also an elaborate support mechanism for its own pampered and cosseted staff – many of whom, in the sad words of former FAO departmental director Raymond Lloyd, 'systematically put their own material security over the risk-bearing ideals for which our organisations were founded'.[93]

One of the worst possible examples of such behaviour occurred in Belgium in 1987 at the offices of UNICEF, the agency established in 1946 'to help protect the lives of children and promote their development'.[94] Jos Verbeek, then the Director of UNICEF's Belgian Committee, was accused of using his position of privilege and trust to organise a child sex ring which operated profitably for several years until he was arrested on charges of 'indecency and incitement to the debauchery of children'. He was subsequently convicted and given a two-year suspended sentence. On appeal, however, the conviction was quashed on grounds of insufficient evidence. The ten-year sentence of another member of staff was upheld. Police discovered a photographic studio concealed in the basement of the building that housed the Committee's offices. The studio was used to take pornographic photographs of children – most of whom were from the Third World. More than 1,000 pictures were seized along with a mailing list of 400 names of wealthy clients in fifteen European countries; the list had been compiled – and was stored – on the UNICEF computer which had also been used to set up a catalogue of teenagers available for sex.[95]

This nasty incident occurred in a year in which UNICEF had been taken to task by the UN's Board of Auditors for 'delinquent accounting' and accused by Congress of giving backhanders to State Department officials in return for their support for 'the incumbent management' and for increased US funding of the organisation.[96] Such isolated scandals and dramas, however, are less significant than the system-wide corrosion of basic principles that has taken place slowly – over almost half a century – and that has reduced the ideals of the United Nations to little more than empty words on forgotten scraps of paper.

SOUND AND FURY, SIGNIFYING NOTHING

From time to time, of course, an appearance of great motion and enthusiasm can still be created in honour of some sacred cow. A closer look, however, usually reveals that nothing much is actually happening – that what is involved is just the ritual celebration of polite inaction. Take, for example, The Week of Solidarity with the Peoples of Namibia and All Other Colonial Territories, as well as those in South Africa, Fighting for Freedom, Independence and Human Rights.[97] The United Nations increasingly favours 'calendar events' of this type and is constantly creating more such pieces of vacuous liturgy:

* The International Day of Innocent Children Victims of Aggression;

* The International Day of Peace;

* World Development Information Day;

- The Week of Solidarity for the People Struggling Against Racism and Racial Discrimination;

- The International Year of Shelter for the Homeless;

- The Transport and Communications Decade in Africa;

- The International Drinking Water Supply and Sanitation Decade;

- The Third United Nations Development Decade;

- The Second Decade to Combat Racism and Racial Discrimination.[98]

None of these observances, past or current, has made the slightest difference to the state of the world we live in. Few outside the international civil service have even heard of them. Nevertheless, their proliferation within the United Nations system tends to be confused with action. In 1987, for example, during the Second Disarmament Decade, much ado was made about the International Conference on Disarmament[99] organised by the UN in New York: a flurry of documents was released, solemn speeches were made, and thousands of delegates were enabled to feel that they had participated in an event of historic importance. In the same year, UN member states spent more than ever before arming themselves to the teeth – an estimated $800 *billion* – while the world body itself devoted *less than one tenth of one day's share* of this massive amount of money to tangible 'peace-related activities'.[100]

What underlies such paradoxes and hypocrisies is an insidious mechanism by which people lose interest in the validity of mere results and concentrate their efforts instead on the *processes* supposedly devised to achieve these results.[101] An important part of this in the United Nations is that the accepted indicators of a job well done have ceased to be, for example, material benefits delivered to the poor; rather, 'success' is defined by bureaucratic or ceremonial factors like the number of conferences, studies and meetings that take place to discuss the subject of global poverty, the number of Days, Weeks, Years or Decades of 'solidarity' with the disadvantaged that are celebrated, the number of 'keynote' publications prepared, the sophistication of the language in which 'back-to-office reports' are couched – and so on. In such a fashion, as Maurice Bertrand puts it: 'The way in which the mill operates becomes more important than the quality of the flour it produces.'[102]

This certainly seems to be the case at the United Nations Conference on Trade and Development – a permanent body founded in 1962 to foster the growth of developing-country trade. UNCTAD managed recently to spend an impressive $36,282,700 on its own offices and staff plus a further $4,186,700 on 'conferences' and more than $1 million on 'consultants'; in the same year 'encouraging economic co-operation among developing countries' got just $3,501,500 of UNCTAD's money (which comes from the UN's regular budget) and 'programmes to promote and expand world trade' got only $1,138,000.[103]

The UN's fascination with processes rather than with results achieves its apotheosis, however, when the processes actually *become* the results. This seems to be what has happened at the Department of Conference Services which, with 2,527 full-time employees and a budget in excess of $280 million per biennium, has grown into an unstoppable juggernaut. In an average two-year period in New York alone the Department boasts that it will service 7,600 separate meetings, handle 65,500 separate 'interpreting assignments', translate, edit or revise 377,650,000 words of text, type 397 million more, and reproduce a total of 1.5 billion page impressions.[104] The Department's other principal bastion – in Geneva – has a similar volume of 'output':[105] here storage of document copies for reference purposes requires 17.5 kilometres of shelves.[106]

What is all this in aid of? At one conference, on the Law of the Sea, the UN employed ninety mimeograph operators to work around the clock at twenty-seven machines spewing forth 250,000 pages of documents a day. Each document was produced in three – and sometimes five – languages by teams of translators and typists from the Department of Conference Services. Indeed, so great was the volume of paperwork generated that the list of documents itself ran to 160 pages. After seventy days of talk in the pleasant surroundings of Caracas, Venezuela, delegates made just one firm decision: a resolution to hold another conference on the same subject.[107]

Some get-togethers seem to consign themselves to muddle and inaction from the very start: take, for example, The United Nations Seminar on the Existing Unjust International Economic Order, on the Economics of Developing Countries, and the Obstacle That This Represents for the Implementation of Human Rights and Fundamental Freedoms,[108] or the equally bewildering United Nations Conference to Review All Aspects of the Set of Multilaterally Agreed Equitable Principles and Rules for the Control of Restrictive Business Practices.[109] As far as the poor of the Third World are concerned it is probably true to say that the learned palaver that goes into such events, the reams of supporting documents, and the miles of expensive storage are just irrelevances. For the peasant picking mortar shrapnel out of his arid field in northern Ethiopia, or the artisan fisherman in Sri Lanka whose catch has just been stolen by a Japanese factory ship, the majority of United Nations conferences might as well take place on the astral plane as on planet earth.

The truth of this is borne out whenever a conference is devised that *could* have some direct and measurable impact on the reduction of human suffering: on such rare occasions the United Nations hastily distances itself from the upstart and unusual event. An example occurred in Paris when Amnesty International obtained permission to use the splendid facilities at UNESCO's headquarters to stage a conference on the subject of torture. The venue was quite appropriate since UNESCO is entrusted by its Charter with the task of furthering 'universal respect for human rights and fundamental freedoms'. Things went wrong, however, when – horror of horrors – Amnesty *named names* in a position paper on the widespread use of torture by governments. The next morning, in response to pressure from delegates of precisely those governments that Amnesty had pointed its accusing finger at, UNESCO ordered that the conference be taken elsewhere.[110]

The same type of craven behaviour can also be seen at work in other areas of the UN. In 1988, for instance, the High Commissioner for Refugees, Jean-Pierre Hocke, ordered an entire issue of his agency's monthly magazine to be destroyed, at a cost of more than $50,000. This was done because the edition in question was sharply critical of West Germany's asylum procedures for refugees and of conditions in three refugee reception centres in the Federal Republic. The West German government provides 10 per cent of UNHCR's annual budget and was thus judged by the Commissioner to be above criticism.[111]

In the never-never-land of the international civil service, craven behaviour of the type that closes worthwhile conferences and pulps hard-hitting publications is often the *only* response to the sometimes horrific events that occur in the real world. Outrages are met with a prim silence and where silence is for some reason impossible then safe platitudes, mealy-mouthed generalities and hot air are substituted. Of the period 1984–6 when Africa was devastated by famine Joseph Reed, a former US Ambassador to the United Nations, had this to say: 'We turned out resolutions while children went without food, water and medicine. We requested reports while families huddled in devastating poverty. We hurled accusations back and forth while desperate people became more resigned to their plight.'[112]

This harsh epitaph to what Reed calls the 'frenzy of playing the UN game' looks even bleaker in the context of the world body's 150 committees, commissions, sub-committees, sub-commissions and working groups all supposedly dealing with the problems of the poor.[113] Added to these are the fifteen or so fully funded development agencies – each of which, in its turn, is orbited by numerous other linked entities: twenty in the case of the World Health Organisation; eighteen in the case of FAO; more than ten at UNESCO and the ILO; thirteen in the case of UNDP – and so on.[114]

Rather than testifying to the strength and diversity of UN efforts to assist poor countries to develop, this fantastically complicated administrative superstructure symbolises the extent to which international civil servants have been allowed to build up disparate personal empires at the expense of focused and single-minded efficiency. Thus, instead of a concerted effort to provide agricultural education in the developing countries, we have the unedifying distraction of a long-running territorial dispute between FAO and UNESCO over whether this work should most properly be in the domain of the one or of the other.[115] Similarly, in the place of agreement and well-programmed action to improve standards of health care in poor communities we find a persistent conflict between UNICEF's focus on specific goals (vaccination, promotion of breastfeeding, etc.) and WHO's endeavours to support more comprehensive policies within the framework of the 'primary health care approach'.[116]

Such squabbles can at times seem inexcusable. During precisely the famine to which Joseph Reed referred, an Office for Emergency Operations in Africa was set up – in New York – to harness the UN's scattered empires under one yoke, to bring together for the duration of the emergency all the different agencies and organs that might have something to contribute. This virtuous objective, however, did not inhibit Edouard Saouma at FAO from making a formal complaint when the OEOA accepted a sum of money from the Netherlands government to buy rice seed for Chad: the basis of this objection was that seed-buying was FAO's job. Throughout the famine years Mr Saouma also continued a long-standing argument with the Director of WFP about which of them had the final responsibility for authorising food aid shipments to Africa. Finally, Saouma refused to attend a special meeting of donors called by the OEOA with a view to integrating their assistance programmes; two weeks later, at FAO, he held his own donors' meeting. As Douglas Williams, a former Deputy Secretary of the UK's Overseas Development Administration, comments: 'There was neither any organisation nor any individual within the UN system with the authority to make a single organisation the leader in all these activities, even in the face of a major international disaster of chronic character and unprecedented proportions. The waste of effort and scarce resources was considerable.'[117]

Wastage occurs at all levels of the system. Within individual agencies, for example, and even within particular departments of these agencies, there is an established tendency for staff members to want to protect and nourish their own programmes and to resist tooth and nail any suggestion that these should be cut back or phased out. In 1982, at least 100 such programmes were judged by the Secretary General of the United Nations to be 'elderly', non-productive, or redundant by virtue of duplication. He recommended that all should be terminated, with an anticipated annual saving of $35 r ˸ᵗion. Four years and $140 million later, however, an independent study ˸vealed that not one of these senile and unnecessary 'pets' had yet been put down.[118]

A STATE OF CONFUSION

In a bureaucratic universe where old programmes never die and where new ones are constantly being created, chaos can be expected to be the natural state of things. As Maurice Bertrand puts it:

> The vagueness of the terms of reference, the similarity of jurisdiction between organs as important as ECOSOC, UNCTAD, the Second and Third Committees of the General Assembly – and the number and repetition of 'general debates' preceding the examination of agenda items repeated in committee after committee whose relative status is not clearly defined – have created a state of confusion which it has been found difficult to remedy.[119]

He adds that, in the field, the sectoral approach favoured by UN agencies – and the tendency of each to defend its own 'patch' – has 'complicated the task of the developing countries instead of simplifying it'. This is mainly because, to pick a few examples: 'The industrialisation goals of UNIDO, FAO's goal of increasing agricultural production, the food strategies of the World Food Programme, the ILO programmes on employment or the development of social security, and UNESCO's plans for the development of education, *are not integrated into a coherent system of analysis.*'[120]

This criticism is one that is readily acknowledged by international civil servants. Most will freely admit that the extreme complexity and fragmentation of the United Nations system is counterproductive; most, furthermore, will agree that something should be done about it: as a result an entire industry has grown up aimed at co-ordinating the monster. Instead of less complication, confusion and muddle, however, the net achievement of this industry has – predictably – been to create more: more committees, more organs and entities, more unreadable reports and more jobs for the boys. Thus we have, inter alia:

- The Administrative Committee on Co-ordination;

- The Economic and Social Council (which may 'through consultation, co-ordinate the activities of the specialised agencies');

- The Committee on Programme Co-ordination;

- A Post of Director General for Development and International Economic Co-operation – with responsibility for 'exercising overall co-ordination within the system in order to ensure a multi-disciplinary approach to the problems of development on a system-wide basis';

- An Office for Programme Planning and Co-ordination ('to examine problems of co-ordination at the level of the system, and to propose studies and analyses of intersectoral programmes');

- A Consultative Committee on Substantive Questions ('to enable the organisations and the United Nations to co-ordinate the preparation of their programmes');

- Resident Co-ordinators with responsibility for 'co-ordination of operational activities for development carried out at the country level';

- The World Food Council, consisting of thirty-six members, with instructions 'at the ministerial level to establish its own programme of action for co-ordination of relevant United Nations bodies and agencies'.[121]

According to the Joint Inspection Unit (itself, incidentally, mandated by the General Assembly with the task 'of achieving greater co-ordination between organisations'):

> This mass of efforts has in no way improved co-ordination. 'Joint planning' has remained wishful thinking; development strategies applied by each organisation have continued to diverge; and 'country programming' and 'field co-ordination' have never been anything more than meaningless terms . . . The notion of an 'integrated approach to

development', although ritually repeated . . . has remained an empty formula.[122]

Many other attempts to streamline the United Nations system and improve its efficiency have failed to achieve their objectives; like co-ordination, they, too, have often only served to create yet more highly paid jobs for yet more international civil servants; they, too, have provided the excuse for yet more committees to be established, yet more meetings to be held and yet more reports to be issued.

An example of this process at work concerns the group of eighteen 'High-Level Intergovernmental Experts' convened in December 1985 on the orders of the General Assembly to 'review the efficiency and the administrative and financial functioning of the United Nations'. Between February and August 1986 this 'Committee of Eighteen' – as it came to be called – met sixty-seven times. The upshot was a weighty series of recommendations encapsulated in a report which ran to more than forty pages.

The report itself pulls very few punches. Phrases picked out from page ten, for example, which deals with the 'Structure of the Secretariat' include: 'reduced productivity'; 'duplication of work'; 'reduced quality of performance'; 'too top-heavy'; 'too complex'; 'too fragmented'; and 'dispersion of responsibility'.[123] The overall tone of the document is pejorative and some of its recommendations are undoubtedly sound, amongst them:

A vacant post should not be filled merely because it becomes vacant . . . The total entitlements (salaries and other conditions of service) of staff members have reached a level which gives reason for serious concern and should be reduced . . . The number of conferences and meetings can be significantly reduced and their duration shortened without affecting the substantive work of the Organisation . . . United Nations offices are at present established at the same location in many cities and countries. In most cases they may be consolidated with no loss of efficiency and with resulting economies both in personnel and general costs . . . A substantial reduction in the number of staff members at all levels, but particularly in the higher echelons, is desirable . . . To this end the overall number of regular budget posts should be reduced by 15 per cent within a period of three years and the number of regular budget posts at the level of Under Secretary General and Assistant Secretary General should be reduced by 25 per cent within a period of three years or less.[124]

Other noteworthy recommendations made by the Committee include: a halt on the construction of new conference facilities (a clear reference to the proposed $73 million conference centre in Addis Ababa that had sparked off the Kassebaum Amendment to the US Foreign Relations Authorisation Act in 1985); a suggestion that the contingency fund in the regular budget of the United Nations (used for meeting 'emergency' expenditures) should be capped at 2 per cent of the total; and a proposal to cut down on the number of committees and 'intergovernmental bodies' since it is evident that the proliferation of these within the international civil service has 'resulted in duplication of agendas and work'.[125]

Despite the uncharacteristically to the point and 'no-nonsense' tone adopted throughout the report, the Committee of Eighteen firmly reinstated itself in the mainstream of at least one time-honoured UN tradition when it recommended that the actual work of cutting down on the numbers of intergovernmental bodies should be done by – believe it or not – yet *another* intergovernmental body.[126] This little hint as to the real nature of the entire exercise was borne out in the way that the United Nations responded to the majority of the Committee's other recommendations as well. After due consideration, a 'reform resolution' (No 41/213) was adopted by the General Assembly on 19 December 1986. It showed little resolve, however, and less in the way of real reforms. To take just a few examples of things that didn't happen:

- Neither the across-the-board staff-cut of 15 per cent nor the more dramatic recommendation for a 25 per cent cut in top-level Secretariat posts was accepted for implementation within three years as suggested; instead both were rather hazily redefined as 'targets' – with the added proviso that the Secretary General should be 'flexible' in taking action to avoid any 'negative impact' on programmes and on the 'structure' of the Secretariat;[127]

- The 2 per cent cap on the contingency fund in the budget was not implemented – and, by the end of December 1986, the Assembly had agreed to no less than $48 *million* in budget add-ons;[128]

- Far from halting the construction of new conference centres, the Assembly agreed that the extravagant Addis Ababa project should now be restarted. It also gave the thumbs-up to another postponed conference centre – a $44 million boondoggle in sunny Bangkok.[129]

When you subtract from the 'achievements' of the UN all the silly conferences, all the ineffectual meetings, all the inane committees and sub-committees, all the reports produced by learned groups recommending that more learned groups be convened to produce more reports, all the co-ordination mechanisms that have only complicated things further, and all the reform measures that have left things as they were – then, what remains? Specifically, what remains to justify the billions of dollars that tax-payers all over the world continue to plough into the United Nations and its agencies year in year out?

Public Relations

Huge sums of our own money are spent on efforts to convince us that a great deal remains. During the last decade, funding for the UN's Department of Public Information (DPI) has grown at twice the pace of the rest of the world body's budget.[130] This has happened for only one reason: in the 1980s, as Maurice Bertrand puts it, criticism of the UN has 'reached the status of a political phenomenon'.[131] Frightened bureaucrats have accordingly voted to strengthen the DPI so that it can better defend their privileges and their interests.

The results have occasionally verged on lunacy. In 1987, for example, the Department actually attempted to suppress screening of the television show 'Amerika' – a political fantasy in which UN peacekeeping forces police the United States at the behest of Soviet occupiers. The highly paid PR men of the DPI felt – in their wisdom – that such fiction would be bad for the 'image' of the United Nations and litigation was mounted to keep the show off the air. As the *Washington Post* commented at the time: 'It seems to have escaped the United Nations' attention – as does so much else – that the proper use of law in a democratic society is to widen the openings for speech, not to narrow them.'[132]

When it comes to presenting a positive image of the UN, however, suppression is replaced by overkill. In an average year the Department, which is headquartered in New York but has sixty-four overseas offices, will issue 12,000 press releases, send out 16,000 'information cables' lauding UN achievements, and prepare a wide range of newspaper articles, radio tapes and films.[133] It has also been known to 'buy' positive opinion in the international media: handsome subsidies to fifteen newspapers totalled $432,000 in one year.[134] In addition to this the Department produces its own brochures, leaflets and books, all of which seek to present the UN in a favourable light and are distributed worldwide – for example, *United Nations: Image and Reality*, which has a print-run of 100,000 copies in English plus separate Spanish, French, Russian, German and Japanese editions of between 5,000 and 10,000 copies in each case.[135]

All this costs a small fortune: DPI spent $75.7 million on 'information work' during 1986–7.[136] This sum, however, does not by any means represent the entire public-relations budget of the UN system – each of the specialised agencies and other organs has its own information department also busily at work producing yet more brochures, leaflets and books, all industriously blowing their own trumpet of course.

There have been a number of occasions when UN organisations have taken the drive to maintain a positive image even further and have actively 'cultivated' friendly members of the press. One British journalist, for example, a regular contributor to the influential *Guardian* newspaper, produced a series of favourable reports on UNESCO in 1985. One typical instance of his work was entitled 'Why Britain Should Keep Faith with the UNESCO Dream', and was published in the *Guardian* on 4 October 1985. This article argued strongly that the British government should maintain its financial contribution to the bloated and over-bureaucratised specialised agency. It was no doubt entirely coincidental that, at the time he wrote this campaigning piece, the journalist in question was benefiting from a lucrative private contract with UNESCO's

Office of Public Information. He subsequently – a full year later – admitted that he had neglected to mention this contract to his editor and that this had been a 'mistake'.[137]

UNESCO is not alone in its fascination with the world of information. Shortly after he took office, UNDP's new Chief Administrator William Draper advocated making 'better use of the services of journalists' and added: 'One of my first managerial rôles has been to initiate the redirection of our public information effort. We will concentrate on presenting the human face of development.'[138] Perhaps this is why, in its publication *Generation*, UNDP claims to have 'played a leading rôle' in the 'social and economic advancement of two-thirds of humanity'.[139]

Likewise in *UNICEF News* we are told: 'There is a phrase in English which has no equivalent in any other language. It is "to be kind". This phrase captures the spirit which has pervaded UNICEF through forty years.'[140]

Like cuttlefish, United Nations agencies have the ability to conceal themselves in clouds of ink.[141] A trawl through the literature produced by FAO, WHO, UNHCR and others will yield a colossal catch of self-congratulatory phrases to add to the umbrella judgement of the Department of Public Information that 'the United Nations system's various programmes and agencies have brought food, shelter, protection and medical assistance to those who most dearly need it: mothers and children in the poorest countries, refugees around the world, the victims of famine and natural disasters'.[142]

How much truth is there in such claims?

EXPENSIVE ADVICE

UNICEF, UNHCR, and the World Food Programme et al. do indeed deliver relief supplies during emergencies; the quality, timeliness and relevance of these items, however, as we have seen in Part One, often leave a great deal to be desired. Meanwhile the hundreds of 'duty stations' in the Third World and the thousands of 'development projects' and 'programmes' that also bear the UN's imprimatur are the main ingredients of its other efforts on behalf of the poor. Here, as we saw in Part Two, capital aid is hardly involved at all;[143] indeed, on close examination, the bulk of the 'long-term development work' done by the United Nations turns out to add up to little more than the provision of *advice* to developing countries on how to achieve certain specific technical objectives. Often the quality and usefulness of this advice are questionable.

At the broadest level of long- and medium-term plans, for example, UNESCO tells us that it intends to 'help member states to mobilise the financial and human resources needed for the execution of development projects'. Likewise FAO tells us that it hopes 'to assist member states in improving the food and nutritional status of their peoples'. While all this sounds helpful enough, what it boils down to in practice is two or three P-graded staff in each case sitting at headquarters and drawing up reports on the subjects mentioned – or at best organising one or two training courses for a few dozen individuals.[144] In the case of the United Nations Medium Term

Plan for the period 1984–9 a Programme of Transport Development is set out in which the world body grandiosely commits itself to: 'overcome the bottlenecks and constraints of transport and communications facing the developing countries, to identify critical issues confronting developing countries, and to foster and promote co-operation and co-ordination regarding these issues . . .' The administrative unit of the Secretariat entrusted with fulfilling all these and many other pledges, however, has only a single professional-level worker![145]

'Advice' is also the main component of assistance at project level: here it takes the form – mainly – of the provision of 'expert services'. To give a specific example, UNDP finances about 1,000 new projects each year, of which the average cost is $393,000. This does not at all mean that at each of 1,000 different locations $393,000 is reaching the poor in any edible, drinkable, wearable, plantable, or drivable form. Far from it! What is actually involved in a typical 'project' is the supply by UNDP of three or four foreign experts – each costing upwards of $100,000 per annum to keep in the field.[146]

In all of this it simply seems to be taken for granted by the UN that the experts and advisers it sends to Third World communities at the expense of Western tax-payers are not only competent and able but are also well motivated and appropriately experienced. The key questions never get asked. Are these 'guiders and managers' really equipped to render direct and useful services to the poor? Do they have sufficient humility and insight – which, presumably, are at least as important as technical know-how? Perhaps most important of all, do the poor actually *require* the kind of guidance and management that wealthy foreigners can provide? Do they really want 'to be helped to help themselves' – or any of the other familiar stock phrases of that ilk? The assumption that they do, that this is what they are asking for, does rather pre-judge the shape of the development process and set its priorities. As with so much else in the world view of the aristocracy of mercy, however, it is an assumption that is deeply flawed.

PART FOUR

THE MIDAS TOUCH

I think you aid people are like the old king. Everything you touch turns to gold and the poor shits on the receiving end can't eat gold.

Jill Tweedie, *Internal Affairs*

LONG AFTER THE EXPERTS and professionals from the United Nations or the EEC or USAID or the World Bank have packed their bags and their cute ethnic souvenirs, boarded their aircraft and fled northwards, the ill-conceived development projects that they have been responsible for continue to wreck the lives of the poor.

During the past twenty years millions of rural people in Africa, in Asia and in Latin America have been forcibly removed from their homes to make space for the expanding reservoirs of giant hydroelectric dams; like ghosts not yet laid to rest, troubled but invisible, the dispossessed *still* wander from place to place in search of recompense. In Ethiopia's Āwash Valley, Afar nomads whose traditional dry-season pasture lands have been sown with cash crops and surrounded by barbed wire are today reduced to absolute penury, their independence gone, their way of life shattered, their dignity destroyed as they queue in rags for food handouts. Brazilian Indians whose rainforests have been felled in the name of progress now face genocide; their unique knowledge and skills are about to be lost to mankind for ever. In Indonesia's 'thousand island' paradise, tribal peoples are remorselessly being extinguished and priceless ecological resources turned to ash and mud amidst the folly of the largest resettlement programme in human history . . .

For increasing numbers in the Third World, as later sections of this part will illustrate in some detail, 'development' has come to mean little more than loss, danger and alienation. Today, as a result, we are seeing the emergence of a new phenomenon – poor people who no longer want to be 'helped', who mistrust and reject the poisoned gifts thrust upon them by outsiders.

It is with the authentic conviction bred of years of sad experience that Chief Raoni of the Brazilian Xingu tribe insists: 'We want nothing from the white man. He has brought us only death, illness and murder. He has stolen our forest. He wants to destroy it all.'[1] Francisco Mendes Filho, a rubber worker and leader of a rural union in Brazil, also opposed the destruction of the rainforest before gunmen hired by the 'pro-development' lobby shot him dead on 22 December 1988: 'In places where there are supposed to be rubber trees there is now only cattle pasture,' Filho had protested shortly before he was murdered. 'Much of the Amazon basin is already turning into desert; it is only a handful of wealthy ranchers who benefit.'[2]

Meanwhile the peoples of the Cordillera Mountains in the Philippines protest at the way in which their land is used as 'a resource area for extractive industries such as mining and logging, hydroelectric dams and other projects'. Representatives of the 500,000 inhabitants of the Cordillera recently stated unequivocally: 'We oppose these programmes and policies because they threaten our very existence.'[3]

In far-off Mexico, community activist Gustavo Esteva seems to be saying almost exactly the same thing when he observes with some bitterness:

> Around us, for a long time, development has been recognised as a threat. Most peasants are aware that development has undermined their subsistence on century-old diversified crops. Slum dwellers know that it has made their skills redundant and their education inadequate for the jobs that were created. If they do succeed in installing community life in the shanties they build or in the abandoned buildings, bulldozers and the police, both at the service of development, will relocate them . . . If you live in Mexico City today you are either rich or numb if you fail to notice that development stinks.

Far from being the fulfilment of a dream of progress and prosperity, development, in Esteva's view, is a 'malignant myth':

> Development means to have started on a road that others know better, to be on your way towards a goal that others have reached, to race up a one-way street. Development means the sacrifice of environments, solidarities, traditional interpretations and customs to ever-changing expert advice. Development, for the overwhelming majority, has always meant growing dependence on guidance and management.[4]

FOREIGN EXPERTS

The increasing reliance on outsiders that Esteva sees in the Mexican 'slums, villages and boondocks' where he works is also a trend that is well established in many other countries and regions. The 'guiders and managers' to whom he refers are in fact the vanguard of the development industry – the thin end of the wedge. They have become so pervasive that Africa, for example, has more expatriates living in it today than it ever did during the era of colonisation and settlement:[5] there are an estimated 80,000 foreign 'experts' working on development projects in the world's poorest continent.[6] To this substantial total must be added the legions of short-stay visitors – agency staff on project-appraisal missions, VIPs from donor countries, consultants conducting feasibility studies, and, of course, researchers. During the 1970s, when Tanzania's *ujamaa* villages were at their most fashionable as examples of successful grassroots development, there were occasions when some villages had more researchers than villagers.[7] Much more recently the small and hungry West African country of Burkina Faso hosted no fewer than 340 separate 'missions' from United Nations agencies in a single year. According to

Maurice Williams of the World Food Council, this deluge of bureaucrats caused 'confusion at all levels and a loss of resources and efficiency . . . the government was not always able to keep up with management and co-ordination requirements'.[8]

The experts and consultants showered down upon the developing world do not, by any means, all come from developed countries. The United Nations hires on a strict quota system from all its member states. 'The result', according to Professor Paul Streeten of Boston University, 'is that a mediocre Indian, who might be useful within his competence in India, is recruited by the UN to work in Sierra Leone at ten times the salary he would earn at home, on a job for which he is ill-qualified, while a Sierra Leonean advises India.' Streeten, who himself acts as a consultant for the World Bank, adds that 'the high salaries and high living standards of these experts alienate them from the societies in which they work. They are like rootless flowers that wither away.'[9]

Every year the United Nations Development Programme sends 8,200 such experts 'into the field' to guide and manage the poor.[10] Reviewing its achievements since the mid-1960s, it boasts that it has 'financed the assignment of 193,000 experts of 164 nationalities to work in nearly every sector in 170 countries and territories'.[11] Other multilateral agencies, notably the World Bank, have similarly impressive records. Meanwhile the eighteen member states of the Development Assistance Committee of the OECD send out some 80,000 'experts, teachers and volunteers' to the Third World each year as part of their bilateral aid programmes.[12] According to informed estimates, a total of at least 150,000 'external advisers, consultants, seconded expatriates and other experts' are employed in the developing countries at any one time.[13]

The expense of hiring them and keeping them in the field eats up a surprisingly large slice of official aid budgets. Even if the minimum cost of a United Nations expert – $100,000 a year[14] – is taken as the average for bilateral and multilateral agencies as a whole, then the bottom line for 150,000 such people can be no less than $15 *billion*: that figure is in the region of *35 per cent* of all official development assistance.[15] Experts from the World Bank, however, cost significantly more than those from the UN, and one bilateral agency now budgets $150,000 per annum per expert.[16] If this higher figure is used, then 150,000 experts could cost in excess of $22 billion a year to keep in the field – nearly half of all the money allocated to official development assistance.

THANKS FOR NOTHING

Are foreign experts really worth so much? Clearly the aid agencies must think so – otherwise they would not go on spending such vast sums. But some recipients have a different perspective. Jacques Bousquet, formerly UNESCO's Chief Educational Adviser in the Ivory Coast, lists the typical complaints that he became familiar with during his stay in that West African country: experts are accused by Ivoireans of earning big salaries and even then 'always wanting more . . . they have the nerve to demand free housing and are constantly claiming extra dispensations for the cars they import and re-sell';

they make money illegally out of tax-free liquor, and smuggle antiques out of the country; they never mix with the local population: 'If you want to know what they think of us, just look at the way they treat their servants . . . basically they are racialists.'[17]

Similarly in Nepal, a country that has been described as 'over-advised and under-nourished',[18] there is a widely held view that experts and consultants are dishonest, lazy, unimaginative, insensitive to local priorities and, as a result of all this, unable to come up with useful insights and suggestions. According to one Nepalese, foreign advisers 'demonstrate a lack of commitment . . . Since most are employed by donors directly, they are always beholden to the wishes of their supervisors in capitals other than Kathmandu . . . the busiest days of those expatriates are when their bosses visit Nepal.'[19]

Even stronger feelings of resentment and dislike, however, get stirred up when foreigners are appointed to jobs that could be done by nationals of the countries concerned. Many educated and qualified Nepalese feel that their own skills, experience and motivation are better than those of any expatriate – and certainly more appropriate. They also point out that, on a rough estimate, aid agencies could hire thirty to fifty Nepalese experts with the sum of money required by just one foreign adviser.[20] Similarly, in French-speaking West Africa a professor brought in from Paris by UNESCO on a teaching assignment will be paid up to ten times as much as a local academic – even though the local man may be doing the same job and may even have the same degree from the same university as the foreigner.[21]

It is sometimes difficult to explain why such things continue to happen. That they do is by no means entirely the fault of the aid agencies. For governments in the Third World even the low cost of local staff can sometimes be too high; the ready availability of foreign experts paid for by foreign donors can thus look like a very attractive option. A programme director in one underdeveloped country found that:

> Many of the advisers assigned to ministries were purely and simply filling the posts of local employees without the government having any plan whatsoever for their eventual replacement. We discovered that, for more than 75 per cent of the posts filled by foreign technical advisers, the appropriations for recruiting their counterparts and subsequent successors had been deleted from the budget.[22]

A second reason for the hiring of expatriates is that there are some jobs which local staff refuse to do. A problem frequently encountered is that of the government employee who will not accept a field assignment because, in the project area, there is no adequate health care or schooling for his children. The job then goes to a foreign expert who can afford to have his children brought up and educated elsewhere.[23]

Another important factor is that, consciously or unconsciously, government officials in the Third World tend to favour and support the continued hiring of foreign experts for personal reasons: stated simply, foreigners can provide them with valuable 'kickbacks' of a kind that they could never hope to get from locals. According to Hari Mohan Mathur, Secretary to the government of India in the state of Rajasthan:

> Many senior officials are beholden to foreign experts for favours they can confer on them, such as a study visit abroad. This may seem to be rather a small thing, but in fact it is not. Visits abroad are highly valued in many Asian countries because the salaries of civil servants are incredibly low. Often savings from daily subsistence allowances at the UN rate on a visit lasting just one week, work out to be as much as salary would be for a month.[24]

Government preferences for foreign experts are bolstered by the practices of the aid organisations. Most bilateral agencies refuse to hire local experts, preferring to spend their money on their own nationals – even when, as one authoritative study found, this means that 'individuals with demonstrated technical failings or an inability to work well in foreign environments' are retained in the system.[25]

In the multilateral sector, recruitment according to geographical quotas as practised by the United Nations does result in the employment of large numbers of Third World personnel. Perversely, however, as Paul Streeten has observed, these people are usually given posts far from home: whether it is by accident or by design, the fact is that only 10 per cent of UN professionals work in their own country.[26]

Other multilateral agencies appear simply to mistrust local brainpower and to doubt the competence of Third World consulting firms: the European Development Fund, for example, relies on teams of foreign experts supplied by Western consultancies to design and implement 90 per cent of its projects in Africa, the Caribbean and the Pacific.[27] The World Bank – by far the largest multilateral donor – tells us frankly that it, too, leaves the design and implementation of the billions of dollars' worth of projects that it finances in the developing countries very largely to people who are foreign to those countries. It notes patronisingly that 'for some activities, such as contacts with local farmers, local staff are essential'. However: 'Only a few developing countries (such as Brazil and Mexico) have a local consulting industry capable of providing most of the wide range of services called for in project work, and many countries have hardly begun the process.' The result, frequently, is that 'only consultants from developed countries may be qualified . . . In such cases the higher price that expatriates command will be more than offset by the unique contribution they can make to the success of the project.'[28]

Exactly how unique this contribution is remains a matter of some controversy. For example, in one series of World Bank-assisted agricultural projects in Nigeria (with a total combined cost of $1.5 billion) there has been extensive use of expatriate experts – indeed, no less than *1,040 staff years* of technical assistance have been provided by the Bank and its consultants. Despite this massive use of expensive foreign skills, however, official audits of the projects concerned have shown that the results have been 'very disappoint-ing' with almost zero productivity increases.[29]

Neither is this an isolated case. An extensive survey of project aid carried out by the OECD's Development Centre concluded: 'We see very few advantages in the consistent use of foreign consultancy firms, except as a way of spending aid money.' Amongst the reasons given for this rather uncompromising statement were the following:

● Claims by Western consulting firms that they are able to make a special contribution to projects because of the wealth of field experience accumulated by their staff are more rhetorical than real. Most such firms in fact employ few permanent staff, the teams they send out are recruited only for the duration of the specific contract on which they are working and, normally, the members of these teams have *not* worked together before.

● Western consultancies are selling their skills; it is therefore not in their interests to communicate their expertise to others. As a result, even when contractually obliged to do so, the vast majority pay no regard to the enhancement of consultancy skills in recipient countries. The net effect is that these firms 'gravely inhibit the development of local capabilities'.

● Likewise, individual foreign experts employed on projects have a strong vested interest in ensuring that their local counterparts never become capable of taking over from them – since such a take-over would mean the termination of their own lucrative contracts. One device that experts use is to make themselves 'indispensable' by unnecessarily complicating and extending the tasks that they perform; in this way they can often outlast a series of counterparts.

● Foreign experts and advisers, with their high cost, may be a less effective way of spending project money than, for example, material inputs. A Western consultant heading one rural scheme complained bitterly that locally hired staff seemed to feel they had a 'right' to make use of project vehicles, and admitted that this issue was 'souring the atmosphere of co-operation'; the vehicles, he said, had been intended for the expatriate advisers only. When interviewed, however, one of the local staff had this to say: 'Improving our efficiency in the field often depends on factors quite removed from what a foreign expert can teach us. Here we don't have the petrol, spare parts or sometimes even the vehicles to go round the nearby farms as regularly as we should. A minute fraction of the salary of one single expert would have settled that problem for five or six of our administrative staff and given them more opportunity to operate effectively.'[30]

Other doubts about the so-called 'unique contribution' that foreign experts can make focus on their attitudes and on the ways in which they conduct their daily lives. For example, the fact that few of them stay long enough in any developing country to learn the languages spoken there effectively cuts them off from any real contact with large numbers of people who should matter to them a great deal – the poor. More often than not, says Hari Mohan Mathur, experts' contacts are 'confined to élite groups in the capital and major towns'.[31] Jacques Bousquet agrees with this observation and adds that experts and consultants frequently come to look on their overseas assignments more as extended tourist trips than as anything else. 'We thought they were here to help us,' the former UNESCO Educational Adviser was told by one Ivoirean, 'but not a bit of it! They want to see the country.'[32]

PACKAGED POVERTY

Development tourism, of course, is done not only by experts and consultants but also by all the other prosperous, propertied, healthy, educated and influential people who make their living from portraying, writing about, launching emotional appeals on behalf of, studying and administering the lives of those who are penniless, vagrant, diseased, illiterate and politically impotent. Bureaucrats from aid agency headquarters in Washington, New York, Paris, Geneva, Vienna or Rome, and certain breeds of academic, researcher, journalist, broadcaster and pop star, are amongst those who do very well thank you, who make their fortunes or their reputations – or both – because of the poor and the dispossessed. Together with the experts and consultants resident 'in the field', it is outsiders like these who shape the ways in which the poor are seen, define their problems, and formulate all the policies, projects and programmes intended to alleviate their poverty. Local and central government officials from the developing countries are also allowed to play a rôle – but these people are as much aliens in the universe inhabited by the poor as are the visitors from afar.

The tendency for those who are *not* poor to become mere sightseers in the world of those who *are* is one of the central problems of international development. It is at its most noticeable during famines and other catastrophes when the distinction between the haves and the have-nots of this world ceases to be merely a matter of relative wealth and poverty and becomes instead a matter of life and death. Whether we are aid workers, journalists, or priests our ability to make excursions to these places, see, smell, touch, interview and possibly feed the dying, and then return to our own comfortable homes and hotels, must surely rank amongst the most bizarre paradoxes of modern times.

At the height of the famine that took more than a million Ethiopian lives in 1984–5, it was perfectly possible during the course of a single morning to travel by light aircraft from the luxury of the Addis Ababa Hilton to the surreal horror of the relief camp at Korem where tens of thousands of gaunt and ragged people lay strewn like the casualties of some brutish medieval battle across a blasted heath. One could then take pictures, take notes, or otherwise appraise and evaluate the situation, and then fly back to Addis Ababa again in time to catch an hour of sunbathing at the side of one of the finest swimming pools in the world.

I was in Ethiopia as a journalist, but journalists were not the only foreigners queuing up to rubberneck the apocalypse. The country, although short on food, was long on relief workers and aid personnel of all kinds: every possible voluntary agency had sent people in to see if they could sniff out likely projects; FAO, UNICEF and WFP were all over the place; ICRC had several ashen-faced representatives in situ radiating appropriate amounts of gloom, doom and selfless devotion to duty; even the Secretary General of the United Nations turned up at one point to find out for himself what starving children looked like – and to be photographed doing so. By 8 a.m. each day the lobby of the Hilton would thus be crammed with bureaucrats in safari suits, some self-consciously clutching lunch boxes from the coffee shop, waiting for the minibus that would take them to the airport to catch the morning shuttle to hell.

Meanwhile celebrities and VIPs by the dozen had also appeared: Charlton Heston, Senator Edward Kennedy, Bob Geldof and Cardinal Basil Hume were just a few of the 'personalities' who came, saw and commented. There were swarms of less important visitors, too – ghoulish holidaymakers for whom the conventional East African attractions of safaris, sun, sand, sea and sex were apparently no longer enough. Typically these were young, middle-class Europeans and Americans with a few Japanese and Australians thrown in. The women wore earnest expressions, but not bras, and favoured jeans and open sandals displaying large dirty feet. The men, fresh-faced but with aggressive beards, were equally casual and equally earnest. Some had got off their Nairobi-bound planes on impulse when they stopped over at Addis Ababa and could give no good reason for wanting to visit the famine areas. Peeping Toms and disaster groupies, the truth was that they were driven by a depraved, voyeuristic urge: they wanted to 'get in touch' with poverty.

It was easy to despise them, but they were not very much more obnoxious than the rest of us on the scene. The aid agency officials who had come to Ethiopia to help (or more often to 'assess the scale of the problem'), the professional communicators who had come to inform world opinion (or more often to mislead it), and the luminaries who had come to lend their prestige (or more often to boost their own egos) were also keen to get in touch with poverty – and were just as unlikely actually to do so. We, too, in our own ways were all voyeurs; we, too, were tourists of a macabre kind.

I got to see the famine in a single-engined Cessna that had been chartered by two aid workers from Washington, DC. With us as well was a rather dour official 'minder' from the government-run Relief and Rehabilitation Commission, sent along, I believe, to make sure that we did not subvert any peasants. We must have looked, when we set off, like rather a diverse team – two Americans, one Brit, and an Ethiopian civil servant; the truth was, however, that we had a great deal in common with one another. We were, for example, all relatively affluent, we were literate, and we were city dwellers; we were also chronically well fed, as were our children; none of us had dysentery or intestinal parasites; all of us had homes and jobs to return to at the end of our mission. In short, we were as different from the starving and destitute beings we were shortly to encounter as, say, Easter is from a motor car, or next Saturday night from a hillside in Provence. We were one category of object and they – the poor – were quite another.

What followed was a package tour. We went (of course) only to places where our aircraft could land and, from there, only to other places that could be reached relatively quickly by car. When we talked to famine victims we did so through an interpreter and this had the effect of producing rather stilted exchanges – less conversations than interrogations. Mostly, however, we got our information from other aid workers, other journalists, Red Cross nurses, and from Ethiopian government officials (who showed us impressive-looking charts on the walls of their offices). We gravitated, in other words, to anyone obliging enough to speak English – to people like us, to outsiders, to the non-poor.

After a few days of this, having touched base at the port of Assab (to see food aid shipments arriving) and having wandered around the relief camps at Korem, Makalle, and Bati (to see people dying like flies), we flew back to Addis in our smart little Cessna. We were, after all, busy men with pressing appointments elsewhere. The upshot was this: I wrote my stories and, eventually, a book. My two American companions wrote their back-to-office reports and, eventually, got some sort of project started. Our Ethiopian minder returned to his desk at the RRC and, eventually, won a scholarship to study agronomy at a technical college in the United States. As for the poor – well, they stayed poor, they are still poor now, and they probably always will be.

I was profoundly moved by much that I saw in northern Ethiopia, but I cannot say that I learned a great deal there. Neither did the aid workers who were with me: they came back equally touched by sentiment and equally out of touch with poverty. Ours was a short, sharp visit, a sightseeing excursion – and absolutely nothing more than that.

Excursions like these, however, take place all the time and not just (or even mainly) during emergencies: major development projects absorbing vast sums of Western tax-payers' money and affecting the lives of billions of people in the Third World for years to come are routinely conceived, planned, supervised and appraised on the basis of visits that are equally brief, hurried and superficial. Robert Chambers of the Institute of Development Studies at Sussex University estimates that there are 'tens of thousands of cases daily' of such jaunts by aid workers, officials, experts and consultants who may differ 'widely in race, nationality, religion, profession, age, sex, language, interests, prejudices, conditioning and experience', but who, nevertheless, usually have at least three things in common: 'they come from urban areas; they want to find something out; and they are short of time'.[33]

SOMETHING FISHY

At the UN's Food and Agriculture Organisation, staff and experts paid to promote food self-sufficiency in the Third World are sometimes *so* short of time that they never visit, supervise, or assess the impact of their projects at all. In one developing country external auditors examined four projects financed by the agency, all nearing completion; at three no FAO personnel had ever been anywhere near the site.[34] A consultant who has been involved in FAO rural development schemes says frankly: 'Projects are dreamed up in two or three weeks.' Thereafter, even if there are 'huge holes in them' they are 'rarely investigated'.[35] Questioned about allegations like these, a disillusioned information officer admitted: 'After nine years in the FAO I have difficulty understanding what it does in the field.'[36]

FAO's recent sorties into fish-farming – known technically as 'aquaculture' – provide some indications of the extent of the agency's incompetence. Its efforts to develop the recognised potential of this relatively new and exciting area of food production have, from the outset, been marred by a series of stupid and expensive blunders, many of which are attributable to hubris and shoddy 'smash-and-grab' research by its own experts.

According to Douglas W. Cross, himself an experienced aquaculture consultant,[37] several fish-farms in Egypt financed and managed by FAO during the 1980s have been unmitigated disasters: to date more than $50 million has been wasted. The farms owe their existence to a single FAO expert who made a very brief field visit and then proposed the establishment in the delta region 'of deepwater ponds rearing several species of fish'.

The idea, which suggested that large-scale units might achieve 'astounding yields', looked good on paper and was taken up enthusiastically by the giant UN agency and by the Egyptian Ministry of Agriculture. What was not realised at the time – because nobody bothered to find out – was that the soil of the delta region is totally unsuitable for building almost any sort of fish-pond structures. As Cross explains: 'Whilst it seems to be strong and stable when dry, it is composed of a sodium montmorillonite clay which, when wet, absorbs up to 110 per cent of its volume of water, turns to a slurry and collapses completely.'

Proper field studies would have identified these soil characteristics. No such studies were done, however, with consequences that have since become painfully apparent. At the FAO farm at El Zawiyah, for example, Cross recently found that:

> Huge ponds had been built with banks two metres high and ten metres or more thick. Only half held water, no more than one metre deep, and their banks were collapsing and eroding at rates of two or three metres a year. At harvest time the loose unstable soil formed a liquid mud which smothered the fry before they could be moved into growing ponds . . .
> Despite overwhelming evidence to the contrary the FAO official responsible for running the farm stated that he still believed an engineering solution would be found to the problem.

Meanwhile, not far away, a group of 'un-aided' smallholders who had established their own much less ambitious ponds in the wetlands of the Lake

Manzalah area were in no need of any expensive high-tech 'solutions'; far from having problems they were successfully harvesting 27,000 tonnes of fish annually at no cost to Western tax-payers. When Cross suggested that FAO and the Ministry of Agriculture might learn something from these farmers, he was told by one official: 'Do not waste your time talking to people like that. They are uneducated. They know nothing.'

This description, however, would seem to apply better to FAO itself. In the southern African country of Malawi, at Kasinthula, the agency has financed another aquaculture project, the centrepiece of which is a demonstration fish-farm – unfortunately located next to a bird sanctuary. As a result, says Cross:

> the ponds support an astonishingly large population of fish-eating birds ranging from small kingfishers to a flock of fish eagles. There have been wonderfully involved quarrels between the sanctuary's bird warden and fish-farm staff when the latter attempted to control some of the worst excesses of the birds in their efforts to clear the ponds of fish before the men could harvest them . . . A less appropriate site for a fish-farm would be hard to find.

FAO now receives over 200 applications per week from fisheries and aquaculture specialists keen to register as highly paid consultants. In Cross's experienced judgement, the applicants – many of whom eventually get contracts – are typically:

> highly qualified but relatively inexperienced graduates, claiming to be at the leading edge of specialisations such as induced breeding and sex control, nutrition, vaccine application and complex recycling technology. All these have their place in the development of aquaculture, but mainly in the devising of luxury products for the richer nations. Aquaculture in the developing countries does not call for such exotic skills. They are irrelevant to the needs of poor people who simply want to gain a little more control over their lives without at the same time increasing their risks. Consultants who are appointed purely because of their impressive academic and technical qualifications are in fact often a menace to the societies in which they yearn to demonstrate their knowledge.

FAO is not alone in taking on consultants like these and then inflicting the silly projects that they dream up on the poor of the Third World. USAID's excursions into aquaculture are also frequently characterised by poor planning and an over-reliance on inappropriate technology. One fish-farm financed by the American agency at San in the baking-hot West African country of Mali was designed on the assumption that it could be kept filled from a nearby irrigation canal. Not so, however! AID's consultant knew a great deal about fish but failed to acquaint himself with the elementary fact that the canal only contains water for five months a year; since the ponds must be kept full during the other seven months as well an expensive diesel-powered pump now has to be used in the dry season to bring water from more than two kilometres away.

A second equally serious problem afflicts USAID's Mali venture: no suitable fish-food is available locally. The result, as Cross explains, is that 'feeds have to be bought in – this in a country which faces desperate problems even feeding its own people'. To add insult to injury, the quantity of fish produced by the farm is extremely low; if account is taken of the value of all the inputs, then the actual cost of the farm's fish works out at roughly $4,000 *per kilo*!

DON'T ASK THE POOR

Mistakes like these are inevitable, however, in a big agency that often appears neither to have the time to talk to poor people nor the humility to tap their local knowledge – of dry seasons, for example. In one recent and unfortunately typical USAID mission, a senior official based in the Indonesian capital of Jakarta went 'up country' – supposedly to learn about a project for mothers of malnourished children in a remote rural area. On arrival the visitor was greeted by a large group of mums and kids. They had dressed in their best clothes and had prepared, in the words of one observer, 'a big table groaning with food . . . they were poor, but they wanted to honour this guy'. The USAID man, however, refused to leave the protection of his vehicle and insisted that 'under no circumstances' would he eat with 'such people'. Asked by a junior colleague if he would at least take a cup of tea he again refused and suggested: 'You could tell them that the important American was just too busy.' All in all, although three full days were spent driving out to the project and then driving back to Jakarta, less than half an hour was spent at the project site itself and none of the beneficiaries were talked to.[38]

Such a scale of priorities would raise few eyebrows at Britain's Overseas Development Administration which allows many of its projects in the Third World to be ruined because it is 'too busy' to talk to local people. Examples include the Victoria Dam on Sri Lanka's Mahaweli River where auditors found that 30,000 people were resettled with undue haste and in an unsatisfactory manner as a result of lack of advance planning and inadequate consultation. In Nepal a rural access road supposedly designed to alleviate poverty in fact made the poor worse off because it stimulated urban development and allowed government bureaucracy to expand in the area.[39] In Belize the upgrading of the Northern Highway entirely overlooked the danger that increased traffic and increased speeds would pose for villagers living near the road. In consequence, several young children were killed and maimed within a few months of completion of works; local people then rightly insisted on the installation of speed bumps to slow down traffic. 'These', as the auditors note, 'have reduced the economic benefits of the road'.[40] Indifference to 'social factors' has been identified in so many other ODA projects that it seems to be almost standard operating procedure to ignore the wishes, the opinions and the possible contributions of the poor.[41]

The same is true at the World Bank which, after more than forty years' experience in the field, is only prepared to admit that *in certain circumstances* 'active involvement of the intended beneficiaries *may* improve the prospects of a project'.[42]

The Bank, which puts more money into more schemes in more developing countries than any other institution, claims that 'it seeks to meet the needs of the poorest people';[43] at no stage in what it refers to as 'the project cycle', however, does it actually take the time to ask the poor themselves how they perceive their needs; neither does it canvass their views on how they feel these needs might best be met. Indeed, from the identification of a possible Bank project right through to its *ex post* evaluation, the poor are entirely left out of the decision-making process – almost as though they did not exist. As a Senegalese peasant commented after one mission of high-powered development experts had made a cursory tour of his village: 'They do not know that there are living people here.'[44]

To explain arrogant behaviour like this, it is not necessary to produce psychological profiles of the high-flying economics graduates who make up almost 70 per cent of the Bank's professional staff.[45] The simple truth is that borrowing is done by governments and it is therefore to government officials that the Bank talks in the main. The only other people whose views seem to matter are foreigners: United Nations experts, for example, or the representatives of large private corporations.

The World Bank's own description of the project cycle makes all this quite clear. In the beginning, we are told: 'Governments propose projects for financing . . . Sometimes a Bank mission supervising an earlier project will suggest a new project . . . Some projects may be suggested through the work of UN agencies. Some are brought forward by private sponsors, such as mining enterprises seeking to develop new resources.'[46]

Once a project has been *identified* in this way, it has to be *prepared*. 'The borrower' does this, helped of course by 'Bank staff, UN agency personnel, and outside consultants' who 'frequently play a major rôle' in designing the technical, managerial, economic and financial dimensions.[47]

Next comes *appraisal*, which is 'solely the Bank's responsibility . . . The appraisal includes a visit by a team of Bank experts to the country, typically lasting from three to five weeks.'[48] If all is well, the project will then be *approved* subject to the signing of a binding loan-agreement between the borrowing government and the Bank.[49] Thereafter, from time to time, *supervision* missions will pop out from Washington to 'ensure that funds are spent in the manner agreed on', and 'that the project achieves the objectives for which the loan was made'.[50]

What is conspicuously absent from all this is any requirement, or opportunity, for professionals and experts to undertake in-depth field investigations amongst the poor who live around the project site – let alone to tap these people's local knowledge or to encourage them to participate in the project itself.[51] As the Bank's own Operations Evaluation Department admitted in 1988 in a disturbing review of experience since 1965: 'The principles guiding beneficiary participation in Bank-financed projects have been quite abstract and of limited operational impact. Beneficiaries were not assigned a rôle in the decision-making process, nor was their technological knowledge sought prior to designing project components.'[52]

This is so in large part because the Bank has elevated the technique of the 'brief rural visit' to the status of a fine art. During the 'three to five weeks' that the appraisal mission spends in the borrowing country, for example, staff have a strict and rather limited working brief which ensures in practice that they will pass most of their time in the best hotel in the capital city studying documents.[53] When they venture out they will do so mainly in limousines which will whisk them in air-conditioned luxury to meetings with their counterparts in various government ministries. A 'field trip' will of course be made at some point but, typically, will not involve leaving the capital for more than two or three days. During this period the experts will stay in a government guest house or other similar facility close to the project site; there they will study more documents and hold meetings with local officials, district commissioners and the like. What they will *not* do is conduct extensive interviews with the poor; even if there were time for this, which there is not, few staff would have the experience to do it properly and less would have the inclination: 'going on missions to prepare and supervise projects was looked upon by most as a trial,' recalls Catherine Watson, a former Bank official.[54]

A fairly precise picture of the hectic pace at which missions operate can be gleaned from *ex post* audits done by the Bank's Operations Evaluation Department. Such audits normally result from a 'desk review of all materials pertaining to the project'[55] and thus maintain the Bank tradition of not talking to the poor; they do, however, reveal a good deal about the way in which staff continually substitute third-rate development tourism for proper fieldwork.

In Guatemala, for example, one typical agricultural project received an impressive total of sixteen missions at various stages of appraisal and supervision. However: 'Fifteen different experts . . . were involved. Ten of them visited the project once; another three of them only twice. The "burden" of continuity was provided by two experts who paid three and five visits respectively. In seven cases none of the supervision staff had visited the project before.' Only in five cases had one of the supervisors been on the previous mission. 'Thus, field supervision was fragmented, staff continuity very low.'[56]

In another audit of a group of agricultural projects in five Latin American countries, the Operations Evaluation Department notes its impression of work being done

> in haste by individuals with heavy travel schedules, few of them able to pay more than one or two visits on any series of projects to any single country . . . only one out of every four individuals made more than one mission on any one series of projects, and only one out of seven made more than two . . . fifty-three out of the seventy-three individuals never got back on a subsequent mission to look at the programmes.[57]

This kind of dilettante approach can lead to glaring errors and oversights. In Sri Lanka, for instance, inadequate appraisal of an agricultural scheme, and total lack of contact with (or knowledge of) the beneficiary population, resulted in 'a faulty project design which dispersed Tamil settlers amongst Sinhalese villages'. Given the ethnic tensions in Sri Lanka at the time – amounting virtually to a state of civil war between Tamils and Sinhalese – this was foolish in the extreme.[58] Meanwhile, in Mexico, no fewer than *nine* successive Bank missions failed to do anything to remedy a basic technical fault at one Mexican irrigation scheme which was suffering from a leaking reservoir. Each mission noted the puzzling fact that the reservoir was empty when it should have been full but made no investigation of the problem – on the assumption that the next mission would handle this irksome task. 'The Bank concentrated its supervision efforts almost entirely on enforcing the covenants on agricultural services and water charges,' notes the internal audit. As a result, 'the main problem confronting the project' was ignored.[59]

Not all supervision is done by such short-stay missions. Although 80 per cent of the Bank's 6,000 staff are based at headquarters in Washington[60] the remainder are posted in the Third World. Bangladesh, Benin, Bolivia, Burkina Faso, Burundi, Cameroon and Colombia all have the benefit of a permanent Bank office, as do Ethiopia, Ghana, India, Indonesia, Ivory Coast, Kenya, Madagascar, Mali, Nepal, Niger, Nigeria, Pakistan, Peru, Rwanda, Saudi Arabia, Senegal, Somalia, Sri Lanka, Sudan, Tanzania, Thailand, Togo, Uganda, Zaïre and Zambia.[61] Whether these offices are able to contribute a great deal more than visiting missions is, however, open to doubt: a recent confidential evaluation of 116 projects found that the Bank constantly rotated its overseas staff with the result that few officers were able to acquire in-depth expertise in any one country or region. Furthermore, there was 'no provision for systematic country orientation . . . sometimes not even an appropriate reading list'.[62]

There would probably be little demand for such facilities, even if they were available. As Catherine Watson observes, staff actively resist foreign appointments, which 'are spoken of as a term of exile in an uncomfortable place'.[63] This perhaps explains why those who do have the misfortune to end up living overseas endeavour to make themselves as comfortable as possible while they are there. All permanent offices are in the capital cities of the countries in which they are located, usually in the plushest business districts. Staff residences, too, are to be found in the very best areas, as far away from the poor as it is physically possible to get, and sometimes designed to cut off all contact with them. In Nairobi, Kenya, for example, the Bank has its own exclusive compound with a barbed-wire perimeter guarded by furious attack dogs; burglar alarms in every house are connected to all the others and there is a hot-line to a security company that can send in teams of uniformed men armed with cudgels in the event of a break-in.

Such a siege mentality can hardly be conducive to feelings of trust and understanding between the World Bank and the ordinary people who its projects are supposed to serve. Rather, it seems to suggest that there is a great gulf fixed between the 'developers' and those they have come to develop: on the one side rich men in their castles; on the other paupers and peasants at the gate. After several decades of such élitism 'it is not surprising', says one observer, that in many countries the poor now see development 'as an alien process, something done to them and a waste of effort'.[64]

An Eerie Philosophy

The World Bank shares this view to some extent. Although, of course, it does not regard what it does as a waste of effort, it certainly no longer defines development as something that is done *for* poor people (let alone *by* them or even with their consent); on the contrary, the tendency is to treat the poor as cogs in a wheel that is rolling towards some greater end.

Projects aimed at alleviating malnutrition, for example, are not seen by the Bank as being intrinsically worthwhile; they are justified because: 'A reduction in mortality generates a value to society equivalent to the discounted value of the future production of each individual saved.'[65] In other words, the function of human life is to produce; people should have enough to eat so that production can continue to grow.

The Bank spells this slightly eerie philosophy out more clearly in its important policy study *Poverty and Hunger*. Subtitled *Issues and Options for Food Security in Developing Countries*, this remarkable document tells us that:

> Food security has to do with access by all people at all times to enough food for an active and healthy life. Available data suggest that more than 700 million people in the developing world lack the food necessary for such a life. No problem of underdevelopment may be more serious than or have such important implications for *the long-term growth* of low-income countries. Attempting to ensure food security can be seen as an *investment in human capital* that will make for a *more productive society*. A properly fed, healthy, active and alert population *contributes more effectively to economic development* than one which is physically and mentally weakened by inadequate diet and poor health.[66]

In the arse-about-face logic of the bureaucrats who write such chilling memoranda, human beings are reduced to capital instruments – to mere means of production. Like lathes, or electric turbines, or smelting plants, their output – and thus their 'contribution to economic development' – will be greater if they are properly fuelled and oiled. This is what the World Bank actually means when it talks about 'investing in human capital'.

Once this point is reached, once abstract concepts like economic growth have been shamelessly reified, it does not take a very great step to put the cart before the horse completely and start seeing some human beings with their silly hopes and aspirations as *obstacles* to the 'development' process. This was certainly the opinion of the Bank consultant in Korea who concluded that that country's export-led growth was '*threatened* by the improvement in the income-share of the workers' that had recently taken place, and advised the government 'to prevent any further rise in wages'.[67]

The obstinate poor may, at times, have to be treated even more harshly than this. In Africa, for example, the Bank is engaged in a messianic campaign for 'structural adjustment' and notes with pleasure that: 'There are definite signs of greater willingness of African governments to consider policy reforms.'[68] Since these reforms involve, inter alia, cuts in public expenditure on 'aspects of education and health' and cuts in subsidies for basic food items, it is inevitable that the most vulnerable sections of the population will suffer – as the Bank admits: 'The urban poor have lost out through higher food prices and deteriorating services,' it tells us, while 'rural dwellers in areas of low potential' have also 'not benefited'. Such people may even *object* to the development that is going on around them and passing them by. This, however, should not be allowed to slow down tough reforms that are taking place in the name of increased productivity and efficiency. Indeed, the Bank defines the main function of external aid as helping to ensure that governments 'sustain reforms against the opposition of those who are adversely affected'.[69]

The policy document in which these remarks are to be found is described as a 'Joint Programme of Action' – joint in the sense that the Bank wants others to participate with it in implementing its agenda for Africa. 'We are keen to join,' it says, 'with the United Nations and its agencies, with the European Community, with the African Development Bank, with the Economic Commission for Africa, and with other international and national organisations to assist the countries in sub-Saharan Africa in their development efforts.'[70]

What this means in plain English is that a gang of vainglorious economists and bureaucrats in Washington who have never in their lives had any direct experience of poverty want to pull donors together so that they can effectively control all aid-flows to the world's poorest continent; once they have done that they will be in a strong position to cow recalcitrant governments and prevent them from playing one donor off against another; they will also be able to support those governments which are willing to 'reform' by bearing some of the economic and political costs of the necessary repression.[71]

That such an approach can in any way be described as 'developmental' without provoking howls of outrage and derision is a tribute to the enormous influence that the Bank has had on the thinking and behaviour of other aid institutions – most of which have *already* 'joined' with it on numerous occasions not only in Africa but also in every other region of the Third World. The global lender undertakes extensive co-financing with virtually all the main bilateral and multilateral agencies and frequently selects, defines, appraises and supervises projects on their behalf. It has forged close and continuing relationships with key United Nations organisations (notably FAO, WHO, UNIDO, UNESCO and UNDP). In addition its vast resources make it a powerhouse of research. Statistics, position papers like those that I have referred to above, and country reports emanating from Bank headquarters in Washington are drawn upon extensively by the rest of the donor community and play an important rôle in shaping the development process and defining the place of the poor within it.[72]

Increasingly this is a marginal place – not because there is a cruel conspiracy astir but, rather, because the Bank and other aid donors see the poor only dimly. Such selective myopia is the inevitable by-product of a philosophy in which economic growth is treated as an end in itself rather than as a means to an end. That same philosophy, however, can only remain unchallenged – and maintain its intellectual credibility – because of work methods that blur perceptions of the human casualties of 'development'. The brief rural visit, the hurried appraisal, the absence of proper fieldwork, and the unshakeable conviction that 'we' know what is best for 'them' are all factors which have important implications for the kinds of project that eventually get handed down to the poor. A great many of these projects are abject failures. Some are irrelevant and help nobody. Others are harmful: in the name of development they trample vulnerable people underfoot and, frequently, do irreparable damage to the environment.

In India, for example, on the borders of the states of Madhya Pradesh and Uttar Pradesh, the Singrauli Power and Coal Mining Complex has received almost a billion dollars in World Bank funding since 1977 – the most recent loan being for $250 million. Here, because of 'development', 300,000 poor rural people have been subjected to frequent forced relocations as new mines and power-stations have opened. Some families have been obliged to move as many as five times; today, unable to put roots down anywhere, they are utterly destitute.[73]

This scandal was recently the subject of emotional testimony heard in the US Senate by the House Subcommittee on International Development Institutions and Finance. According to Bruce Rich, Senior Attorney with the Environmental Defense Fund:

> The management of the Bank-financed power plant and coal-mine is gravely deficient. The cooling channel for the power plant has never functioned properly and 60 per cent of the water flows out through a rupture in its walls, periodically flooding the land of an adjacent village; human settlements exist right on the edge of the plant's ash dumps; overburden from the coal-mine is actually being dumped on the grazing land of a tribal village, menacing the houses of the inhabitants – who refuse to leave because the Bank-financed coal company will not offer them compensation.

In all directions around Singrauli, as far as the eye can see:

> the land has been totally destroyed and resembles scenes out of the lower circles of Dante's inferno. Enormous amounts of dust and air and water pollution of every conceivable sort have created tremendous public health problems. Tuberculosis is rampant, potable water supplies have been destroyed, and chloroquine-resistant malaria afflicts the area.

Once-prosperous villages and hamlets have been replaced by 'unspeakable hovels and shacks on the edges of the huge infrastructure projects . . . Some people are living *inside* the open pit mines.' Furthermore, over 70,000 previously self-sufficient peasant farmers – deprived of all other possible sources of income – now have no choice but to accept the indignity of intermittent employment at Singrauli for salaries of around 70 cents a day: below survival level even in India.[74]

VICTIMS OF DEVELOPMENT

In the name of progress, lives have been destroyed in virtually every country of the Third World. In Brazil a massive 'colonisation' and resettlement scheme known as 'Polonoroeste' has transformed many poor people into refugees in their own land and stands out as being particularly callous and ill-conceived. The project, which by 1985 had attracted loan commitments totalling $434.3 million from the World Bank, has subsequently been the subject of consider-able public controversy, despite determined efforts to hush things up.[75]

Brazil is a country in which a wealthy few – just 1 per cent of the population – own 48 per cent of all arable land; it is also a country where at least 2.5 million people are landless and where an estimated 1,000 children die every day from hunger-related causes.[76] As a development project, it seems that the main function of Polonoroeste has been to provide a safety-valve for the political and social pressures that such stark contrasts generate by the simple expedient of moving the poor. Holding out the tantalising prospect of free land and a 'new start' amidst the dense-canopy rainforests of the north-west, the scheme has persuaded hundreds of thousands of needy people to migrate from central and southern provinces and to relocate themselves as farmers in the Amazon basin – where, conveniently, they are out of sight of their more prosperous compatriots.

The World Bank's backing for this project between 1982 and 1985 was crucial to the very rapid progress that it made in that period and contributed directly to what is now recognised – even by the Bank itself – as 'an ecological, human and economic disaster of tremendous dimensions'.[77] It was $250 million of the Bank's money that paid for the speedy paving of Highway BR-364 which runs into the heart of the north-western province of Rondônia. All the settlers travel along this road on their way to farms that they will slash and burn out of the jungle. The highway has also encouraged rapid commercial penetration of the region by mining and logging companies and by cattle ranchers.

The consequences of this combined onslaught have been devastating. Already 4 per cent deforested in 1982, Rondônia was 11 per cent deforested by 1985. Since then NASA space surveys show that the area of deforestation has doubled approximately every two years; if the destruction continues at this pace, then less than 20 per cent of the province's unique jungles will remain by the turn of the century.[78] Neighbouring Mato Grosso (the name means 'thick forest') had lost only 3,900 square miles of its 310,000 square miles of virgin forest in 1975. By 1987, however, almost all of the jungle was gone. In that year satellite photographs showed 6,000 forest fires burning across the entire Amazon basin – every one of them started deliberately by land-clearers. Many of the fires were burning close to Highway BR-364.[79]

Such developments have created deep concern amongst environmentalists. Rainforests like those in Rondônia and Mato Grosso today occupy only 7 per cent of the earth's surface but are thought to be home to 80 per cent of plant and animal species. More important, they play a crucial rôle in the maintenance of *all* life on earth. One probable consequence of continued wholesale clearances will be an acceleration of the 'greenhouse effect' – the name given to the process whereby carbon dioxide, no longer being absorbed by trees, builds up in the atmosphere and causes global temperatures to rise.[80] Brazil contains one-third of all tropical rainforests and now has the dubious distinction of destroying more of this precious and irreplaceable resource than any other country in the world: over 3.6 million acres are felled each year.[81]

Polonoroeste has made its own significant contribution to such short-sighted desecration. The project, however, is seriously flawed not just because of its dire ecological implications but also because of the violence that has been visited upon those indigenous Indian peoples of Rondônia who have attempted to resist the incursions of outsiders. Some tribes have been virtually wiped out; others, herded into insanitary reservations, have been decimated by malnutrition and by diseases – like measles – that are new to them.[82]

In 1985, as a result of a well-organised international campaign mounted by environmental and human rights groups, the World Bank was forced to impose a temporary halt on payments of the undisbursed balance of its Polonoroeste loans; the flow of funds was only renewed after the Brazilian government had given guarantees that the environment, and the rights of tribal peoples in Rondônia, would in future be respected.

Although these guarantees have, by and large, been honoured, there is a limit to what the government can do now that the Pandora's Box of development has been opened in the Amazon. The settlers, who continue to pour into the north-west at the rate of 13,000 a month,[83] come because of land hunger. The cruel reality, however, is that the land they receive is wholly unsuitable for agriculture of any sustained kind. Within two to five years at most, soils that have previously been covered by tropical rainforest cease to be able to support enough food crops to provide even basic subsistence to smallholders, let alone a saleable surplus. The typical characteristic of such soils is that they have been leached of their nutrients by thousands of years of heavy precipitation and high temperatures. No problems occur while they are still forested and while vitality is preserved by the complex inter-relationships of above-ground plant and animal life. After logging and burning, however, the newly created fields become ever more barren and useless with each season.[84]

The smallholdings of many settlers in Rondônia have already failed and tens of thousands are now pressing on into the neighbouring province of Acre; there the cycle of deforestation and destruction to no useful end is being repeated.[85]

Life for almost all the migrants has proved to be infinitely worse than before they were persuaded to begin the trek to the Amazon. Their prospects for supporting themselves are virtually zero and, in addition, more than 200,000 are estimated to have contracted a particularly virulent strain of malaria, endemic in the north-west, to which they have no resistance.[86]

It is fair to say that, today, under the watchful eye of international environmental groups, the World Bank is making considerable efforts to promote measures and actions to mitigate the deforestation and human suffering caused by the earlier stages of the Polonoroeste project.[87] Surprisingly, however, it seems bent on repeating elsewhere the same mistakes that it made in Brazil.

A FINAL SOLUTION FOR THE POOR?

In Indonesia, the world's largest-ever exercise in human resettlement is currently under way – an exercise that is similar in many respects to Polonoroeste and that has attracted multi-million-dollar backing from the Bank. Known as the 'transmigration programme', it is transferring peasant farmers from overcrowded Java to the more thinly populated outlying islands of the vast archipelago. At least six million people have already been moved,[88] and several million more are scheduled for relocation by 1994.[89]

The Bank first became involved in 1976. By 1986 it had committed no less than *$600 million* directly to support the transmigration programme – some 20 per cent of all its lending to Indonesian agriculture during this decade. In addition, a further $680 million has been committed to the linked Nucleus Estate and Smallholder scheme – a long-term project which is settling some 95,000 families of whom about one quarter are transmigrants.[90] USAID, the government of the Netherlands, the government of France and the government of the Federal Republic of Germany have also been generous in providing funds and technical assistance for resettlement, as have the EEC, UNDP, FAO, the World Food Programme and Catholic Relief Services[91]

Such unquibbling backing from so large and respectable a group of Western bilateral, multilateral and voluntary agencies is difficult to explain or understand – particularly in the context of the experience of Polonoroeste which illustrated most starkly the dangers of resettlement in rainforest areas. Like Polonoroeste, furthermore, transmigration in Indonesia has entailed a breathtaking combination of human rights abuses, environmental destruction and bad development. To give some examples:

- Land rights enjoyed under traditional law by the tribal people on outlying islands like Irian Jaya, Sulawesi and Kalimantan have been subordinated to transmigration. The relevant clause in Indonesian government legislation reads as follows: 'The rights of traditional-law communities may not be allowed to stand in the way of the establishment of transmigration sites.'[92]

- Transmigration to the island of Irian Jaya has fuelled a growing conflict between the Indonesian armed forces and nationalist Irianese. According to Marcus Colchester of Survival International: 'Local resistance to the takeover of traditional lands has been met with brutal violence by the Indonesian military.' Indeed, the violence has been so extreme that more than 20,000 Irianese have so far fled their homes and sought refuge in neighbouring Papua New Guinea.[93]

The World Bank seems unconcerned: its principal internal policy document on transmigration states unequivocally that 'well-planned settlement . . . must be encouraged' in Irian Jaya.[94] The document adds that there is a clear need for the Indonesian government to be 'sensitised to the rights of isolated and unassimilated people'. What we are not told, however, is how this is to be achieved[95] – nor does it seem likely that it will be an easy task: Irianese refugees report that their villages have been bombed by the Indonesian air force, that their settlements have been burned by the military, that women have been raped, that livestock have been killed or driven off, and that numbers of people have been indiscriminately shot while others have been imprisoned and tortured.[96]

- Meanwhile, the Indonesian government continues to implement a policy of 'sedentarising' and 'assimilating' into the mainstream all of Indonesia's tribal peoples. According to the Minister of Transmigration: 'The different ethnic groups' of Indonesia 'will in the long run disappear . . . and there will be one kind of man'.[97]

This rather chilling objective has been described by one Australian critic as 'the Javanese version of Nazi Germany's *lebensraum*'.[98] To achieve it, Indonesian government plans call for Irian Jaya's entire indigenous population of 800,000 tribal people to be moved – forcibly if necessary – from their traditional homesteads and villages and into resettlement sites on the island by 1998; this programme of 'internal transmigration' is being carried out at the rate of approximately 13,000 families per year.[99]

'Apart from causing severe conflicts over land rights,' says Marcus Colchester, internal transmigration – which is also taking place on several other islands – 'has proved socially and economically catastrophic for the tribal communities involved. Many communities have faced the double indignity of having their lands taken over for the creation of transmigration sites and then of being forcibly resettled back on their own lands where they find themselves a minority, despised for their "primitive" customs such as eating sago and pigs.'[100]

- According to a report presented to the United Nations by the London-based Anti-Slavery Society, at least one supposedly vacant island given to migrants was actually already inhabited; the Indonesian army cleared land for the settlers by burning the indigenous people's crops.[101]

- East Timor – seized by the Indonesian army in 1975 – has since been the target of considerable resettlement from Java. An estimated 150,000 of the 700,000 indigenous inhabitants of East Timor have been killed in the subsequent fighting, or have died of hunger.[102]

- In addition to the human damage that it has done, the resettlement programme has also been responsible for much destructive clearing of Indonesia's unique and extensive tropical rainforest. This forest, as the World Bank tells us in its own policy document on transmigration, 'is one of the most biologically diverse areas in the world and has more than 500 species of mammals, 1,500 species of birds, and a botanical diversity which includes 10,000 species of trees. For this reason, Indonesia's forests and wildlife are a matter of international interest, and Indonesia's stewardship of them a matter of utmost importance.'[103]

In the light of this remark the Bank's continued support for the transmigration programme seems grotesque. An authoritative survey recently carried out by the Indonesian government's own Forestry Department (jointly with the Washington-based International Institute for Environment and Development) concludes that transmigration is 'the single sectoral activity with the greatest potential to advance forest destruction [and] can only have negative implications for forest resources'.[104] Sulawesi and Sumatra – both major focuses of transmigration – have suffered particularly badly. On the latter, 2.3 million hectares of land formerly under canopy forest are today defined as 'critical' – i.e. so degraded that they are unable to sustain even subsistence agriculture or to fulfil normal soil functions such as absorbing water. More than 30 per cent of Sulawesi has been reduced to this same 'critical' state as a result of transmigration.[105] Over Indonesia as a whole, current plans envisage the destruction of a great many more millions of hectares of irreplaceable rainforest to make way for resettlement sites.[106]

Despite these and other profoundly negative aspects of transmigration in Indonesia, the long-term involvement of the World Bank and other donors would perhaps be comprehensible if the programme were achieving its own stated objectives – i.e. if it were greatly improving the quality of migrants' lives or, at the very least, making them less poor than they were before they left their original homes. Tragically, however, this is not the case.

A principal reason why – as aid agencies acquainted with Polonoroeste could not have failed to realise from the outset – is that the soils of new settlements that have been hacked and cleared out of rainforest cannot support sustained agriculture. The result, observes United States Republican Senator Robert Kasten – who has strongly opposed American financial support for transmigration – is that the migrants, after a few short years, 'are left with little choice but to move back to the cities, or to begin illegal logging and slash-and-burn farming, which destroys even more forest lands'.[107]

The move back to the cities is already well advanced. There are documented cases of migrant families attempting to sell their children in order to raise the money to pay for a return to Java.[108] Meanwhile, on Irian Jaya alone, more than 7,000 settlers are known to have abandoned transmigration sites and to have flocked to towns such as Jayapura and Sorong in search of urban employment – which is often not available. Prostitution and the spread of venereal disease are growing social problems which have been directly linked to the failure of transmigration to provide a sustainable economic base for settlers.[109] Nationwide some 300,000 people are now estimated to be living in 'economically marginal and deteriorating transmigration settlements' and are recognised by the Indonesian government itself as 'a potential source of serious political and social unrest in the future'.[110]

These 300,000, however, are probably just the visible tip of a much larger iceberg of settlers who have found their farms disappointingly unproductive. 'Dumped on deforested land without tools, without a community,' in the words of one former aid worker, 'the migrants have been unable to make a go of it.'[111] As a result they are presently obliged to rely on 'off-farm' work for up to 80 per cent of their incomes[112] – a precarious state of affairs since, as the World Bank admits, these off-farm earnings will fall when 'wage-income associated with site development ceases'.[113] The Bank also notes the probability that any further 'slowdown in government investment in receiving areas . . . could result in declining migrant incomes and employment opportunities'.[114]

The cumulative effect of factors like these – in a period that has indeed seen reduced spending by the Indonesian government – has been considerable. Despite all the emotional cost, stress and upheaval of leaving their homelands, by far the majority of the migrants have *not* had their dreams for a better life or their aspirations for higher incomes fulfilled. On the contrary, as the Bank makes clear in its confidential *Transmigration Sector Review*: 'Migrant incomes in the settlement areas are, on average, slightly lower than those in rural Java and significantly lower than those in the rural outer islands.'[115] Worryingly, the lowest incomes are not found amongst the least experienced settlers on the newest sites – which might be expected – but, rather, in places where migrants have been settled for six years or more.[116]

Because of such disturbing findings, and also in a long-overdue response to protests from environmentalists and human rights groups, some Western donors have reassessed the scope and nature of their involvement in the transmigration programme. Since 1987, for example, the World Bank has been claiming that it is no longer *directly* financing the movement of people: its money is going instead into planning and preparing the sites to which settlers will be moved and into upgrading existing sites. A case in point is the Transmigration Second Stage Development Project which has received two loans from the World Bank, the first for $160 million and the second – in 1988 – for $120 million.[117] According to a letter dated 6 May 1988 from Russel Cheetham, a senior Bank officer, this project aims through the 1990s to 'improve the incomes and welfare of transmigrant families and local people living in the immediate surroundings [of transmigration sites] by upgrading infrastructure, improving food-crop production, introducing cash crops and improving social and environmental aspects'.[118]

Likewise, in a telex that I received on 30 June 1988 from the chief of the Bank's Agriculture Operations Division, I was told that the latest transmigration project to receive a loan 'does not have a settlement component. It addresses the economic, social and environmental aspects of transmigration through extensive studies for settlements, as well as technical assistance for planning, construction, environment and land tenure issues.'[119]

While such assurances are welcome, there are elements of sophistry in the Bank's attempts to detach the particular operations that it now finances from the murky underbelly of resettlement in Indonesia: arguably support for *any* aspect of transmigration must be helpful in a fairly direct and tangible way to the programme as a whole, particularly when large sums of hard currency are involved. By the summer of 1988 the simple fact was that the Bank had only cancelled $63 million out of a total lending programme well in excess of $1 billion and had already disbursed $324 million in support of transmigration.[120]

Disbursements on this very large scale continue, justified by a virtual blizzard of reassuring statements to the effect that tribal communities will in future be protected and that the Indonesian authorities are now 'showing sensitivity'.[121] Meanwhile, however, Dyaks on Central Kalimantan are tricked into giving up their land rights by signing blank pieces of paper,[122] and the Governor of Irian Jaya describes the indigenous Irianese as 'living in a stone-age-like era'.[123] Having launched a programme to separate Irianese children from their parents,[124] this flamboyant individual called in December 1987 for a further *two million* Javanese migrants to be sent to Irian Jaya so that 'backward' local people could intermarry with the incomers – thus 'giving birth to a new generation of people without curly hair'.[125]

Likewise, while the Bank tells us that its advocacy is helping the Indonesian government to pay more 'attention to the environment, including forests',[126] the truth is that transmigration continues to cause immeasurable ecological damage. In late 1987 forest fires, set off by transmigrants and loggers, raged unchecked over large parts of Kalimantan, Sumatra and Sulawesi – with an estimated 2 million hectares destroyed by October.[127] Meanwhile, on East Kalimantan, logging alone had resulted in the destruction of a further 2.9 million hectares of forest by September 1987.[128] Associated with site development for transmigration, much of this work continues to be carried out in a very careless and ill-disciplined way, leaving logged areas strewn with debris. The result is that when fires get out of control in densely settled areas they spread rapidly through the logging zones. In addition, trash and discarded logs dumped in dried-up stream beds have turned even these natural fire-breaks into fire hazards.[129] 'In these circumstances,' says Stephen Corry, Director of the respected British charity Survival International, 'the promotion of further transmigration into Kalimantan would seem highly irresponsible.'[130]

In 1988 Corry put this concern to Barber Conable, the World Bank's President.[131] The reply, however, was that there was no intention of withdrawing 'assistance at this crucial stage'. On the contrary, Corry was told, the Bank's 'continued dialogue with the government' will 'lead to a better-managed programme'.[132]

There are good reasons to doubt this optimism for the effectiveness of 'dialogue' – particularly since the Bank admits in its own internal documents that the Ministry of Transmigration, with which the so-called dialogue is in fact being conducted, has only 'limited capacity to influence policies' in Indonesia.[133] Furthermore, whatever the future holds, the fact remains that many hundreds of millions of dollars have *already* been disbursed by the Bank and other donors, thus inextricably associating Western tax-payers with a spectacularly expensive scheme that appears to have contributed virtually nothing to Indonesia's long-term development. On the contrary, at great cost to human rights and to the environment, transmigration's only 'success' has been to export poverty from Java – where it is visible – to the remote outer islands where it is hidden from view.

BEING PART OF THE ACTION

In this respect, as in so many others, transmigration and the Polonoroeste project have much in common. Unsurprisingly, then, the thing that immediately strikes most observers who have seen the Indonesian outer islands and north-western Brazil is the depressing similarity of the destruction that Bank-financed development has wrought in both of these widely separated places:

> It is hard to view without emotion [comments one such witness], the miles of devastated trees, of felled, broken and burned trunks, of branches, mud and bark crisscrossed with tractor trails – especially when one realises that in most cases nothing of comparable value will grow there again. Such sights are reminiscent of Hiroshima. Brazil and Indonesia might be regarded as waging the equivalent of thermonuclear war upon their territories.[134]

Accused of being an accessory to such brutality Barber Conable has a ready answer: 'Where development is taking place,' he says, 'it cannot be halted, only directed. The Bank cannot influence progress from the sidelines. It must be part of the action.'[135] Indeed, when cornered, the President's strategy – understandably enough – is to deny vigorously that the institution he heads is in any way violent or destructive. On the contrary, the Bank is wise, gentle and far-sighted: by engaging in 'policy dialogue', therefore, and by 'being part of the action', it can guide even the most vicious and recalcitrant governments towards the path of virtue.

The record, however, suggests otherwise. At best, the Bank's guidance seems to be a case of the blind leading the blind. At worst, and far more frequently, it participates in a kind of destructive synergy: working as a team with its client of the day it can make things much, much worse for the poor – and for the environment – than would have been possible otherwise.

Polonoroeste stands out as the classic example of this kind of rampant and calamitous folly: colonisation of Rondônia, genocide of the province's 'backward' native peoples, and wholesale forest clearances were little more than glints in a crazed and bureaucratic eye prior to agreement between government and global lender. It was the paving of Highway 364 – paid for by the Bank – that made all these things immediately possible. Today, with thousands of people dead, hundreds of thousands hungry and desperate, and countless millions of trees felled, even Mr Conable describes the Polonoroeste experience as 'sobering' and admits in hushed tones that the Bank 'stumbled' – that it 'misread the human, institutional and physical realities of the jungle and the frontier'.[136]

It has been said that 'pride, perceiving humility to be honourable, often borrows her cloak'.[137] The Bank's willingness to come clean on the mistakes that it has made in the Brazilian north-west may be a case in point – because there are very few signs that it has *learned* from those mistakes: in Brazil, tropical forests covering an area bigger than Belgium were burnt by settlers and cattle ranchers during 1988. Commenting on this in 1989 Orlando Valverde, a leading conservationist, said: '1988 was a black year for the Amazon. The destruction was incredible, the worst in Brazilian history.'[138]

Thus, together with most of the other members of the international consortium of aid donors with which it co-operates, it seems fair to say that the Bank has a very brief and selective institutional memory and can conveniently forget its more embarrassing and painful errors. Such corporate amnesia, however, has an ongoing price both for the environment and for the poor.

This price is not only being paid in Brazil and Indonesia.

BIG RANCHES AND BIG DAMS

In 1972, in the southern African country of Botswana, the Bank contributed $1.65 million to the total of $5.4 million subscribed by international aid agencies to finance cattle and sheep ranches in the environmentally sensitive Western Kalahari. The project – which was eventually completed with a budget over-run of $2.9 million – resulted in dangerous overgrazing of the fragile savanna grasslands but, unfortunately, produced no benefits at all. Despite optimistic projections of a 21 per cent yield, the final economic rate of return proved to be below zero. Undeterred, however, the Bank and other donors were back in Botswana in 1977 to finance 'Livestock II' in the same region – a $13.4 million scheme to establish 100 ranches on collectively owned lands. Bringing with it further overgrazing and desertification, this project was finally completed in 1984; audited, its economic rate of return was judged to be 'inconsequential'.[139]

Perhaps to prove that bad things always come in threes, the Bank has now approved a further $10.7 million loan for yet another project of the same type in the same area. It is already clear that 'Livestock III' will benefit only a few large ranchers: small farmers struggling to survive on increasingly stressed communal grazing lands receive no help at all. In addition the very existence of the project contravenes the advice of the Bank's own livestock consultants who argued against it on the grounds that it would have 'such negative social effects as widening the income gap between rich and poor, permanently concentrating the country's land resources in the hands of a tiny percentage of its occupants, and depressing the already limited subsistence capabilities of its poorer citizens'.[140]

Worldwide $1 billion has been 'wasted over the past fifteen years on ill-conceived projects' in the livestock sector, according to FAO.[141] Vastly more, however, has been spent in another area of development – large-scale irrigation and hydroelectric schemes based on the expensive infrastructure of big dams.

In the last forty years literally thousands of dams have been built in the Third World, absorbing colossal amounts of aid. The experience thus garnered, however, has not been correspondingly immense. On the contrary, with the commissioning of each new dam, it seems the agencies are destined to reinvent the wheel: to be genuinely surprised by the human, ecological and economic damage that this kind of project can cause, and to do nothing in advance to mitigate the harm.

An early lesson should have been learned in Ghana. Here in the 1950s and 1960s the World Bank took the lead amongst the group of aid agencies that planned, implemented and provided the soft loans to pay for the giant Akosombo Dam on the Volta River. Certainly, very substantial benefits have since been extracted from this project by foreign interests – notably the US-owned VALCO aluminium plant which, for more than twenty years, has been supplied with hydroelectric power at substantially below production cost. To the detriment of the local economy, however, VALCO's operations are based on the smelting of imported alumina which has previously been refined in Louisiana from Jamaican bauxite; Ghanaian bauxite is *not* used.[142]

The dam has also benefited wealthy Ghanaians: driving from Accra to Akosombo one cannot help but notice how the transmission-lines that run from the hydroelectric plant to the most prosperous districts of the capital simply pass over the many impoverished villages en route – as though they did not exist. It is, however, the inhabitants of these same poor villages, still without electric light, who have paid the real price for the project:

- It is they who now suffer in the largest numbers from endemic onchocerciasis (river blindness) which affects 100,000 people, of whom 70,000 have been rendered totally sightless since completion of the dam;

- It is amongst their ranks that at least 80,000 more people have been permanently disabled as a result of schistosomiasis, a parasitic water-borne disease carried by two species of snail that are now the commonest molluscs in the Volta reservoir;

- And, almost needless to say, it was these poor rural people – not the inhabitants of Accra – who were amongst the 1 per cent of Ghana's population displaced (virtually without compensation) when the Volta reservoir began to fill up in the 1960s.[143]

For these reasons, and for some time – probably since at least the mid-1970s – one thing has been clearly understood by all the aid agencies which financed the Volta dam: while contributing little or nothing to the Ghanaian economy, this mega-project has infinitely worsened the predicament of the Ghanaian poor.

Detailed studies in other countries have, furthermore, made it quite clear that the Volta fiasco was not an isolated incident: the same kinds of problems crop up so frequently with large dams that they can now be regarded as inevitable by-products of the genre.[144] These problems are typically long-term and in some cases are so severe as to counteract completely any economic benefits that dams may produce. As one authoritative paper from the Washington-based World Resources Institute puts it:

> Diseases have spread, whole communities have been displaced and valuable crop and forest lands have been flooded . . Tens of millions of hectares of agricultural land have been lost through waterlogging and salinisation . . . In India, 10 million hectares have been lost to cultivation through waterlogging, and 25 million hectares are threatened by salinisation. In Pakistan more than half the Indus basin canal system command area, some 12 million hectares, is waterlogged, and 40 per cent is saline.

All in all, the mania for building large dams has meant that, today, 'half the world's irrigated land is salinised badly enough that yields are affected'.[145]

Worse still, the Damoclean sword of sedimentation hangs over all dams: sooner or later any reservoir, however large, will fill up with the silt and other detritus which the dam prevents from flowing downstream.[146] When that happens, of course, the dam must be decommissioned: without its reservoir, it is no more than a useless slab of concrete. This is not mere speculation. To give just a few examples:

- In India the projected siltation rate of the Nizamsagar Dam in Andra Pradesh was 530 acre-feet a year. The actual rate has turned out to be 8,700 acre-feet a year. As a result the dam's reservoir has already lost more than 60 per cent of its storage capacity. Virtually every reservoir in India is currently suffering from similar problems.[147]

- In Haiti, the Peligre Dam on the Artibonite River was completed in 1956. Built to last fifty years its reservoir has silted up so quickly that it was decommissioned in the mid-1980s.[148]

- In China, the Sanmenxia Reservoir, which was completed in 1960, had to be decommissioned in 1964 owing to premature siltation. Another reservoir, Laoying, actually silted up before its dam was completed![149]

Although such cautionary data are available to the aid community, nothing much has changed. The World Bank and other donors consistently postpone serious investigation of alternatives to big dams and, in the mean time, continue gleefully to commit huge sums of money to ecologically and economically unsound water-development schemes – many of which bear strong family resemblances to old projects that have failed. Recent schemes which are either about to receive or have already received funding from the Bank and/or other Western aid donors include the Three Gorges Dam on China's Yangtze River, the Diama Dam and the Manantali Dam in Sahelian West Africa, the Bakolori Dam in Nigeria, the Tucurui Dam in Brazil, the Balbina Dam, the Itaparica Dam and the Paradao Dam, also in Brazil, the Itaipu Dam on the Parana River in Brazil/Paraguay, several major dams on the Mahaweli River in Sri Lanka, the Tarbela and Kalabagh Dams in Pakistan, the proposed Bardhere Dam in Somalia, and the proposed Chico Dams in the Philippines.[150]

It is India, however – with its 10 million hectares already waterlogged, with its 25 million more threatened by salinisation – that continues to be the happiest hunting ground for aid agencies looking for super-dams to finance. The long-term and heavy emphasis placed by successive Indian governments on the expansion of hydroelectric power and of large-scale irrigation has resulted in the construction of more than 1,000 dams in the past ten years.[151] Amongst these, a recently launched project – the Sardar Sarovar Dam on the westward-flowing Narmada River – looks set to repeat many of the best-known and most avoidable mistakes in water-development.

Sardar Sarovar received a loan commitment of $450 million from the World Bank in 1985, despite the fact that India's Department of Environment and Forests had at that stage not granted environmental clearance for the project because major studies relating to environment and resettlement had not been completed. These studies were still not complete when the Indian government forced through the legislation in the spring of 1987 that gave the dam the needed environmental clearance.[152]

Filling of the reservoir is displacing over 70,000 poor rural people from their homes, against their will and without adequate compensation: in most cases no provision has been made to resettle them and they must simply re-establish their lives wherever they can.[153] Apart from the human rights abuse that this implies there is, according to the Washington-based Environmental Defense Fund, 'substantial risk of unsustainable ecological stress from the movement of these displaced people up into the hills surrounding the reservoir. These areas are already suffering from deforestation, sheet erosion and other environmental degradation.'[154] In addition, included in the 900 square kilometres to be flooded by the dam are some 12,000 hectares of pristine rainforest. 'Along with the forest many rare species, flora and fauna, as well as an entire life rhythm – cultural and social – will be lost,' warn six of India's leading scientists and environmentalists in a letter to Prime Minister Rajiv Gandhi.[155]

A study by the Indian Council of Science and Technology predicts that completion of work at Sardar Sarovar will result in increased malaria, cholera, viral encephalitis, and other water-borne diseases for millions of local people.[156] Meanwhile, there is no guarantee that the project will justify itself in the long term, even on purely economic grounds. Serious questions have been raised by non-governmental organisations, environmentalists and scientists regarding the cost–benefit analysis which the World Bank and the Indian government have relied on to validate the dam.[157]

The Greater Narmada Programme, of which Sardar Sarovar is only a part, ultimately envisages the expenditure of billions more dollars on at least twenty-nine other major dams along the Narmada River; several of these are already being actively appraised for funding by the World Bank even though it is known that their construction will involve the displacement of more than 1.5 million people – mostly of tribal and minority origin. Alternatives such as energy-efficiency improvements, and the building of smaller-scale dams which would be environmentally, socially and economically less risky, have not even been considered by the global lender in its Gadarene rush to commit ever larger sums to India's most grandiose 'development' scheme.[158]

LEND BIG, LEND FAST

Of course the Bank is in the business of lending money for development. If it stops doing that, then it ceases to have a rôle. Conversely, the more lending that it does the more important its rôle becomes. This creates a pressure within the institution to make loans big and to make them quickly and, frequently, leads to important little details being neglected – quality control, for example, attention to the usefulness of projects, efforts to establish whether they will do harm, and so on. What gets forgotten most often and most easily is the welfare of the poor: too much time spent worrying about peasants and paupers, too much effort spent carefully devising projects that take people into account, would definitely slow down the flow of money.

Thus the Bank's mounting enthusiasm for structural adjustment loans, evident since these were first introduced in 1980 (see Part Two for further details), is almost completely explained by the fact that twice as many dollars per staff week of work can be disbursed by SAL as by any other instrument.[159] As Sheldon Annis of the Washington-based Overseas Development Council observes, the result of this is that 'ambitious Bank staffers' increasingly 'gravitate towards work on structural adjustment rather than towards poverty-focused projects'.[160]

It is as part of precisely the same internal dynamic that young men and women seeking to 'go places' are drawn by the powerful lure of big, high-profile, high-tech schemes, like Sardar Sarovar, and by schemes which involve a particularly grand design – Indonesian transmigration, for example, which envisages nothing less than the restructuring of an entire society. Projects of this kind have the capacity to absorb very large loans very quickly – characteristics that must appeal strongly to zealous staff in a World Bank where top executives hand out merit awards exclusively on the basis of the gross amounts of money that the departments under their supervision are able to commit;

quite literally, the more you spend, the 'better' you are judged to have done. Thus, speaking of the operations of the IBRD in July 1987, Bank President Barber Conable was able to say with some pride: 'The 1986–7 fiscal year, which ended on 30 June, was a *success*; our commitments represented $14.2 billion as against $13 billion in the previous year.'[161]

In the Soviet Union an apocryphal story is told of a factory which met its annual production target of 50,000 tonnes of nails by producing fifty nails each weighing 1,000 tonnes. Too often Mr Conable's World Bank is like that plant and its projects are like those nails: large, cumbersome, useless and possibly dangerous. Not all members of the Bank's staff, however, are indifferent to the implications of a régime that defines 'success' in purely quantitative terms; indeed, at almost exactly the same moment that the President was crowing about spending $1.2 billion more in 1987 than in 1986, the Bank's own Operations Evaluation Department was cautioning that 'the drive to reach lending targets' is 'potentially damaging' and is 'a major cause of poor project performance'.[162]

Like Cassandra, the Trojan seer whose fate it was to prophesy truly and not be believed, the OED has made almost identical observations virtually every year since 1975 when it began compiling its *Annual Review of Project Performance Results*. To this day, however, the drive to fulfil lending targets – to 'succeed' by spending ever more money – maintains its primal importance for the staff of the World Bank and continues to harm the poor while short-changing Western tax-payers.

A recent extensive internal audit done by the OED described one disastrous rural development project in the impoverished Caribbean island of Haiti as 'an example of the effects of Bank pressure for rapid project launching, despite scant Bank acquaintance with the country'.[163] The desire of staff to win pats on the back from senior management for lending quickly and in large amounts also lay behind the cancerous growth of the Papaloapan Integrated Rural Development Project in Mexico. Here the auditors found that, although relatively good work had been done at an early stage, 'the initial design (based upon pilot activities) was completely changed by the appraisal mission – the project area was extended sevenfold to cover the entire Papaloapan basin, with costs increasing from $26 million to $111 million and later to $138.5 million'. This expensive project closed three years behind schedule with barely half of its original components implemented and was judged by the auditors to have been a catastrophic failure – a failure attributable almost entirely to 'the Bank's pressure for quick action'.[164]

Mexico and Haiti were not the only Third World countries to be lent large sums of money for something that they didn't need by Bank officers zealously promoting their own careers. At the Morondova Irrigation and Rural Development Project in Madagascar, for example, the auditors detected 'an unseemly pressure to lend', highlighted an appalling 'lack of consensus between the Bank and the borrower' and stated their regret that the government, which in fact had 'serious reservations', was nevertheless 'pressured to accept the project'.[165] The conclusion of the Operations Evaluation Department is that 'it is neither in the Bank's nor in the individual borrower's interests to embark on non-viable undertakings on the basis of lending targets'.[166]

Year in year out, however – and in true Soviet-factory style – this is precisely what the Bank continues to do. It is thus probably not entirely coincidental that, out of a representative sample of 189 of its projects audited worldwide, no less than 106 – almost 60 per cent – were found in 1987 either to have 'serious shortcomings' or to be 'complete failures'.[167] A similar proportion of these projects – including many judged in other senses to be 'successes' – were thought unlikely to be sustainable after completion.[168] Furthermore, it is in the poorest countries of the world, and amongst the poorest segments of the populations of these countries, that the Bank does worst. In sub-Saharan Africa, for example, 75 per cent of all agricultural projects audited were found to have failed.[169]

An even more extensive series of audits produced by the Operations Evaluation Department in 1988 again found high failure rates, particularly in the poorest regions,[170] and drew special attention to the increasingly serious issue of *sustainability*. Out of a total of 246 projects reviewed, fully 50 per cent were found to have 'unlikely, marginal or uncertain' sustainability, with this figure rising to 70 per cent in, for example, impoverished West Africa. Another recent OED report – which has not been distributed because its findings are so damning – looked at the fate of twenty-seven agricultural projects approved by the Bank between 1961 and 1975 (all of which were judged to be successful at the time disbursements were completed). The report concludes that only nine of these projects achieved any kind of longer-term sustainability, ten failed outright, and eight had marginal or uncertain results.[171] In accounting for this worrying lack of sustainability, the auditors point to the 'generally too optimistic outlook' on the part of staff presenting project loans for approval by the Board, and again criticise the priority that the World Bank seems to put on meeting lending targets rather than 'on supervision'.[172]

The Bank is by no means the only major aid institution at which staff can earn Brownie points from their superiors by spending big and spending fast, even when such behaviour results in bad projects. A former employee of the Canadian International Development Agency says that, in government circles in Ottawa, CIDA's performance is measured almost entirely by its ability to spend the funds allocated to it within the allotted time. 'So, too,' he adds, 'is the performance of individual staff members . . . progress is measured by the quantity of disbursements.' Unsurprisingly, therefore, CIDA officers tend to attach themselves to 'those channels and projects where rapid disbursement potential is maximised'.[173]

Likewise, David Deppner, a former USAID official, recalls:

The entire management system at AID was based on how much money we spent; we were paid or promoted according to the size of our projects. No administrator wanted to lie awake at night worrying about a dozen little projects when he could spend his time moving money around in big blocks. Since it's just as easy to administer a twenty million dollar project as it is a twenty thousand dollar project, the logic is – why not go for the biggie?[174]

SMALL IS DIFFICULT

Somewhat ironically the tendency to 'go for the biggie' is to be seen at work even on those rare occasions when the American agency is making conscious efforts to introduce small-scale projects and 'appropriate' or useful technologies to impoverished parts of the Third World. This has proved to be the case, for example, with its much vaunted Renewable Energy Programme. Auditors from the US government recently inspected a solar-powered electrical system that AID's experts had installed at a cost of $713,000 in a poor rural village in India. The system included exceptionally complex solar thermal collectors, a steam engine, associated controls, motors and pumps which could only be operated and repaired by highly trained technicians.

> A more *inappropriate* technology for a remote site occupied by uneducated villagers [the auditors concluded] is hard to imagine . . . Electricity has the potential for drastically altering the lives of the rural poor. It can give them light, entertainment, new appliances and new opportunity to earn income. But an electrical plant that is much more difficult to maintain and far more costly than a diesel set, and that requires three trained engineers in residence, is not the solution.[175]

Other projects of this type that the auditors looked at – in India, the Philippines and the Dominican Republic – were found to have involved excessive equipment costs. Some individual components, which in the event of a breakdown would have to be replaced by the 'beneficiaries' at their own expense, had price tags ranging from $25,000 up to $615,121. These included, inter alia:

● A rice-hull-fed thermal power plant in the Philippines – cost $528,000;

● A solar drier in the Dominican Republic – cost $500,000;

● A small-scale hydroelectric system in India – cost $467,000.

'The rural poor cannot afford such costs,' the auditors rightly concluded, noting in addition that the computer system required in the Indian hydroelectric project (to distribute power between uses such as irrigation and household lighting) was so complicated that normal commercial software could not be used; as a result it had been necessary to develop specialised programmes. The auditors also expressed serious concern about the long-term durability and reliability of a microcomputer used twenty-four hours a day in a location that was far off the beaten track, and noted that the technical expertise to maintain this complex system was not available in the village.[176]

Many more of the supposedly small-scale and appropriate projects in which

AID has invested US tax dollars with the explicit objective of assisting the rural poor in developing countries were found at audit to have been devised without any understanding of the problems that poor people actually face. As a result, most of these projects were abject failures. For example:

- The anaerobic digestor component of a $4.5 million project in Mali was 'not suited to the needs of the poor'. The purpose of the digestor was to produce gas from animal dung; the end product, however, was 'too expensive for intended small-scale uses such as cooking'. Worse still, inputs of water and dung required for continuous operation were scarce, and daily filling and cleaning of the digestor required exhausting and time-consuming physical labour from people already weakened by malnutrition.

Likewise:

- Because of persistent economic and technical problems, a $3 million sub-project in the Philippines involving biomass gasifiers was 'unacceptable' to the villagers who were supposed to benefit from it. At the time of the audit only two of the total of 103 gasifiers installed in one region of the Philippines were in fact operational.

All in all, the auditors' judgement of USAID's renewable-energy projects is damning: they were not helpful to the poor because they were 'not simple and inexpensive to build, use and maintain', they required 'large capital investments', and they involved 'high operating costs'.[177]

Other audits of more conventional development projects that the agency has financed and implemented around the world illustrate the same kinds of mistake being made again and again – an addiction to highly priced technologies and to grandiose and irrelevant schemes, a culpable lack of empathy for the poor on the part of staff and consultants, and repeated failures to take into account in project design the harsh realities of Third World existence.

In Egypt USAID disbursed $108 million during 1986–7 to pay for the construction of a huge grain silo complex at the Red Sea port of Safaga. The complex incorporated ultra-modern offloading equipment and other advanced design features intended to save operating time and reduce grain losses. As the project neared completion, however, the Inspector General for Audit uncovered a crucial oversight: locally available electricity supplies were completely inadequate for the proper running of the space-age complex with its vast daily demand for power. The only possible solution, therefore, was to spend more money: $6.5 million to cover the cost of four diesel generators with a capacity of 3,000 kilowatts each. This USAID promptly agreed to do; however, it was thought unlikely that the new units could be imported, installed and functioning before 1989. 'For about two years after completion,' the audit notes with regret, 'the complex will have to be operated on a reduced basis – thus mitigating to a large extent the benefits contemplated when the project was approved.'[178]

Another typical USAID scheme where the anticipated benefits have been substantially 'mitigated' by hasty design and implementation is the $23.1 million Integrated Rural Development Project in Peru. Here a recent audit uncovered a series of prize snafus – amongst them a road which was supposed to connect the villages of San Marco and El Azufre. The road was listed as being 7.2 kilometres long; after the auditors had travelled no more than half a kilometre on it, however, they found that it 'abruptly ended at the edge of a river'. It transpired that a bridge was to have been built here but work had been prevented because of strenuous opposition from local peasants who farmed on the land around the river banks. Such opposition would not have been encountered, the auditors discovered, if the road had been cut from a different angle approximately 2.5 kilometres further up-river. USAID had not looked into this option. At considerable expense, however, as the auditors could see when they peered across the fast-flowing waters, the agency *had* completed construction of the road on the other side of the river – despite the impossibility of ever building the bridge to link the two sections.[179]

CATHEDRALS IN THE DESERT

Roads that end in rivers and then continue blithely onward on the other side, silos without power supplies, highly sophisticated equipment that no one can use installed in remote places, aquaculture projects producing fish at $4,000 per kilo for consumption by African peasants who do not even earn $400 a year, dams that dispossess thousands and spread fatal water-borne diseases, resettlement schemes that make the migrants poorer than they were before they left home, that destroy the environment and that obliterate tribal peoples – such blunders are *not* quaint exceptions to some benign and general rule of development. On the contrary, they *are* the rule. In consequence, the Third World today is littered with the festering carcasses of many prodigious white elephants.

A classic example is provided by the Kenana sugar complex in the Sudan, a country that, fittingly enough, has hunted all its genuine four-legged elephants to extinction. The result of a feasibility study done in 1974, which put total costs at a containable $150 million, Kenana eventually started producing refined sugar in 1981. By then the final bill for the plant had risen to an awesome $613 million.[180]

Believed to be the largest scheme of its kind ever created, there is almost nothing about Kenana that looks right in the Sudanese context. The 40 megawatt power-station, the network of conduits and canals (the main one twenty miles long), the pumping station to lift the waters of the Nile 150 feet from the canals to the fields, and the factory capable of crushing 17,000 tonnes of sugar a day[181] – all these ingredients and many more seem to belong in some futuristic vision of an advanced agro-industrial economy rather than in the heart of one of the very poorest countries in a destitute continent.

Neither does the feeling of unreality, of something being seriously wrong and out of place, end here. In line with the World Bank's insistence that Sudan should earn more foreign exchange, Kenana was originally intended to export sugar on a large scale. Unfortunately, however, the project site – at Kosti on the White Nile – is separated from the nearest port by more than a thousand miles of bleak and burning desert. Since there is a huge surplus of sugar on world markets, and since this state of affairs keeps the international price for the commodity low, there is just no margin for heavy transportation costs. As a result, although sugar is produced at Kenana today, it is sold almost exclusively in the Sudan itself – and at a price significantly higher than that of imported sugar.[182]

The main beneficiaries of the project are the 400 expatriates who run the entire show. Each of these managers receives a very substantial salary, of which the bulk – almost 70 per cent – is denominated in foreign currency payable abroad. There are also some 15,000 Sudanese labourers; most, however, are migrants from quite far afield and live in dormitories around the site. By contrast only 2 per cent of the indigenous Kenanian tribe have found work: they are paid at the rate of approximately $3 per twelve-hour day.[183]

Kenana is matched in both scale and unsuitability by another Brobdingnagian Sudanese scheme – the Jonglei Canal, which was intended by the consortium of aid agencies that backed it to draw water off from the Nile's swamps in order to irrigate much of the southern part of the country. Construction of the canal, which began in 1978, called for the use of nothing less than the largest mobile excavating machine in the world.[184] This juggernaut was bought second-hand and required constant maintenance by costly teams of foreign technicians; it also had an insatiable appetite for spare parts, consumed lakes of imported fuel, and crawled forward so slowly that, after two years of digging, the Jonglei had fallen seriously behind schedule – so seriously in fact that the Sudanese government defaulted on its own share of the payments to the French company that had won the construction contract.

Fresh infusions of international aid made it possible for the excavations to continue, presumably on the tried-and-tested donor principle that no opportunity to throw good money after bad should ever be wasted. By this time – 1980 – it was already being estimated that the canal would cost at least three times as much to complete as had originally been budgeted.[185] An even more fundamental problem had also emerged: hostile opposition from southern Sudanese peasants who feared that an invasion of wealthy northern farmers would follow the Jonglei's slow but remorseless progress. Aid agencies ignored the frequent protests that were made, but were soon to regret doing so. When the long-anticipated civil war finally broke out between north and south in 1983, the first action of the newly formed Sudan People's Liberation Movement was to hit the Jonglei Canal. Foreign workers were kidnapped and the giant digger was closed down. It remains closed to this day – a monument to bad development.

Similarly, on the Thai island of Phuket, one recent World Bank project – a $44 million tantalum-processing plant – was regarded as such a fiasco by the local inhabitants that they burnt it down. Keen to disburse funds rapidly, and indifferent as ever to the opinions of the poor, the Bank had not taken the trouble to canvass local opinions of the scheme before going ahead with it. The islanders, however, knew that the huge ore-refinery would be messy, noisy and would thus represent a serious threat to the tourist trade which provided the majority of their incomes. When it became clear in addition that the plant was capital intensive – and would create only a few new jobs – a rational decision was taken by all concerned to get rid of it; accordingly it was razed to the ground shortly before its doors were due to open for business.[186]

This example of poor people taking action against a project which did not offer them any benefits – indeed, imperilled them – and seemed largely to be in the interests of faraway investors and consumers, is rare indeed. Usually the money of international development agencies, combined with the muscle of borrower governments, is enough to enforce acceptance of any scheme – however irrelevant, cruel, unusual or hare-brained it in fact may be.

Britain's Overseas Development Administration has a consistent track record of working closely with Third World governments to devise projects that by-pass or actually harm the poor. In Karnataka, India, a forestry scheme funded by the ODA has planted a great many quick-growing eucalyptus trees. The original purpose of the project was to provide fuel-wood and animal fodder for landless peasants and small farmers in the area; the eucalyptus, however, is a tree that is not at all suitable for such purposes. Cattle will not eat its bitter aromatic leaves and it is thus quite useless as a source of free fodder. Likewise, its stem grows straight up for several feet – well above the height of a man – and there are no side branches within reach that can be broken off and taken away by villagers for firewood. Neither does felled timber from the Karnataka scheme help the rural poor. Because of commercial pressures, most now goes to provide pulp for the Mysore paper mills. The little that remains is sold in the markets of Bangalore as fuel for better-off urban consumers.[187]

Another ODA project – at Cajamarca in Peru – has had equally dubious results. This scheme encouraged small farmers to invest in dairy cows by providing them with loans and veterinary services. There was only one customer for the milk produced, however: a major multinational company which was able to use its monopoly position to preside over a sharp fall in the price paid for milk at the farm gate. The farmers today are caught in a poverty trap: their earnings are too low even to repay the original loans and they cannot sell their cows since nobody wants to buy the valueless beasts.[188]

So often, development initiatives that begin with the best intentions end up going as sour as the milk produced by those cows in Peru. In the Mayan Indian highlands of Guatemala, for example, a giant hydroelectric dam, the Chixoy, stands today as a salutary reminder of the misguided folly of so many 'developers'. Originally budgeted at $340 million, the construction costs had rocketed to $1 billion by the time the dam was opened in 1985. This money was lent to the Guatemalan government by a consortium of Western aid agencies, with the World Bank and the Inter-American Development Bank taking the lead; however, it will have to be paid back by the Guatemalan people out of taxes. To this burden must be added the 70 per cent price-hike for domestic electricity that has been imposed since the dam's hydro power began to provide three-quarters of the nation's electricity needs. According to Robert Balsells, whose misfortune it is to be President of the state-owned electricity company at this time, the implications for the average Guatemalan are grim. Indeed, paying for the Chixoy will mean 'going without medicines and food . . . We were poor before, now we are miserable.'[189]

Irredeemably out of touch with poor people, and with the tedious day-to-day realities of their lives, it is little wonder that the World Bank and its partners in development so consistently come up with bizarre and extraneous projects like the Chixoy Dam – projects that are worthless, or even harmful, to those they are intended to benefit. More often than not big, fanciful, extravagant, and high-tech, such schemes do, however, meet the bureaucratic needs of the agencies themselves, the psychological and career needs of their staff, and the commercial needs of suppliers from whom equipment and services are procured.

As the saying goes, it's an ill wind that blows nobody any good.

PART FIVE

WINNERS
AND LOSERS

Public money is like holy water;
everyone helps himself to it.

Italian Proverb

IN AFRICA, a complex and very expensive irrigation scheme on the banks of the Niger River at Namarigounou has recently been abandoned and its ultra-modern equipment lies derelict: the government that was given the project as aid cannot afford to meet the astronomically high running costs. Meanwhile, just a few kilometres away, international donors are paying $17,000 per hectare to construct another virtually identical scheme. Western contractors providing the equipment, and Western consultancies responsible for the design and supervision, are probably going to be the only long-term beneficiaries of the total investment of $25.5 million.[1]

This is already clearly understood by all concerned, but no one seems to mind very much – after all, since the funds have been provided by Western tax-payers it is fitting that they should circulate back to Western businesses. There is, of course, an argument that smaller investments in rain-fed agriculture, making full use of established local skills, might actually grow more food; such grassroots initiatives, however, offer little mileage for rich-country suppliers.[2]

Here is a rule of thumb that you can safely apply wherever you may wander in the Third World: if a project is funded by foreigners it will typically also be designed by foreigners and implemented by foreigners using foreign equipment procured in foreign markets.

Thus British trucks, Russian tractors, German combines and Japanese machinery are all to be found on farms run by the Bangladesh Agricultural Development Corporation, and it is quite normal for each item to be accompanied by an expert or technician from the donor country. The British are particularly active, with Technical Co-operation Officers and VSO workers installed on every farm to look after the British equipment. Similar arrangements are also in force in virtually all other sectors of an economy where an impressive 90 per cent of the national development budget is contributed by foreign aid.[3] UK assistance alone runs at around £40 million per annum;[4] in some years, however, less than 1 per cent of this total amount is actually spent in Bangladesh – the rest is used to import British goods and to pay the salaries of British experts.[5]

In nearby Nepal, the extent of foreign involvement in the national development effort is so great that, in some schemes, it is genuinely difficult to discern whether the real beneficiaries are even *intended* to be the Nepalese poor, or whether, in fact, the whole exercise has been designed around the needs and interests of expatriate corporations.

The Rapti Area Rural Development Project, financed by USAID, is a case in point. Here just one foreign contractor – PADCO, the Washington-based firm that is providing technical assistance – has succeeded in taking 20 per cent off the top of the $24 million expended so far.[6] PADCO has also been intimately involved in another AID venture, the 'Town Development Fund'. Based in Kathmandu, this owes its existence to recommendations that came out of an earlier 'Urban Development Assessment', which was also paid for by AID and also carried out by PADCO. With the preliminary $1.3 million 'management-support' phase only recently under way the project has already given inces-tuous birth to yet more business for PADCO, as well as for another US consulting firm. Further lucrative work for a number of American companies is in the pipeline: the size and complexity of co-ordination required in running the scheme are thought to rule out any effective Nepalese participation.[7]

AID AND TRADE

From Kathmandu to Quito and from Thailand to Timbuktu, a stirring and egalitarian emblem has, for many years, been the symbol of America's altruism: two hands – one black and one white – shaking above the logo 'Gift of the People of the United States'. Often, though you would never guess it from the packaging, the 'gift' in question is a loan. Even when it is an outright grant, however, the generosity involved is qualified. During the period 1960–70, for example – John F. Kennedy's idealistic 'First Development Decade' – studies showed that 99 per cent of all the funds provided by AID for development in Latin America were in fact spent in the USA, and on products that were priced on average at 35 per cent above their world market value.[8] Even today 70 cents out of every dollar of American 'assistance to the Third World' never actually leave the United States.[9] The Agency for International Development spends an awe-inspiring $7 billion a year purchasing goods and services directly from domestic companies and contractors: New York, Pennsylvania, North Carolina, Illinois and Texas get the lion's share of the patronage, but no state is ever entirely left out.[10] In the process, as AID itself claims, 'thousands of jobs' are created 'here at home'.[11]

The story is the same in virtually every aid-giving country. The UK allocates some £850 million a year to its bilateral aid programme.[12] Out of this substantial sum, around 80 per cent is typically spent on the purchase of British goods and services[13] – a share that approaches 100 per cent in the case of some recipients, like Bangladesh.

The already high level of domestic procurement routinely financed by British 'overseas' aid is, furthermore, increased by a special tranche of money concealed within the bilateral budget that is used solely and specifically to help UK exporters to secure contracts in the developing world. Known as the

Aid–Trade Provision (ATP), this slush fund was originally established in 1977 and has since become increasingly important: in 1984, despite widespread famine and other emergencies, ATP handouts to UK firms used up almost twice as much of Britain's official development assistance as did disaster aid, food aid and debt relief for the whole of sub-Saharan Africa.[14]

From an administrative point of view, ATP is a joint creature of the Overseas Development Administration and the Department of Trade and Industry. The former provides the money (out of tax revenues) but it is the latter that decides how the money should actually be spent. The financing arrangements for normal aid projects are agreed directly between the Overseas Development Administration and the recipient government in the Third World; ATP funds, however, have to be sought initially by the aspiring British exporter, who makes an application to the DTI. Thereafter, the amount of aid eventually offered is based almost exclusively on the Department's estimate of the size of subsidy needed to win the contract (rather than on any merits or drawbacks that the project may have from a developmental point of view). Furthermore, it is stipulated very clearly that ATP is *not* 'available for business which could reasonably be expected to be won on normal commercial terms'.[15]

In virtually all international forums, and for many years, the British government has declared itself to be staunchly in favour of free enterprise; it thus seems odd to discover that a growing slice of the official aid budget, rather than being used to help the poor, is in fact earmarked for a determined effort to subvert global market forces. 'Lame duck' companies that fail to trade competitively should, Prime Minister Margaret Thatcher has insisted on a number of occasions, be allowed to 'go to the wall', yet ATP uses public money to give a competitive edge in circumstances where, otherwise, none would exist.

The British are not kept well informed about the Aid–Trade Provision. One detailed report on the subject, commissioned by the Overseas Development Administration, was judged to be too critical and was suppressed just prior to publication; it is now covered by the Official Secrets Act.[16] Careful research has revealed, however, that a surprisingly small number of large corporations have been the main beneficiaries of the scheme. Between 1978 and 1985, £328 million in aid was allocated as ATP; of this more than half – £166 million – went to just four companies. GEC and NEI, both major electrical engineering firms, got respectively £49 million and £47 million from the British tax-payer; Davy McKee and Balfour Beatty each got about £34 million during the same period.[17] In 1986 the Biwater Group of Dorking, Surrey, benefited from the largest single allocation ever made under the Aid–Trade Provision – £60 million in support of a water-development project in Malaysia.[18]

THE GENEROUS MULTILATERALS

Neither is the harvest that UK industries reap from official aid budgets confined to bilateral allocations. Approximately 40 per cent of total development assistance is channelled through multilateral agencies like the UN's Food and Agriculture Organisation and the World Bank. Although these can spend the money where they like, the record shows that Britain gets a very good return indeed on its 'investment' in the multilateral sector – in fact it repeatedly wins procurement contracts worth significantly more than it puts in. Thus in a recent year British tax-payers provided multilateral aid agencies with £495 million; in the same year, however, British firms received contracts worth £616 million from those agencies.[19] In another year the multilateral institutions received £531 million of British money and £637.2 million boomeranged back in the form of business placed with British companies.[20] According to the Overseas Development Administration, multilateral agencies can normally be relied upon to purchase British goods and services with a value equivalent to 120 per cent of Britain's total multilateral contributions.[21]

The spending of the United Nations Development Programme bears this out. In a typical year, when Britain's contributions to the agency totalled £17.5 million, UNDP purchased UK goods and services worth £23.54 million: a net gain of £6 million. Among the recipients were British Leyland (£444,000 for the supply of Rover cars), Racal Decca (£459,000 for survey equipment) and George Wimpey International (£688,000 for construction works in Tanzania).[22]

Not included in any of the official calculations of the benefits that Britain receives from its participation in the multilateral aid effort are the salaries paid to the many thousands of UK nationals employed as 'experts', 'professionals', 'administrators' and so on by the agencies concerned. UNDP alone has 1,223 British citizens on its payroll;[23] excluding fringe benefits, the combined value of the salaries earned by these people will not be less than £30 million a year. Likewise remunerating the British staff at FAO headquarters in Rome costs that giant multilateral agency seven times as much as it receives from the UK in the form of contributions to its regular budget.[24]

Of course, Britain is by no means the only industrialised country to reap more than it sows where multilateral aid is concerned. To stay with the example of FAO for a moment, the cost–benefit ratio is 1:5 for Holland, 1:2 for France and 1:7 for Belgium. Italy, as the host country, does particularly well: for every dollar it contributes to the Organisation sixteen come back. In one bumper year Italy's share of the FAO's regular budget was just $5.7 million; meanwhile Italian staff received $73 million in salaries and Italian firms won $19 million worth of orders.[25] In a similar fashion UNDP, which has its headquarters in New York, puts back 45 per cent more into the American economy than it takes out in the form of budgetary contributions from the United States.[26]

Few UN offices of any size are to be found in the Third World; again it is the industrialised countries that benefit from the spending involved – $120 million a year in the case of UN Geneva, for example, and almost $100 million a year in the case of UN Vienna. These sums of money alone are larger than the respective annual contributions that Switzerland and Austria make to the budgets of the world body.[27] New York, as the preferred headquarters location for several UN 'development' agencies, does particularly well: although the pampered legions of international civil servants and diplomats cost the city $125,000 a month in unpaid parking fines, their lavish patronage of restaurants, theatres, bars and department stores pumps at least $800 million a year into the Big Apple's economy.[28] On top of this New York benefits from about $400 million of annual spending that comes directly out of the United Nations budget.[29]

At World Bank headquarters in Washington, DC, $400 million is the sort of sum that you would expect to find in the petty-cash box. This giant amongst multilateral institutions disburses literally billions of dollars for 'development' purposes every year; with an eye to continued support from its wealthy member states, however, the global lender is the first to admit that out of every $10 that it receives around $7 are in fact spent on goods and services from the rich industrialised countries.[30] Thus in fiscal 1986 IDA and IBRD procurements from Japan, the Federal Republic of Germany, and the United Kingdom totalled, respectively, $1.14 billion, $762.3 million, and $604.7 million. In the same financial year procurements from the United States were worth $1.02 billion.[31] In fiscal 1987 the USA did a great deal better, winning procurement orders worth $1.810 billion. West Germany got $954.3 million in that year, the UK got $894.8 million and Japan got $1.322 billion.[32]

In terms of the relationship between what it puts into the World Bank and what it takes out Japan has consistently done a better deal for itself than other industrialised nations – notably the United States. This frustrates and angers American politicians.[33] Nevertheless, the USA does manage to claw back a good chunk of the 'multilateral aid' that it channels through the Bank: for every tax dollar contributed, 82 cents are immediately returned to American businesses in the form of purchase orders.[34]

All in all, multilateral agencies provide huge volumes of lucrative work for contractors in the industrialised countries. One UN periodical, *Development Business*, aims to lubricate this trade. 'CASH IN ON $24 BILLION WORTH OF BUSINESS,' proclaims a flyer soliciting subscriptions at $295 per annum:

> Fortnightly *DB* lists procurement notices and bid invitations that give you early access to billions of dollars of business from multilateral lending organisations . . . *DB* features Monthly Operational Summaries from the World Bank and the Inter-American Development Bank. These sources of information alert you to consulting, contracting and supply opportunities from the moment projects are first proposed. You will also find indispensable information on securing contracts in developing countries and timely articles aimed at making your business easier . . . Let *DB* work for you.

An accompanying letter from the editor claims: '*DB* is a unique business tool . . . According to a recent independent survey, one out of three subscribers submitting bids on procurement notices listed in *DB* won those contracts.'[35]

As well as permitting the publication of its Monthly Operational Summaries, the World Bank offers some special facilities exclusively to the corporations it does business with. Project Appraisals, Reports to the Executive Directors, and other internal documents, are strictly withheld from the general public, from community groups concerned about the environmental and social impact of the activities of the global lender, and from people in the Third World whose lives are directly affected by those activities. Many of these same 'confidential' documents, however, are filed at the Department of Trade and Industry in London and at the US Commerce Department Library in the Herbert C. Hoover Building, Washington, DC. At either location they can be inspected freely by employees and consultants of large Western corporations once bona fides have been established and the appropriate forms have been filled in. Potential suppliers of goods and services are thus deemed to have a legitimate 'need to know' about the most intimate details of any project they may have an interest in; meanwhile, those who actually live in the project area itself are kept in the dark until the bulldozers move in. It would be hard to find a clearer illustration of the privileged links between private business and public money – links that are the matrix for so much that passes as 'development'.

NEITHER FISH NOR FOWL

Although normally recondite on the subject, aid agencies do make a considerable song and dance about their contributions to business prosperity when – as is now frequently the case – they are attacked by critics on the right of the political spectrum and accused of recklessly hurling tax-payers' money into the bottomless and undeserving pit of the Third World. The US Agency for International Development, for example, proclaims: 'Foreign aid doesn't cost Americans, it pays!'[36] Likewise, across the Atlantic, the UK's Overseas Development Administration wants its critics to know that it 'seeks to ensure that the aid programme is as helpful as possible to those who may be able to do business as a result of it'.[37]

The problem, however, is that aid is not really supposed to be a sort of hidden subsidy for commerce and industry in the donor countries. Because the agencies know this they still devote the bulk of their PR literature, and their oratory, to stressing the poverty-focused and humanitarian aspects of their operations in the developing nations. 'The central challenge to the World Bank,' says Barber Conable, the President of that multilateral institution, 'is the central concern of our world: to mobilise the will and the resources of the affluent and the afflicted alike in the global battle against poverty.'[38] The 'principal purpose' of US aid is 'to meet the basic needs of poor people in the developing countries', a former Secretary of State told the Senate's Foreign Relations Committee.[39] 'Increasing the wellbeing of people in the developing countries is a central objective of US assistance policy,' says AID. 'Many projects are designed to help the poor to help themselves.'[40] Similarly, Britain's Overseas Development Administration wants to make it clear that it will continue to concentrate its aid 'on the poorest countries'[41] and on 'the poorest people in those countries'.[42]

Thus, if the publicists are to be believed, aid can be all things to all people: it can please both the right and the left, it can win the support both of the general public and of the business community, it can make the poor prosperous and the rich richer still, it can reconcile opposites, it can transform obvious conflicts of interest into harmony and mutual gain, it can leap tall buildings at a single bound, it can block the path of a speeding train . . . in short, like Superman it can do just about anything it sets its mind to.

Unfortunately, like Superman also, aid is neither bird nor plane, neither fish nor fowl. This ambiguity, this hermaphrodite quality, is apparent in many statements that are made about it. Towards the end of his second term in office, for example, President Ronald Reagan said: 'Our foreign aid is not only a symbol of America's tradition of generosity and good will, but also a servant of our national interest.'[43] At about the same time Christopher Patten, Britain's Overseas Development Minister, asserted: 'We should not be coy about the extent to which to do what is right can also be to do what is good for Britain.'[44] Clarifying this point, his Ministry adds: 'Most British bilateral aid has to be spent on British goods and services but this does not mean that we cannot provide worthwhile help to the poorest groups in developing countries. By choosing projects carefully we can ensure that benefits go to them at the same time as offering valuable opportunities to British firms.'[45]

There is something undeniably seductive about this kind of argument, but also something seriously wrong. In logic, saying that aid benefits the giver because some of it is spent on his own goods and services is like saying that a shopkeeper benefits from having his cash-register burgled so long as the burglar spends part of the proceeds in his store.[46] As the eminent British economist Lord Bauer puts it: 'A businessman does not prosper by donating money to people, some of whom later purchase his products.'[47]

If we are to have subsidies – a dubious proposition in itself – then let them at least be efficient. Surely any government of an industrialised country that is minded to oblige its tax-payers to donate funds to profit-making corporations would be able to do so far more effectively if the transfer of wealth from public to private pockets were direct – rather than filtered through the medium of the Third World? If the subventions were out in the open, rather than deviously concealed within the aid budget, then – at the very least – they could be scrutinised much more closely and distributed with greater equity. Instead of going to a few big corporations, for example, they might be diverted to benefit a large number of smaller businesses.

Using Western aid to create profits for Western companies thus looks like a flawed and misguided policy, even in its own terms. It is, moreover, a policy that seriously impairs the ability of development assistance to do its *other* job – namely to provide 'worthwhile help' to the poor of the Third World.

NORTHERN EXPORTS, SOUTHERN POVERTY

A case in point is the human and ecological disaster of the Singrauli Power and Coal Mining Complex in India, examined in Part Four. After ten years of operations, involving the allocation of $850 million of multilateral aid, the World Bank belatedly decided to carry out an environmental and social-impact assessment of this catastrophic scheme. Its short-list of consultants to do the vital job, however, did not include any of the several Indian environmental groups actually in day-to-day contact with the poor communities harmed by Singrauli. All six of the candidates considered were large electrical-utility and engineering firms and all hailed from countries that were important contributors of funds to the Bank – specifically France, Canada, Australia, the United Kingdom, and the United States.[48]

It is in bilateral aid programmes, however, that the pressure to subsidise business in the donor countries most often results in projects that are badly conceived and that fail to deliver any obvious benefits to the poor.

For a start, goods and services purchased with 'tied' aid tend to be priced well above their actual market value, with artificial mark-ups of 20 to 30 per cent being quite normal and even higher margins exceedingly common.[49] Bangladesh, for example, found that railway carriages that it was obliged to buy from British suppliers were 50 per cent more expensive than comparable equipment available from other sources. Carriages purchased with tied aid from Denmark also turned out to have been excessively over-priced – they were three times more expensive than comparable equipment available elsewhere.[50] When the aid involved in such purchases takes the form of a loan rather than an outright grant – as is frequently the case – then it is not only the tax-payers of the donor country who are being cheated but also the poor in the Third World.

Price is just part of the problem: when a greater priority is put on meeting the needs of the supplier than on meeting the needs of the recipient then the quality of goods delivered often turns out to be second rate – or worse.

A classic illustration was the provision of fifty buses to Zambia under Britain's ATP. The £1.76 million contract had a positive impact on the bank accounts of two UK companies: British Leyland – which provided the chassis parts – and Willowbrook International, which provided the bodies. Unfortunately, however, the buses were entirely unsuitable for Zambian road conditions. In a matter of months after going into passenger service the Willowbrook bodywork had collapsed and, despite costly attempts at repairs, had to be scrapped. Within two years most of the BL chassis – which had by then been rebodied in older buses already to hand – had also become unserviceable; within five years only three were still in operational condition.[51]

Similarly British forklift trucks supplied to Sudan as part of the UK's aid programme to that African country turned out to be of a design that was wholly inappropriate for operation in hot conditions; as a result the recipients were saddled with expensive recurrent costs for maintenance. To add insult to injury, the manufacturer had fitted all the trucks with tyres of the wrong size.[52]

According to Overseas Development Minister Christopher Patten: 'Virtue can bring its own reward . . . it's not a crime to be popular.'[53] The tendency to give priority to commercial considerations, however, means that British aid has become increasingly *un*popular with its recipients, many of whom are at a loss to find any virtue in it at all.

Egypt, for instance, is today saddled with a set of gas turbines for electricity generation supplied at a cost of £28 million by Rolls-Royce. Although the turbines came with the lure of a £10 million subsidy under the ATP they have subsequently proved very expensive to run and represent a real and on-going burden to Egypt. The project proposal originated with Rolls-Royce itself and was hurried through by the Department of Trade and Industry and the Overseas Development Administration. Neither ODA nor DTI took the time to consider other more suitable alternatives that might have had lower running costs. There is, in addition, documentary evidence that both were fully aware throughout that the Rolls-Royce turbines were inappropriate for Egypt's needs. The proper concerns of the aid programme – development in Egypt – were simply overridden in the stampede to assist a British supplier.[54]

Problems like these arise increasingly frequently, whether ATP is involved or not. Timothy Raison (Christopher Patten's predecessor at the Overseas Development Administration) was so determined to win benefits for British business from the regular aid programme that, in 1985, he virtually forced the government of India to accept twenty-one Westland W-30 helicopters.[55] The sum of money involved, £65 million, was a pure grant courtesy of the British tax-payer; however, it was not ATP and thus was to be deducted from India's normal allocation for that year. The Indians objected. The money, they argued, could be better and more effectively spent in other ways. In addition, Mr Raison was proposing that the helicopters should be put into service with India's Oil and Natural Gas Commission to provide transport to and from offshore oil-rigs. The Westland W-30 was an unsuitable machine for this purpose.

Raison was incensed by these reservations and warned the Indian authorities that failure to place an order would *not* result in the funds earmarked for the helicopters being reallocated to other projects but, rather, would 'mean the loss of £65 million of British aid over the next two years' unless there was a last-minute change of mind.[56]

Inevitably that 'last-minute change of mind' did occur and the order was duly signed in New Delhi on 15 March 1986.[57] Westland, which was then in serious financial trouble – and could in fact have been bought up lock, stock and barrel for £65 million[58] – immediately placed triumphant advertisements in Fleet Street newspapers lauding itself for its business acumen. Anyone reading the copy in these ads ('three years of negotiation is over; two years of manufacture is about to begin') could have been forgiven for believing that Westland had pulled off a triumph of salesmanship. Nowhere was it mentioned, however, that this 'deal of the century' had been done entirely at the expense of Britain's overseas aid budget or that the Indian poor had been short-changed as a result.

The unsuitability of the Westland helicopters for their intended duties – foreseen by the Indians – quickly became apparent. Most of the W-30s delivered by April 1988 had, from the outset, performed below specification and had failed to cope with the heavy-duty nature of service in the oil and gas industry. With fifty-five major engine malfunctions recorded, and one fatal crash in which seven people were killed, it was little wonder that by August 1988 the Oil and Natural Gas Commission had 'redeployed' to lighter duties all but five of the twenty-one helicopters. It was, furthermore, an appropriate symbol of the real rôle of aid in the lives of the poor that these redeployed machines were now being used as air taxis by senior politicians, VIPs and wealthy businessmen. Even these privileged people might wish to reflect on an additional item of information about Britain's 'gift horse' helicopters: at the Westland plant in Yeovil, Somerset, production of W-30 ceased with completion of the last machine for India.[59]

Between 1982 and 1988 India received approximately £1 billion in aid from UK tax-payers – rather more than half as bilateral assistance, the rest through multilateral institutions.[60] This high level of funding, explains Christopher Patten, is accorded to the subcontinent 'because we recognise India's capacity to put British assistance to good use'.[61]

The Minister claims that projects aimed at alleviating poverty play an important rôle in the overall programme and would clearly prefer to regard the Westland incident as an aberration.[62] It is far from that, however, because the commercial distortions to which British aid is subject militate strongly against support for small-scale, local-level schemes of the sort that can be directly helpful to the poor. As John Toye, who is Professor of Development Policy and Planning at University College, Swansea, observes: 'Not much imagination is necessary to see that poverty-focused projects in the urban or rural sectors of developing countries may do relatively little for British exports or technical links.'[63] The converse is also true: not much imagination is needed to understand the attraction of large high-technology schemes to an aid programme that is as intent as Britain's is on giving kick-backs to export-hungry industries.

It is not coincidental that major construction works and advanced power-stations are particularly prominent amongst the items that British aid pays for in India: UK firms that specialise in these fields *have* to sell their products and services abroad if they are to survive at home. The availability of concessional finance is vital to achieving this task. As Graeme Anderson, Deputy Chairman of Northern Engineering Industries, explains candidly: 'No longer do we sell on the basis of the excellence of our plant, or its reliability . . . Unless we are able to match the finance offered by our competitors the customer will not buy from us.'[64]

NEI, which has consistently been amongst the principal beneficiaries of the ATP slush fund, is forced to sell in the developing world because of a lack of domestic orders.[65] It has done particularly well in India, but its work there has been the subject of growing acrimony.

At Rihand, for example, one of India's most remote areas, the company has for some years been engaged on the construction of a huge power-station which is to be fuelled with coal from the notorious Singrauli mines. The Indian government, however, is irritated by NEI's performance which has fallen badly behind schedule – mainly because the British firm proved itself to be inadequately prepared for conditions in one of the poorest parts of the subcontinent. Ridiculous as it may seem, what NEI set out to do at Rihand when it started work there in 1983 was to build a straight clone of the kind of plant that might have been ordered from it in the UK by the Central Electricity Generating Board. Subsequently – and painfully – it has learned that it could do no such thing. Today the company admits: 'There were problems at the start of this project.' Optimistically, however, it adds that 'these are now being worked out'.[66]

What cannot be worked out at Rihand is any kind of positive rôle for the £230 million power-station in the lives of the poor rural people who reside in the area. There has been some temporary employment provided – tribal women wearing dust-covered saris and clutching babies to their breasts are to be seen working on site, carrying piles of bricks or baskets full of concrete. However, there are no other obvious benefits at all: local villagers in their wattle-and-daub huts could not afford the electricity that will eventually be generated, even if it were to be offered to them.[67] They will, however, be exposed to the inevitable pollution from the plant which, like most bad things, will come free of charge.

Prem Bhai, a social worker who is struggling to improve conditions in the area, says pointedly: 'Development passes over these people and their villages like the electricity cables soaring overhead. They remain in poverty, sometimes ousted from their land, and facing ill-health from tuberculosis.'[68]

A fact much advertised by the Overseas Development Administration is that over 80 per cent of British aid goes to the poorest countries;[69] as Prem Bhai knows, however, this does not mean that it is the poorest people in those countries who benefit. Another and typical project that UK tax-payers financed in India was the complete renovation and updating of Calcutta's traffic-light system.[70] It is almost – but not quite – needless to say that the Indian poor do not drive cars (although they do get run over by them from time to time).

In Africa, where the population is still overwhelmingly rural and where incomes are amongst the lowest in the world, the 1980s saw a steep decline in British allocations for rural development – from about £10 million a year to just £200,000 a year.[71] To the detriment of both the rural and the urban poor, however, the decade also saw a steady rise in the importance of big infrastructural schemes.

In the Sudan, for example, British aid has focused in recent years on the construction of two power-stations to provide unbroken supplies of electricity to the more prosperous northern suburbs of Khartoum, the capital city. These projects, which have resulted in a bonanza of procurement for British companies, cost tax-payers £78 million – more than 75 per cent of *all* UK bilateral aid to the impoverished Sahelian country for the period 1984 to 1986.[72]

Khartoum, which contains only about 15 per cent of the Sudanese population, was founded in the nineteenth century by General Gordon, who patriotically laid it out in the form of a Union Jack. Today the city's best hotel, the Hilton International (owned by the British company Ladbrokes), stands at the confluence of the Blue and White Niles and provides a comfortable venue for British aid workers to mingle with the team of British engineers recently called in to provide the sophisticated skills needed to operate the high-tech British-built power-stations – skills that are not available locally.[73]

Taking their meals from room service or watching imported movies on video, Hilton guests can completely forget that they are in the middle of one of the poorest and most shambolic countries on the face of the earth. Within just a few kilometres of the brightly illuminated hotel, however, dense slums that have never known an electric light huddle together against the elemental edge of the red and encroaching desert. To the refugees, mendicants and prostitutes who squat here (and who are occasionally flooded out when, as in August 1988, the Nile bursts its banks) 'development' means the police who will move them on with bulldozers, if it means anything, and the costly power-stations at Khartoum North and Burri are just irrelevant extravaganzas that belong in someone else's world.

Much the same can be said of the Greater Dhaka electricity transmission and distribution system in Bangladesh, which is costing the British tax-payer £38 million – a significant sum equal to the entire amount of UK assistance to that Asian country in 1986.[74] More than 85 out of every 100 Bangladeshis live in rural areas and thus, by definition, cannot benefit from the electrification of the capital city.[75] Furthermore, even in Dhaka itself, the main users of the system will not be the poor but, rather, the middle classes (and the large foreign community) who can afford to be connected up to the electricity grid. This is why a team of British consultants who have won a £3 million supervision contract in connection with the project are concentrating their efforts exclusively on the wealthy suburb of Gulsham, which has a population density of around eighteen people per acre; by contrast, in the Old City where the poor live but where transmission lines from the new power project are unlikely ever to penetrate, densities of 2,000 per acre are the norm.[76]

Only 4 per cent of the total population of Bangladesh presently has access to electricity;[77] with its marked urban and élite bias, however, the Greater Dhaka scheme is not seriously expected to make any difference at all to this extremely low figure. As a 'development' initiative it would therefore appear to leave much to be desired – even if there were a shortage of other items to spend scarce aid funds on in Bangladesh. This, though, is not the case. Indeed, in a country where 95 per cent of all children under the age of eleven are suffering from malnutrition, there is clearly a great deal that could be done.[78]

Britain's overseas aid is not at all exceptional in favouring large-scale, high-technology schemes like the Greater Dhaka Power Project that by-pass the poor but that provide massive benefits to rich-country contractors. Many similar examples could be cited from the bilateral programmes of other donors and from the operations of the multilateral agencies.

Worldwide, for instance, Japan dispensed $25 billion in aid during 1984-8, with the vast bulk of this being used to fund contracts for Japanese corporations. An authoritative 1988 investigation found that even the relatively small share of the bilateral-assistance budget which is nominally 'untied' is, in practice, always restricted to procurement bids from companies in Japan and in the recipient country: 'The Japanese company wins almost 100 per cent of the time,' the study concluded.[79]

Inevitably, Japanese aid, targeted to reach $50 billion in the period 1989-92,[80] supports the kinds of scheme that Japanese suppliers are able to make money out of – whether or not these schemes are worthwhile from a developmental point of view. For similar reasons, Canada's aid programme has frequently put the poor last as a result of commercial pressures.

An example is provided by Tanzania, where more than 80 per cent of all Canadian development assistance is tied to the procurement of Canadian goods and services.[81] In the 1970s CIDA (the Canadian International Development Agency) gave its support to a scheme supposedly designed to help Tanzania to become self-sufficient in wheat production. By the mid-1980s, however, with $44 million spent, it had become clear that this objective would never be achieved; indeed, the only real beneficiaries of fifteen years of work were Canadian companies that had supplied expensive agricultural equipment, spare parts and technical back-up throughout the life of the project.

Effective as they may be in Canada, the capital-intensive production methods of Western-style agribusiness should not necessarily be expected to work in rural Africa – particularly when delivered by people with no specialised experience of the problems of tropical agriculture or of peasant production.[82] In Tanzania, failure to recognise the implications of these challenges, together with a rather dogmatic emphasis on securing benefits for Canadian firms, resulted in a wasteful and inappropriate project that was of no value whatsoever for the poor.

Excessive use of advanced and complicated technology meant that the 250 Tanzanian staff could only be recruited from the already educated, English-speaking – and thus affluent – middle classes; 70 of these people sent to Canada for technical training failed to continue working on the scheme on their return. Meanwhile, with machines doing most of the menial work, the demand for casual labour was small. At harvest time jobs could be provided for no more than 100 local men who were paid at the rate of just $1.50 per day; their wives were able to earn almost twice as much scavenging for grains behind the combines.

The main problem with the project, however (to which, incidentally, the Tanzanian government and CIDA contributed in equal measure), was that it failed dismally to live up to its promise of bountiful cost-efficient production. The six farms, laid out in prairie style, each required an initial investment of $1.5 million for equipment; subsequently, costs of spare parts for the combine harvesters, plus 100,000 litres of fuel per farm per annum, proved to be a crippling burden – but these costs had to be met if the machinery was to be kept working. By the mid-1980s recurrent running costs had risen to around $4 million a year. At the same time, with the rate of growth in the demand for wheat exceeding 5 per cent per annum, with the project only meeting one quarter of this,[83] and with self-sufficiency still a distant dream, impoverished Tanzania found itself obliged to pay through the nose to import significant quantities of the cereal from Canada and from the United States.[84]

THE DRUG OF FOOD AID

The taste for wheat is a relatively new phenomenon in Africa, but it is an important one. Because of it, traditional home-grown staples like maize are increasingly regarded as 'low-class' peasant fare, and are going out of fashion; indeed, the continent's governments now spend about $2 billion a year on wheat imports.[85] Similar trends are also evident elsewhere in the Third World as refined white flour imposes its stodgy domain from Mexico to Indonesia and from Thailand to Peru. Canada has played its part in creating this nutritionally and economically disastrous situation. It is the aggressive food aid policies of the United States, however, that have most effectively 'hooked' developing countries on the 'fix' of Western farm produce.

Administering America's huge 'Food for Peace' programme under Public Law 480, the US Agency for International Development operates on the streetwise principle that those who accept free handouts today will become paying customers tomorrow. AID's ethics are really very little different from those of a drug pusher when it boasts – as it frequently does – about past recipients of food aid who are now among the top purchasers of US agricultural exports: 'In 1986 seven of the ten leading importers of US farm goods had been Food for Peace recipients. Of the fifty largest customers of American commodities, thirty are developing countries, thirteen have received PL 480 assistance and twenty-one are former beneficiaries.' Furthermore:

> Countries that have received substantial American aid have increased their imports from the United States at a 30 per cent *faster rate* than their purchases from other nations. In 1981 alone, South Korea imported $2.1 billion worth of our agricultural products – more than the value of all US food aid provided to that country between 1955 and 1959 . . . The record shows that food assistance can produce lucrative trade relationships and can generate new commercial markets.[86]

The markets that have been opened up by the Food for Peace programme are in fact 'critical to America's ailing farm economy', as AID admits.[87] Today over 40 per cent of US commercial agricultural exports go to developing countries. The proportion rises to nearer 50 per cent in the specific categories of grain and flour sales, and approaches 70 per cent in the case of wheat.[88] In addition, every year – courtesy of the ever-patient tax-payer of course – US agribusiness benefits from AID procurement orders worth around $1.8 billion.[89] American companies exporting corn and rice receive a further direct bonus, since the aid programme is specifically designed to inhibit the emergence of potential competitors overseas: recipients of PL 480 wheat only get their supplies on condition that they themselves do not attempt to export any corn or rice that they may grow.[90]

What is good for General Mills, Ralston Purina, or Quaker Oats, therefore, is not necessarily good for the Third World. Indeed, in a number of cases, food aid has had an utterly devastating effect on the agricultural output of developing countries. As well as creating expensive addictions to non-indigenous cereals, and discouraging export-production of items like corn and rice in which the USA is expanding its own trade, PL 480 has frequently served as a major disincentive to the efforts of local farmers to grow food even for domestic consumption. Simply stated, the dumping of large quantities of low-priced American grain in Africa or Asia can make it economically impossible for small producers in those regions to compete.

South Korea has been hailed by a former Assistant Secretary for Agriculture as: 'The greatest success story worldwide of the Food for Peace programme in terms of contribution to the growth of that nation'.[91] While it is undoubtedly true that South Korea has grown, the rôle of US food aid in this process is not so clear – and certainly not admirable. In an economy that has been dominated by export-orientated manufacturing based on cheap labour, the main function of US grain imports in the 1950s and 1960s seems to have been to allow the government to maintain a 'cut-price food' policy that put many small Korean farmers out of business. Prices paid to domestic rice producers, for example, were consistently below cost – with the result that millions of rural people were forced to seek jobs in the cities.[92]

In Haiti in the late 1970s, researchers found PL 480 commodities to be available in almost every market-place and in direct competition with locally produced foods.[93]

Well over a decade later the same is true in Somalia. In this country in the Horn of Africa markets in even the most remote rural areas typically offer for sale bags of grain and tins of vegetable oil bearing the familiar Food for Peace logo of friendly, shaking hands. From time to time visiting journalists – and some of the more ignorant members of the aid fraternity – have concluded from this that corrupt Somali officials are selling food aid that is supposed to be *given* to the poor. Reports to this effect, however, are based on a misconception. The fact is that the Somali government (like the government of Haiti) receives the bulk of its US food supplies under Title I of PL 480, which means that it pays for them – albeit on the basis of long-term loans. This being the case, it can of course do what it likes with its purchases and is in fact encouraged to sell on the open market.

In January 1987 the Title I programme in Somalia was subjected to an investigation by auditors whose principal objective was to determine if it 'effectively supplemented Somalia's food supply without discouraging local production'.[94] The conclusions of the investigation are damning.

'Title I food aid to Somalia', the auditors note, 'exceeded annual deficits in food supplies.' In consequence:

> At November 1986, 7,007 metric tons of corn and 2,727 metric tons of soft wheat remained unsold in government warehouses after about fifteen months, and had deteriorated. The audit staff requested a laboratory analysis of the grain, because of concern about the potential adverse impacts of the distribution of unwholesome US-produced food. The analysis determined that the grain was unfit for human consumption, resulting in a loss to the government of Somalia of $1.5 million.[95]

Another problem was the scheduling of deliveries. Shipments of food aid to any country should arrive during the months just prior to the major harvest if they are to be at all effective or helpful. 'At that time', as the auditors note, the cheap imports 'can best stem hunger resulting from crop shortfalls and least depress the prices local farmers get for their production'. In the case of Somalia, however: '100 per cent of the 1985 Title I food grain and 92 per cent of the 1986 grain arrived *during* the harvest period – the worst possible time.'[96]

Blaming this unequivocally on 'poor planning by USAID/Mogadishu', the auditors note two adverse results. First: 'food valued at $16 million in 1985 and $12 million in 1986 was not made available during the critical hungry period'. Second, and worse still, the untimely deliveries, coinciding with the harvest, caused a glutted market when they did arrive. The across-the-board 40 per cent drop in prices that resulted 'discouraged farm production because farmers made less profit'.[97]

The sad epitaph came a few months later when famine struck Somalia's Central Rangelands (see Part One for a full account). By forcing the country's own farmers to compete with dumped American surpluses in the relatively good years of 1985 and 1986, USAID had indeed deprived them of profits – and thus of any incentive to increase their production. When food aid *was* needed during the 1987 emergency, however, the Agency was initially unwilling to supply it and subsequently unable to get it to the hungry with speed and efficiency; thousands died needlessly as a result.

As a hybrid of commerce and humanitarianism, food aid displays the worst aspects of both its parents and seems to have inherited none of their better qualities. The efficiency and single-mindedness of private enterprise might have salvaged something out of the Somali disaster – and would certainly have saved lives; instead incompetence and confusion ruled. The selflessness and devotion to duty of a genuinely welfare-orientated institution might have helped; but the day was won by petty bureaucratic concerns, snobbery and hubris.

Aid can sink lower than this, however – and frequently does.

CANDY FROM A BABY

In Somalia again, that archetypally 'aided' country, I remember being driven – much too fast – down a brutal highway. Its recently macadamised surface only added to the bone-pulverising solidity of an apparently endless series of pot-holes and deep corrugations.

'Dear God,' I protested as my head hit the roof of the Landcruiser for the seventh or perhaps the eighth time in as many minutes, 'who built this bloody road?'

'The European Economic Community,' my Somali companion replied smugly. A moment later, as the vehicle came to a screeching halt on the edge of an inexplicable abyss, he added: 'And this particular stretch was the contribution of Italy.'

In a sense the entire highway, which connects Mogadishu, the capital, with the southern port of Kismaayo, can be blamed on the Italians: it was built during 1982–3 by a Milanese contractor who won the $100 million contract in open tender from the EEC. Somalia will still be repaying the Community's long-term, low-interest loan in the year 2023. This is unfortunate in view of the fact that the road itself had virtually ceased to be serviceable by 1988.

Badly engineered and shoddily surveyed, it is now in such a shocking state of repair that lorries avoid it altogether: by driving alongside it rather than on it they have created deep gullies which greatly increase the rate at which it is being undermined and washed away. In some places it can still carry cars and light trucks, although few vehicles that make the journey arrive at their destination entirely undamaged. Breakdowns are common and there are numerous accidents: several people have been killed as a result of roll-overs resulting from blown-out tyres.

No one has yet computed the cost to Somalia's transport fleet; what is clear, however, is that the government can no longer afford to pay for the continuous maintenance and resurfacing that the road requires. As a result, a project that should have been an asset to the impoverished East African nation has transformed itself into a liability and a reproach. The only winner is the Italian contractor who – although forbidden to work in Somalia again – is free and clear with the fat profit obtained by cutting corners and using sub-standard materials and techniques.

Meanwhile, in the sprawling central African country of Zaïre, General Electric and the US contracting firm Morrison-Knudsen have made handsome sums out of the $1.5 billion Inga-Shaba Power Project with its 1,000-mile high-tension transmission-line. Passing over rough terrain on its way to the Maluku steel mill and copper refinery, the line has been explicitly engineered to preclude the provision of electricity to the many poor rural villages en route; the copper and steel plants that it is destined for, however, are not at present functioning properly and are not thought likely to do so in the foreseeable future.[98]

Most expert observers concur that, as a development project, Inga-Shaba was ill-conceived from the outset: the electricity that it provides could have been generated much more cheaply and efficiently in other ways and without recourse to expensive foreign expertise. In support of this view State Department officials have recently been quoted as saying that the principal reason that the power-line was opted for by Zaïre was that it provided a big construction contract for US industry in return for continued American support for the deeply unpopular government of President Mobutu Sese Seko.[99]

Meanwhile, in north-eastern Guatemala, foreign companies have done well out of the construction of the massive Chixoy hydroelectric dam. This, as we saw at the end of the last part, was originally priced at $340 million; the final bill, however, turned out to be approximately thrice as much.

An important factor in the very dramatic cost-escalation that the project suffered was the collapse in 1983 of a tunnel through which water was supposed to travel to the power-station. It has been suggested that this accident, which extended the construction period by two years and added an estimated $165 million to the bottom line, may well have been the result of poor workmanship by members of the LAMI consortium which built the dam. 'The engineering companies overlooked warnings. They knew it was a lousy site,' complains Robert Balsells, President of INDE, the Guatemalan electricity board.[100]

Now threatening legal action, INDE claims that the members of the consortium – Lahmeyer International of West Germany, Motor Columbus of Switzerland, and the International Engineering Company of California – were negligent. LAMI, however, denies the charge. 'It is a pity for the country,' shrugs one official, Martin Lommatzch, 'but I do not feel responsible.'[101]

The dam was financed by the World Bank which, despite the controversy, is still collecting payments of interest and principal on its massive loan to Guatemala – one of the poorest countries in Central America where 75 per cent of the population earn less than $300 per annum.[102]

The Bank likes to act as though it is above corruption and graft; frauds and financial irregularities, however, occur frequently within the hallowed halls of the largest source of development assistance on earth. Recent instances brought to light include an employee who violated conflict-of-interest guidelines by accepting an expenses-paid trip to Europe from a supplier of computer services; three employees who covered up the fact that the file of a favoured contractor was incompletely documented; and a high-ranking procurement official who awarded business worth $1 million on a sole-source basis in direct contravention of the Bank's own rules and regulations.[103]

Cosy links between the private sector and officials who control the purse-strings of public money can lead to some spectacular abuses: in the case of one World Bank contract an estimated *$3 million more than necessary* was paid to a supplier of pump-sets for a tube-well project in Bangladesh. Lower alternative bids of equal quality were available and had been recommended by staff at the Dhaka office. These recommendations, however, were mysteriously overruled by Washington. Robbing the Bank, as one jaded official put it at the time, was 'easier than robbing a bank'.[104]

The fact is that many Western companies working on aid contracts in the Third World are allowed to get away with daylight robbery. This can happen as a result of collusion between entrepreneurs and corrupt aid administrators or because the officials concerned are simply idle and negligent. Either way, where foreign assistance budgets are concerned it seems that stealing from tax-payers, and from the poor, is just like stealing candy from a baby.

HARD CHEESE IN JAMAICA

One scheme in the Caribbean island of Jamaica illustrates the kind of abuses that can occur, and is worth describing at some length. Financed by the US Agency for International Development it was marred from the outset by wastage and bad management, greed, opportunism, and conflicts of interest. These failings, all involving a private contractor, were only uncovered by AID's auditors after millions of dollars had been lost.

At the beginning of the 1980s a large US agricultural company, Land O'Lakes Inc. (LOL) of Minnesota, won a contract from the American agency to provide technical assistance to Jamaican agriculturalists. In 1983, while working on this project, LOL put in a proposal suggesting that surplus US commodities could be used to create a private non-profit foundation for financing further agricultural development in Jamaica. AID liked the proposal and approved it in 1984. The result was the formation of the Jamaica Agricultural Development Foundation to which the Agency agreed to donate 4,000 tonnes of US cheese and butter every year until 1990.

The idea was simple and innovative: local revenue earned from butter and cheese sales would finance the Foundation's operating expenses and would also provide cash for loans, grants, and equity investments to promote Jamaica's agricultural sector. Neither were the sums involved small: by the end of 1985 the Foundation had received $6 million worth of dairy produce from the USA. Things did not work out quite as planned, however – mainly because Jamaicans did not like, and thus would not buy, American salted butter; besides, there were cheaper alternatives available locally. As a result sales were negligible, storage costs soared and the Foundation quickly got into trouble. Eventually, to avoid bankruptcy, it had to be bailed out by USAID with more than $1.5 million of American tax-payers' money.

The few loans and grants that the Foundation had managed to make in the mean time under its mandate to promote the development of Jamaican agriculture had not gone to the recipients envisaged when AID had approved the project. Large and well-established companies had done well; small farmers and the nascent local dairy industry had got virtually nothing.

Even more worrying to the auditors, however, when they made a thorough study of the project in 1986, was evidence that one of the main beneficiaries of the Foundation's largesse had been Land O'Lakes Inc. Having originated the idea in the first place, and having written the project proposal, it had seemed natural enough in 1984 that LOL should be given a seat on the board of the new entity. This raised the possibility of a conflict of interests – a possibility that loomed large when it was discovered that the American company had been awarded fees of $185,400 by October 1985, apparently as compensation for its 'technical assistance services'.

In addition, when elderly surplus cheese donated by USAID began to deteriorate in the Foundation's warehouses, LOL was quick to recommend an answer to the problem: cheese that was only one to two months old would have to be blended with existing stocks. By a strange coincidence, furthermore, LOL's Minnesota plant just happened to have the required quantity of the right sort of cheese available. Since no young cheese was in the AID pipeline at the time, the Foundation bought LOL's product. The sum of money paid out, $400,000, was found by the auditors to be three times the world market price. Worse still, it was suggested subsequently that the whole expensive operation might well have been unnecessary.[105]

SKIMMING, DELVING AND LEAKING

It would be quite wrong to suggest that Western corporations are alone in putting their fingers into the aid pie and pulling out plums. Many in the Third World also help themselves.

In Bangladesh, for instance, a tiny handful of wealthy local 'commission agents' are reliably estimated to have pocketed a minimum of $136 million from aid transactions during a recent eight-year period.[106] According to the respected Bangladeshi economist Rehman Sobhan, these influential middle-men have now

acquired a material stake in an aid-dependent régime . . . Any trend towards abridging external dependence is likely to be directly inimical to these commission agents of foreign suppliers . . . Their external nest-eggs make it possible for them to travel abroad frequently where they enjoy the lifestyles of the West. They import luxury goods into Bangladesh both legally and illegally and provide a major source of domestic demand for luxury imports.[107]

It is not only prosperous urban intermediaries who skim off large amounts of the aid actually intended for the rural poor of Bangladesh. Out in the field, as in so very many other Third World countries, another set of filters is in place to divert even more resources from those who really need them to those who really don't.

An example is provided by the fate of 3,000 mechanical wells which were financed by a long-term World Bank loan to Bangladesh. According to a press release on the project, each well would serve twenty-five to fifty small farmers joined together in a co-operative irrigation group. In practice, however, as independent researchers discovered, virtually every well was quickly co-opted by the richest man in the village in which it was located (in one case the wealthy individual concerned *bought* 'his' well for $300 and then rented out access to it to his neighbours at an extortionate hourly rate which few could afford).[108]

A Bank official subsequently admitted:

> One hundred per cent of these wells are going to the big boys. First priority goes to those with the most power and influence – the judges, the magistrates, the members of parliament, the union chairmen. If any wells are left over, the local authorities auction them off. The big landlords compete and whoever offers the biggest bribe gets the well.[109]

Corruption at village level in the developing countries, however, is a minor issue by comparison with corruption at the top. In this respect, the case of Guatemala's Chixoy Dam again comes to mind.

General Romero Lucas Garcia's military government, which was in power in Guatemala during the bulk of the construction phase and which signed the contract with the World Bank, is today recognised by political analysts as having been the most corrupt administration in the history of a Central American country that has been afflicted by more than its fair share of venal and dishonest régimes.[110] According to Robert Balsclls, President of the state-owned electricity company, members of the junta pocketed about $350 million out of the $1 billion provided for the Chixoy project. IIe points to insurance documents that put the actual value of the dam at $650 million and suggests with an eloquent shrug: 'Draw your own conclusions.' Another expert observer, Rafael Bolanos, Dean of the School of Civil Engineering at Guatemala's San Carlos University, has a higher estimate of the extent of official theft: $500 million. The dam, he says, was the 'biggest gold mine' that the crooked generals ever had.[111]

The huge sums of international aid and development finance attracted by schemes like the Chixoy are consistently mined, dredged, delved for, dug up and salted away by Third World politicians who have seized power without any kind of popular mandate and who then single-mindedly set about enriching themselves at the expense of the poor in their own countries.

This process is sometimes acknowledged by the agencies concerned. On one occasion, for example, the World Bank admitted that between 10 and 15 per cent of all the money that it had put into projects in Indonesia had been dissipated through 'leakage' – a euphemism for high-level theft.[112]

THE CASE OF IMELDA AND FERDINAND

In the Philippines, another South-East Asian country much favoured by the Bank, an enormous foreign debt of $26 billion[113] had been built up by 1986 when President Ferdinand Marcos was overthrown. Most of the loans had been contracted to pay for extravagant development schemes which, although irrelevant to the poor,[114] had pandered to the enormous ego of the head of state. After Marcos was gone, however, it became clear that his rôle in creating this staggering liability went far beyond a predilection for expensive and inappropriate projects: a painstaking two-year investigation of his dealings established beyond serious dispute that he had personally expropriated and sent out of the Philippines more than $10 billion.[115]

Much of this money – which, of course, should have been at the disposal of the Philippine state and people – had disappeared for ever into Swiss bank accounts;[116] much had been invested in US real estate;[117] much had gone on fripperies: $100 million, for example, to pay for the art collection that former beauty queen Imelda Marcos used to decorate the walls of her favourite properties overseas. Her tastes were eclectic and included six Old Masters purchased from the Knoedler Gallery in New York for $5 million, a Francis Bacon canvas – fetchingly entitled 'Masturbation' – supplied by the Marl-borough Gallery in London, and a Michelangelo, 'Madonna and Child', bought from Mario Bellini in Florence for $3.5 million.[118]

Almost two years after Imelda and Ferdinand went into exile in Hawaii only one of these treasures had been recovered – a Fantin Latour flower painting found in a luxury apartment on New York's Fifth Avenue and auctioned at Christie's in November 1987 for $440,000. By that time another thirty-eight of the total of 155 paintings had also been located. These, however, could not immediately be returned to the Philippine authorities since they were in the possession of a long-time Marcos family friend, arms dealer Adnan Kashoggi. According to Ramon Diaz, chairman of the commission set up to track down the loot, the canvases – thought to include two works by Franz Hals – had been given to the Saudi multi-millionaire in an attempt to conceal their ownership.[119]

During the last decade of the Marcos régime, while valuable art treasures were being hung on penthouse walls in Manhattan and Paris, the Philippines had lower nutritional standards than any other nation in Asia with the exception of war-torn Cambodia. To contain popular unrest, strikes were banned and union organising was outlawed in all key industries and in agriculture. Thousands of Filipinos were imprisoned for opposing the dic-tatorship and many were tortured and killed.[120] Meanwhile the country remained consistently listed amongst the top ten recipients of both US and World Bank development assistance.[121] Mediated through aid, the connection between the great wealth of the Filipino leadership and the great poverty of the majority of the people could not have been more stark or explicit.

It was contrasts like these that, ultimately, led to the ouster of the Marcos régime. History will judge how much better the new administration in the Philippines will be. What is quite clear, however, now and for the foreseeable future, is that the country is going to have to continue to pay out each year between 40 and 50 per cent of the entire value of its exports just to cover the interest on the foreign debts that Marcos incurred.[122]

THE FAT MAN AND THE THIN MAN

Rather than penalising greedy and irresponsible Third World leaders like Ferdinand Marcos, Western aid often condones their behaviour, encourages them in their costly delusions of grandeur, and provides them with the wherewithal to keep up the bad work.

This was certainly the case with Jean Bedel Bokassa, head of state of the

Central African Republic from 1966 until 1979, who once admitted in a moment of rare honesty: 'Everything around here is financed by the French government. We ask the French for money, get it and waste it.'[123] The main bilateral donor, France, in fact provided its run-down and obscure former colony with about $38 million per annum in aid during the 1970s – not a colossal sum by Philippine standards perhaps, but enough to keep things going in one of the poorest countries in Africa if properly spread around. In December 1977, however, and in just one day, Bokassa was permitted to waste on himself no less than $20 million of that year's entire subvention from French tax-payers: he blew the money on a glittering but ludicrous ceremony that transformed him from a mere President into an Emperor. For the occasion, which was attended by thousands of foreign guests, the demented former captain in the French army wore a $2 million crown topped by a magnificent 138-carat diamond and draped himself in robes designed by Guiselin at a cost of $145,000.[124]

The Central African Republic – or 'Empire' as it was renamed after the events of 4 December 1977 – had at the time less than 170 miles of paved roads and a population immersed in abject poverty: average per-capita incomes were in the region of $250 a year.[125] Bokassa, however, felt quite justified in spending as much as he did on his own coronation: 'One cannot create a great history without sacrifices,' he explained, 'and this sacrifice is accepted by the population.'[126]

Africa is a continent that is justifiably renowned for the vast wealth hijacked and expropriated by its élites and for the sacrifices demanded of its long-suffering poor. There are even jokes on the subject – for example, the story of the fat man and the thin man that does the rounds during every crisis of hunger:

> 'You should be ashamed of yourself,' said the fat man to the thin man. 'If a foreigner saw you before he saw anyone else he would think there was a famine here.'
>
> 'And if he saw you next,' replied the thin man, 'he would know the reason for the famine.'

Dr Mahmood Mamdani, an Associate Professor of Science at Uganda's Makerere University, told a version of this joke on 19 March 1985 during a talk he gave at a Red Cross conference on the subject of disaster prevention. The conference was held in Kampala and Mamdani used the occasion to draw attention to some glaring sacrifices that the poor of Uganda were then making for the rich. He recounted tales of prosperous farmers who had bought up land at knock-down prices from desperate smallholders during a recent famine. One profiteer, who had acquired 500 acres, had told him without any shame: 'The famine helped me. People were in need. For the first time they were willing to sell land, cows – things they wouldn't dream of selling in normal times.' Mamdani added that the Ugandan government also appeared to be getting in on the act of making itself wealthy at the expense of the poor. Peasant farmers, for example, were getting from state marketing boards just 25 per cent of the final price of millet and less than 19 per cent of the final price of coffee. As a result of such practices:

> The peasant operates with a permanent handicap . . . his surplus pro-duct is regularly siphoned off. His cash income is barely enough to meet immediate needs – for tax, to replenish a hoe or buy some salt or medicine. He is thus forced to begin the production cycle with roughly the same or even a worse technical base than the previous time around.

In such a context, Mamdani asked, what is the rôle of foreign development assistance? He urged his listeners – who were mainly expatriate aid workers – that, at the very least, they should not behave in such a way as to bolster up the continued exploitation of the poor. Rather, they should seek to 'restore the initiative of the victim . . . to revive the creativity of the people . . . If labour is maimed and shackled by administrative coercion, we must organise to remove that coercion. If products of labour are appropriated through monopolistic market practices, we must organise to change these.' For giving such sub-versive advice Mamdani was deprived of his Ugandan citizenship by the government of the then President, Dr Milton Obote.[127]

A RUMBLE IN THE JUNGLE

In some countries you can lose more than your citizenship for questioning the status quo. Since 1965 Mobutu Sese Seko, Zaïre's terrifying President, has ruled his thirty million people with an iron fist: detentions without trial, torture, murders and disappearances are commonplace and no criticism of the régime is permitted.[128]

Zaïre, in terms of GNP per capita, was ranked the eighth-poorest nation on earth in 1987 – at which time life-expectancy at birth for the average citizen was estimated to be just over fifty years.[129] The hardships faced by ordinary Zaïrians, however, have not prevented Mobutu from becoming one of the world's richest men. His personal assets – most of which he keeps well away from Zaïre – are estimated by Western intelligence sources at between $3 billion and $4 billion.[130] Included in his portfolio are hotels, castles, mansions and luxury apartments in Belgium, France, England, Australia and the USA.[131]

The President has achieved wealth on this scale by the simple expedient of stealing it. According to Erwin Blumenthal, a German banker sent to Zaïre by the IMF, 18 per cent of the national budget is routinely earmarked for Mobutu's personal use. He squanders the money on such extravagances as all-expenses-paid excursions to Disneyland for ninety guests at a time.[132] Other important sources of funds for the President are business contracts, foreign aid grants and long-term loans for wasteful and exotic schemes like the Inga-Shaba Power Project: he has reportedly helped himself to approximately 20 cents off the top of every dollar of foreign assistance that has come Zaïre's way since 1965 when he was brought to power in a CIA-backed coup.[133]

Indeed, he has even robbed the CIA itself: in the 1970s the Agency gave him $1.4 million which he was supposed to use to finance the Angolan FNLA in its fight against the MPLA; instead the money went straight into his own apparently bottomless pocket![134]

In 1982 Blumenthal warned the IMF: 'Mobutu and his government regard the idea of paying their debts as a joke.'[135] This prophecy was disbelieved and Zaïre obtained consistent support from the Fund in subsequent years. In May 1986, for example, an IMF loan worth rather more than $200 million was agreed.[136] In October of that year, however, Mobutu made Blumenthal's warnings come true by announcing a moratorium on repayments.[137] The Fund, which had already assisted Zaïre to extract a world-record total of seven debt reschedulings from the Paris Club of creditors, was not put out by this temerity; instead of taking a tough line with Mobutu in 1987, an *eighth* rescheduling was helpfully arranged and new loans totalling $370 million were put his way.[138]

The irony is that if the President were to return all the funds that he personally has expropriated from Zaïre during his quarter-century in power, then the country's foreign debt, estimated at $5 billion,[139] would be reduced to an almost negligible sum. IMF austerity programmes which, amongst other things, recently led to the dismissal of 7,000 teachers from Zaïre's primary school system for 'budgetary reasons', and which cause great suffering amongst the poor in many other ways as well, are clearly *not* the answer under such circumstances[140] – and neither are new loans or generous rescheduling arrangements. Indeed, the entire rationale of continued Western backing for this free-spending tyrant must remain something of a mystery to the average tax-payer in Brussels, London or New York.

THAT VOODOO THAT YOU DO SO WELL

So often in Africa, and throughout the Third World, the main function of foreign aid seems to be to finance the emergence of 'kleptocracies'. In Haiti in 1981, for example, the IMF paid in $22 million to the Treasury as part of a standby credit; two days later a visiting team of Fund experts discovered that President Jean-Claude Duvalier ('Baby Doc') had withdrawn $20 million of this money for his personal use. It was also noted that a further $16 million had 'disappeared' from various state bodies over the previous three months and that the Central Bank was paying the elegant Mrs Michèle Duvalier a salary of $1.2 million a year.[141] All this happened long before the pro-American Duvaliers finally became such an embarrassment that they *had* to be removed. Indeed, a blind eye was turned to their thefts until 1986 and the IMF acted throughout as though the money it was supplying was actually being used properly; certainly it continued to extract its pound of flesh from the Haitian poor by imposing swingeing austerity measures that would supposedly make the republic better able to repay its foreign debts.

Haiti, by any standards, was a poor country in 1956, and it became steadily poorer during the years 1957–86 when the Duvaliers (*père* and *fils*) were in power. The proportion of the total population judged to be in 'desperate poverty' increased, for example; from 48 per cent in 1976 to almost 70 per cent in 1986 – at which time average per-capita incomes for three-quarters of all Haitians had fallen below $140 a year, only 10 per cent of rural people were functionally literate, 80 per cent of children under six had had at least one bout of malaria, and 75–80 per cent of *all* children were suffering from malnutrition (with over half the recorded deaths in the territory being caused by malnutrition and gastroenteritis).[142]

Interestingly enough, however, Haiti was a major recipient of foreign aid throughout the Duvalier era – with the United States, Canada, West Germany and France prominent amongst the bilateral donors and with the World Bank, FAO, WHO, UNDP and UNICEF the most notable of the multilaterals.[143] With all these 'assisters' on the scene, a question has to be asked: Did the ruin of the Haitian poor occur *in spite* of foreign aid, or *because* of it?

A definitive answer is difficult to arrive at, but one thing at least is immediately clear from World Bank figures on the country's economy: the plentiful availability of aid funds facilitated the Duvalier clan's efforts to maintain an extremely low tax régime for their cronies amongst the Haitian rich. By 1986 the wealthiest 1 per cent of the population had managed to seize 40 per cent of the national income but was required to pay only 3.5 per cent of that income in taxes.[144]

Such a bizarre state of affairs was made possible purely and simply by aid: under the rubric of Official Development Assistance it was Western tax-payers who in fact contributed the bulk of the Haitian government's budgets. Typically, during the 1970s and 1980s, aid financed two-thirds of government investment and also covered more than half of the national import bill.[145]

There was widespread awareness of the corruption and depravity of the régime; little effort was made to impose controls on how aid funds were spent, however. Indeed, the United States – the largest bilateral donor – stated frankly that its strategy was to 'place maximum responsibility on the Haitian government for the selection and design of projects'.[146] It might as well have trusted a thrice-convicted axe-murderer not to kill again, or a kleptomaniac not to steal when left unwatched in a department store.

While AID was being so charmingly credulous, the US Department of Commerce produced figures to show that no less than 63 per cent of all recorded government revenue in Haiti was being 'misappropriated' each year. Not long afterwards – and just before he was dismissed by Duvalier – Haiti's Finance Minister, Marc Bazin, revealed that a monthly average of $15 million was being diverted from public funds to meet 'extra-budgetary expenses' that included regular deposits into the President's private Swiss bank account.[147] Most of the 'public funds' in question had, of course, arrived in Haiti in the form of 'development assistance'.

Meanwhile, in one typical year, the Ministry of Sports allocated $2 million of the little that was left in the Treasury after Duvalier's depredations to pay for a stadium that actually cost $200,000 to build. At about the same time CIDA, the

Canadian aid agency, cancelled a multi-million-dollar rural development programme that it was financing when it discovered that 50 per cent of the 700 Haitian employees on its payroll did not actually work for the project at all – and possibly did not even exist.[148]

Few other donors followed Canada's example: despite flagrant and prolonged misuse of funds, deep-rooted corruption, and the violence and human rights abuses of the feared Tonton Macoutes, the West kept faith with the Duvaliers until the very last possible moment. It was appropriate that when 'Baby Doc' finally fled the country in 1986 to take up his comfortable exile in the south of France he did so in transport provided by the US air force.

MONEY HAS WINGS

The powerful in the Third World come and go; today they are in the Presidential palace doing business with international civil servants, tomorrow, with rebellion in the streets, they fly away to their carefully prepared retirement homes in Hawaii or on the Côte d'Azur. Their embezzled fortunes will long ago have gone out ahead of them, usually to Switzerland or to the United States. As former Treasury Secretary Don Regan accurately put it of America and the mighty greenback: 'We have become a haven currency and a haven country not only for people but also for their money.'[149]

There is a technical term for what is going on here, and that term – 'capital flight' – sounds just like the name of an exciting new board game. This is how the game works: public money levied in taxes from the poor of the rich countries is transferred in the form of 'foreign aid' to the rich in the poor countries; the rich in the poor countries then hand it back for safe-keeping to the rich in the rich countries. The real trick, throughout this cycle of expropriation, is to maintain the pretence that it is the poor in poor countries who are being helped all along. The winner is the player who manages to keep a straight face while building up a billion-dollar bank account.

Of course, in real life, things are somewhat more complex than this. Direct thefts from the aid pot – *à la* Baby Doc – are still rare; much more common are methods of personal enrichment that are indirect, subtle and devious. The really clever players are those who have understood that every dollar of development assistance that comes their way creates an opportunity for undetectable personal enrichment – even when donors insist on closely supervising the expenditure of the particular funds they have provided. Such supervision is not an obstacle to the enterprising fiddler who knows the meaning of the word 'fungibility'.

Food aid, for example, is eminently fungible because it frees the recipient government from the tiresome necessity of ensuring that its own people do not starve. While well-meaning foreigners feed the hungry, the leaders of a country afflicted by famine can spend *other* funds at their disposal on whatever they like: they can buy advanced weapons with them, they can overpay their civil servants, or they can make some more hefty deposits into their Swiss or Californian bank accounts.

Project aid is also fungible and thus creates the same kinds of opportunity: a road or a dam or an irrigation system paid for by someone else is a road or a dam or an irrigation system that does not immediately drain the national exchequer of funds. The President and his Ministers can therefore continue with impunity to treat the Treasury as their personal cash dispenser.

Possibly the biggest break that corrupt officials have ever had, however, as we saw in Part Two, is the new fad for 'structural adjustment': in return for reforms which usually hurt only the poor, such 'policy-based lending' injects millions of dollars directly into the recipient government's hands. Since no 'project' needs to be completed or accounted for, and since no hungry have to be fed, structural adjustment money thus lends itself perfectly to the theft and plunder of capital flight.

All in all, the sums that wing their way out of the Third World are very large indeed. It is estimated, for example, that corrupt Venezuelans have massaged and finessed enough money into foreign bank accounts to pay off their country's entire foreign debt – which stands at around $40 billion.[150] A study done by Morgan Guaranty Trust Company looked at ten heavily indebted developing countries in Latin America between 1983 and 1985: during this period, as the domestic living standards of the poor plummeted, moneyed people in the countries concerned managed to deposit $44.2 billion in Western banks.[151] Another longer-term survey covering the ten-year period 1976–86 came up with the following aggregate figures for capital flight: Argentina, $26 billion; Brazil, $10 billion; India, $10 billion; Indonesia, $5 billion; South Korea, $12 billion; Malaysia, $12 billion; Nigeria, $10 billion; Philippines, $9 billion.[152]

Mexico's flight capitalists drained off a breathtaking $56 billion during the decade[153] – a sum of money that represents almost exactly half of that country's total foreign debt.[154] Aid agencies and financial institutions, however, do not seem to take this apparently unmissable problem into account in their efforts to promote development in Mexico. In World Bank structural adjustment lending, for example, as one senior official admits, there has never been any 'mention of imposing limits on corruption or on capital flight – two of Mexico's biggest problems'. Indeed, the global lender has not even obliged the Mexican government 'to install a decent auditing system to control graft'.[155]

BAD TO THE BONE

Although it is the subject of a pious literature, and is credited with saintly and humanitarian motives, foreign aid – as we have seen – often keeps strange and brutal company. In Mexico and Zaïre, in the Philippines and Haiti, thieves and murderers, psychopaths and cheats have all been amongst its bedfellows. Elsewhere it has consistently bestowed its favours upon the big battalions. Big corporations, big and wasteful projects, big, ambitious, absurd development plans, big ideas, and big bureaucracies have all flourished thanks to aid's bounty. Meanwhile local-level initiatives, relevant and realistic strategies, and the energy and enterprise of the poor in the Third World have been ignored.

Aid is not bad, however, because it is sometimes misused, corrupt, or crass; rather, it is *inherently* bad, bad to the bone, and utterly beyond reform. As a welfare dole to buy the repulsive loyalty of whining, idle and malevolent governments, or as a hidden, inefficient and inadequately regulated subsidy for Western business, it is possibly the most formidable obstacle to the productive endeavours of the poor. It is also a denial of their potential, and a patronising insult to their unique, unrecognised abilities.

Resettlement schemes in Brazil and Indonesia, reviewed in Part Four, have typically absorbed investment at the rate of $12,000 per settler.[156] Such schemes, involving the transfer of huge quantities of Western aid to repressive and irresponsible régimes, have destroyed the environment on a near-apocalyptic scale, have wiped out indigenous tribal peoples, and have made the majority of the migrants materially poorer and more miserable than they were *before* the intervention of the World Bank and other donors. What would have happened, I wonder, if the money had *not* been handed over in bulk to sneering and insensitive bureaucracies, had *not* been used to enrich road-builders, forest-clearers and other corporate contractors, but had instead been divided up into $12,000 dollops and simply given to each of the settlers? What would have happened if even one-tenth of that amount – $1,200 – had been provided to each of them?

They would not, I suspect, have migrated at all if they had benefited from such an unprecedented windfall. To a landless Brazilian peasant or to a smallholder struggling to eke out a living in rural Java, $1,200 is a fortune, is equivalent to perhaps four years of income. I am confident that such people would have made effective use of money on this scale if it had been entrusted to them directly, would have invested it productively and intelligently in their home areas to transform their own lives and would, in the process, have permanently reinvigorated the flagging rural economies of the countries in which they live.

This is just a pipe-dream, however. Whether given for dams in India, resettlement in Indonesia, power-stations in Bangladesh, structural adjustment in Mexico or balance-of-payments support in the Sudan, our aid does not help ordinary people 'to help themselves' and it does not promote broadly based prosperity. On the contrary, it systematically empowers and enriches the very forces that today most efficiently stifle the initiative and resourcefulness of peasants, nomads, slum-dwellers and villagers throughout the Third World.

CONCLUSION

AID IS NOT HELP

His fame and learning and his high position
Had won him many a robe and many a fee . . .
Nowhere there was so busy a man as he;
Yet he was less busy than he seemed to be.

Chaucer, *The Canterbury Tales*

IN THE PERIOD 1950-5 total bilateral and multilateral aid from all sources rarely exceeded $1.8 billion per annum.[1] In the 1960s, however, the scale of the operation increased dramatically: disbursements of official development assistance in 1961, for instance, were 20 per cent higher than they had been the year before.[2] By 1962 total world aid had risen to just a shade under $6 billion and, by 1972, OECD member states alone were giving close to $10 billion a year.[3] By 1984 there had been a threefold increase in this OECD figure, OPEC member states had established themselves as major donors and the Soviet Union was also giving significant quantities of development assistance.[4] Total world aid in 1987 was just over $50 billion[5] – up about 7 per cent on the 1986 figure of $46 billion.

One of the remarkable aspects of aid's busy growth is the way in which giving more has, over the passing years, subtly become equated with doing better, indeed with moral virtue. As a result of the activities of pro-aid pressure groups and of effective public relations by the agencies themselves, 'increased aid' is now a phrase that is used interchangeably with 'improved aid performance'. In almost all diplomatic and economic forums, as the British economist Lord Bauer observes: 'Countries giving a higher percentage of their national income in official aid are described as better performers than others giving a smaller percentage.'[6]

Indeed so. Official development assistance today is a sacred cow which must never be killed; which, preferably, must be nurtured. Within the United Nations, for example – as we saw in some detail in Part Two – the whole debate is framed in terms of 'targets'. Since the 1960s the world body has been urging its member states to give 0.7 per cent of their annual GNP as ODA: those countries that do increase their aid, that do 'meet the target', are 'good' in the UN's terms; conversely, of course, those that decrease their aid are 'bad'.

A campaign launched by the British Labour Movement in 1988 promotes this naïve and simplistic notion. Under the slogan 'Support the Just 0.7 Campaign' a leaflet tells us that Britain in 1979 'was the *most generous* of the top seven industrialised nations' because it was well on its way to 'achieving' the 0.7 per cent target. Since then, however, as a result of the 'shameful record' of the Conservatives, there has been a disgraceful turn-around. Having fallen behind France, Sweden, Denmark, the Netherlands and Norway in the generosity stakes, the UK is now 'on the way to being the *meanest*' nation in the world.[7]

Similar judgements on aid performance are also to be found in the influential reports of the Commission on International Development that met under the chairmanship of Willy Brandt in the 1970s and 1980s. While those donor countries that have surpassed the 0.7 per cent target are fulsomely praised, the failure of many others to reach it is described as 'deeply disappointing' and as a sign of 'a marked lack of political will'.[8] Noting that aid is in fact falling as a share of the GNP of several wealthy industrialised nations – for which 'there is no excuse' – the Commission urges the recalcitrant donors 'to set their sights once more on the fulfilment of the 0.7 per cent target'.[9]

If and when this target is reached – the argument continues – then the people of the Third World will *inevitably* benefit. The notion that increased aid from the North will result in improved conditions in the South is thus treated as though it were a self-evident truth.

It is far from that, however, particularly when what we are talking about is an increase amounting to just a few tenths of a single percentage point of the donor countries' GNP. Aid, after all, is just one amongst many different forms of financial flow – and these flows move from South to North as well as from North to South. To arrive at the real bottom line in the relationship between the rich and the poor nations it is therefore necessary to total up the figures for global ODA with all the other relevant transactions that take place in both directions.

When this is done an interesting and little-advertised trend emerges: since the early 1980s, mainly as a result of a sharp decline in new lending by private banks coupled with ongoing repayments at rising interest rates of old loans, the wealthy countries have consistently been net *recipients* of funds from the Third World – not net donors to it – even when ODA is taken into account. Initially the gain of the North was small – just $300 million in 1983. By 1984, however, it had risen dramatically to $12.5 billion. Since 1985 the poor South's net transfer of finance to the rich nations has exceeded $30 billion per annum;[10] the figure for the year 1 July 1987 to 30 June 1988, for instance, was $39.1 billion.[11]

My dictionary tells me that 'aid' is a synonym for 'help'. The whole notion that the developing countries are being 'helped' by the developed ones, however, seems to me – on the basis of these negative financial transfers alone – to be highly suspect.

This general view is best clarified by some specific examples. During the three years 1986–8 the International Monetary Fund received net payments totalling almost $8 billion from the Third World.[12] And recently the International Bank for Reconstruction and Development has also become a significant drain on the resources of poor countries: in the financial year to 30 June 1988 it was a net beneficiary of $1.9 billion.[13] Negative transfers of this sort in the multilateral sector are, however, dwarfed by those on a country-by-country basis. Between 1982 and 1987 British banks took in more than £80 billion in debt-service payments from Latin America.[14] Averaged out, this meant that every man, woman and child in that impoverished continent had transferred a generous £40 a year to the City of London. By contrast, Britain's bilateral aid to Latin America during the same period was worth just under 8 pence per capita per annum.[15] For the record, India – the UK's largest 'aid partner' – normally receives about 15 pence per capita per annum and Kampuchea, one of the poorest countries in the world, gets 0.0026 pence per capita per annum. Britain's official development assistance to Gibraltar and the Falkland Islands, on the other hand, averages out respectively at £748 per capita per annum and £5,350 per capita per annum.[16]

Such anomalies – found, incidentally, in the ODA of every single donor – illustrate a seminal point: aid is far too small in macro-economic terms to do much good to anyone (except to a few favoured mini-states like Gibraltar, in the case of the UK, or Israel in the case of the US). Neither will marginal increases of the kind envisaged by the Brandt Commission or by Britain's 'Just 0.7' campaign make any significant difference to this state of affairs.

At $60 billion a year, on the other hand, aid is already quite large enough to do harm. Indeed, as this book has argued at some length, it is often profoundly dangerous to the poor and inimical to their interests: it has financed the creation of monstrous projects that, at vast expense, have devastated the environment and ruined lives; it has supported and legitimised brutal tyrannies; it has facilitated the emergence of fantastical and Byzantine bureaucracies staffed by legions of self-serving hypocrites; it has sapped the initiative, creativity and enterprise of ordinary people and substituted the superficial and irrelevant glitz of imported advice; it has sucked potential entrepreneurs and intellectuals in the developing countries into non-productive administrative activities; it has created a 'moral tone' in international affairs that denies the hard task of wealth creation and that substitutes easy handouts for the rigours of self-help; in addition, throughout the Third World, it has allowed the dead grip of imposed officialdom to suppress popular choice and individual freedom.

Aid has its defenders, not least the highly paid public-relations men and women who spend millions of dollars a year justifying the continued existence of the agencies that employ them. Such professional communicators must reject out of hand the obvious conclusions of this book: that aid is a waste of time and money, that its results are fundamentally *bad*, and that – far from being increased – it should be stopped forthwith before more damage is done.

Whenever such suggestions are made the lobbyists throw up their hands in horror. Despite some regrettable failures, they protest, aid is justified by its successes; despite some glitches and problems, it is essentially something that works; most important of all – the emotional touch, the appeal to the heartstrings – they argue with passion that aid must not be stopped *because the poor could not survive without it*. The Brandt Commission provided a classic example of this line of thought: 'For the poorest countries,' it told us flatly in its final report, 'aid is essential to survival.'[17]

Such statements, however, patronise and undervalue the people of the poor countries concerned. They are, in addition, logically indefensible when uttered by those who also want us to believe that 'aid works'. Throughout history and pre-history all countries everywhere got by perfectly well without any aid at all. Furthermore, in the 1950s they got by with much less aid than they did, for example, in the 1970s – and were apparently none the worse for the experience. Now, suddenly, at the tail end of almost fifty years of development assistance, we are told that large numbers of these same countries have lost the ability to survive a moment longer unless they continue to receive ever-larger amounts of aid. If this is indeed the case – and if the only measurable impact of all these decades of development has been to turn tenacious survivors into helpless dependants – then it seems to me to be beyond dispute that aid *does not work*.

On the other hand, if the statement that 'aid works' *is* true, then presumably the poor should be in much better shape than they were before they first began to receive it half a century ago. If so, then aid's job should by now be nearly over and it ought to be possible to begin a gradual withdrawal without hurting anyone.

Of course, the ugly reality is that most poor people in most poor countries most of the time *never* receive or even make contact with aid in any tangible shape or form: whether it is present or absent, increased or decreased, are thus issues that are simply irrelevant to the ways in which they conduct their daily lives. After the multi-billion-dollar 'financial flows' involved have been shaken through the sieve of over-priced and irrelevant goods that must be bought in the donor countries, filtered again in the deep pockets of hundreds of thousands of foreign experts and aid agency staff, skimmed off by dishonest commission agents, and stolen by corrupt Ministers and Presidents, there is really very little left to go around. This little, furthermore, is then used thoughtlessly, or maliciously, or irresponsibly by those in power – who have no mandate from the poor, who do not consult with them and who are utterly indifferent to their fate. Small wonder, then, that the effects of aid are so often vicious and destructive for the most vulnerable members of human society.

All this notwithstanding, what is to be said about aid's much-vaunted 'successes'? Do they justify a stay of execution for the sacred cow?

India is a country that is frequently cited as a glowing illustration of what development assistance can achieve: since independence its overall economic growth rate has been high and, through the 'green revolution', it has transformed itself from a net food importer to a major food exporter. India is, in addition, the world's tenth-largest industrial power: it can boast a complete range of heavy industries and a burgeoning new-technology sector, plus its own space programme. Donors express their confidence in these achievements by continuing to channel very large quantities of ODA to the subcontinent – an impressive total of $5.4 billion in 1988.[18]

The underlying reality of India, however, for the vast majority of its population, is just about as grim as it is possible to find anywhere on earth. While four million television sets may be produced each year for the wealthy middle classes – the richest 20 per cent, who expropriate 49 per cent of total household income – the average per-capita GNP is still a mere $250.[19] This means that after more than forty years of independent 'development', and the absorption of tens of billions of dollars of foreign aid, India is still poorer than neighbouring Pakistan or Sri Lanka – is poorer even than Somalia in the far-off, famine-ridden Horn of Africa.

More than 300 million Indians, fully a third of the whole population, subsist below the official poverty line with even their most basic nutritional needs unmet. Two-thirds of the adult population still cannot read and write, and the infant mortality rate is scandalous – nearly twice as high as that of Vietnam.[20] In India's teeming cities there are an estimated thirty million unemployed. In the countryside conditions have steadily deteriorated for the majority who depend on farming: in 1947, half the national income came from agriculture; more than forty years later this share is down to a third, but about 70 per cent of the workforce is still employed on the land – the same proportion as a century ago.[21]

As for the green revolution, the truth is that its benefits have been very patchy. The relatively affluent north-western corner of the subcontinent – notably the states of Haryana, Punjab and western Uttar Pradesh – together with parts of Tamil Nadu in the south, have benefited disproportionately from the new technology and from heavy public-sector investment in irrigation, and have in addition scooped up the lion's share of agricultural subsidies (mainly for export crops). This perhaps explains why, despite increased farm output, per-capita availability of food grains has declined from 480 grams a day in 1964 to 450 grams a day now. 'You need', as one observer has put it, 'spectacles tinted the deepest possible pink to get excited about India's development record in the last few decades'.[22]

So much, then, for aid's leading success-story. There are others, too. In Africa, for example, one frequently hears that Ivory Coast and Malawi – both with high economic growth rates – represent definitive proof that development assistance is capable of achieving much. Yet the Ivory Coast today has accumulated a national debt of over $8 billion which must be paid by a population of just ten million – hardly an encouraging prospect for the future.[23] In a similar fashion, Malawi's 'economic miracle' also begins to look slightly tarnished when account is taken of the hard facts that face the poor: this country has the fifth-highest infant mortality rate in the world and only 4 per cent of the adult female population can read and write.[24]

Africa contains many lessons for the aid lobby. It has lost the self-sufficiency in food production that it enjoyed before development assistance was invented and, during the past few decades, has become instead a continent-sized beggar hopelessly dependent on the largesse of outsiders – per-capita food production has fallen in every single year since 1962. Seven out of every ten Africans are, furthermore, now reckoned to be destitute or on the verge of 'extreme poverty', with the result that the continent has the highest infant mortality rates in the world, the lowest average life-expectancies in the world, the lowest literacy rates, the fewest doctors per head of population, and the fewest children in school. Tellingly, during the period 1980 to 1986 when Africa became – by a considerable margin – the world's most 'aided' continent, GDP per capita *fell* by an average of 3.4 per cent per annum.[25]

Outside Africa the story is much the same. Indeed, in the Third World as a whole, while total outstanding debt rose by 10 per cent during 1987–8 to reach $1.21 trillion (39 per cent of GDP), economic growth rates fell from 4.2 per cent to 3.5 per cent.[26] Statistics like these translate 'on the ground' into a steady decline in household incomes and a consequent collapse in the standard of living of the majority of poor people. Thus, in Bangladesh, the infant mortality rate has risen from 101 babies per thousand in 1980 to more than 120 per thousand today[27] and, in Bolivia, GDP per capita has fallen by a third in the past decade.[28]

Both Bangladesh and Bolivia are significant recipients of foreign aid. In Nicaragua, by contrast, which has had virtually all its aid cut off since the collapse of the Somoza régime in 1979, things have improved noticeably during the 1980s. Without any of the so-called 'help' that outsiders normally offer, the Government of National Reconstruction has succeeded in reducing illiteracy amongst adult Nicaraguans from 53 per cent to just 13 per cent and has, according to the *New England Journal of Medicine*, achieved more advances 'in most areas of social welfare than in fifty years of dictatorship under the Somoza family'.[29] In 1979 – *with* aid – little more than a quarter of the Nicaraguan population had any access to medical services; by 1982 – *without* aid – three-quarters of Nicaraguans had regular access to health care. Overall agricultural production was 8 per cent higher in 1983 – without aid – than it had been in 1980 with aid. In addition, since aid was withdrawn, Nicaragua's infant mortality rate has dropped from 120 per thousand (in 1979) to less than 80 per thousand (in 1987), the number of vaccinations against killer diseases given to poor children each year has more than doubled during this same 'aidless' period, there has been a staggering 98 per cent fall in the number of new malaria cases, and – at the level of the national budget – total funds allocated by the Government to both education and health care have more than tripled.[30]

It would seem, then, that official development assistance is neither necessary nor sufficient for 'development': the poor thrive without it in some countries; in others, where it is plentifully available, they suffer the most abject miseries. Such suffering, furthermore, as I have argued throughout this book, often occurs not *in spite of* aid but *because* of it.

To continue with the charade seems to me to be absurd. Garnered and justified in the name of the destitute and the vulnerable, aid's main function in the past half-century has been to create and then entrench a powerful new class of rich and privileged people. In that notorious club of parasites and hangers-on made up of the United Nations, the World Bank and the bilateral agencies, it is aid – and nothing else – that has provided hundreds of thousands of 'jobs for the boys' and that has permitted record-breaking standards to be set in self-serving behaviour, arrogance, paternalism, moral cowardice and mendacity. At the same time, in the developing countries, aid has perpetuated the rule of incompetent and venal men whose leadership would otherwise be utterly non-viable; it has allowed governments characterised by historic ignorance, avarice and irresponsibility to thrive; last but not least, it has condoned – and in some cases facilitated – the most consistent and grievous abuses of human rights that have occurred anywhere in the world since the dark ages.

In these closing years of the twentieth century the time has come for the lords of poverty to depart. Their ouster can only be achieved, however, by stopping development assistance in its present form – something that might prove to be in the best interests both of the taxpayers of the rich countries and the poor of the South. Perhaps when the middle men of the aid industry have been shut out it will become possible for people to rediscover ways to 'help' one another directly according to their needs and aspirations as they themselves define them, in line with priorities that they themselves have set, and guided by their own agendas.

References

INTRODUCTION

1 Quoted in *South* Magazine, London, January 1987.
2 P. T. Bauer, *Equality, the Third World and Economic Delusion*, Weidenfeld & Nicolson, London, 1981.
3 Ibid.
4 Ibid.

PART ONE

1 *The Independent*, London, 3 December 1986.
2 *Sunday Times*, London, 30 November 1986.
3 Figures from *Aid for Development: The Key Issues*, World Bank, Washington, DC, 1986.
4 Oxfam estimate.
5 Frank Balance, *State of the Aid Mandate in the United States and Canada*, World Bank, Washington, DC, 1984.
6 The European Omnibus Survey, 1983, conducted on behalf of the European Commission for Agricultural Development by the Paris-based survey group Faits et Opinions.
7 Paul A. Laudicina, *World Poverty and Development: A Survey of American Opinion*, Overseas Development Council, Washington, DC, 1973.
8 Total official development assistance in 1984 was just short of $36 billion, up 5 per cent in real terms on the 1983 figure, largely as a result of 'exceptional emergency efforts for drought-stricken countries in Africa'. *Twenty-Five Years of Development Co-operation: A Review*, OECD, Paris, 1985.
9 B. E. Harrell-Bond, *Imposing Aid: Emergency Assistance to Refugees*, OUP, Oxford, 1986.
10 *The Independent*, London, 15 and 17 August 1988.
11 *Sunday Times*, London, 15 June 1986.
12 National Charities Information Bureau, New York, 29 April 1986.
13 *Sunday Times*, London, 7 December 1986.
14 *Daily Mail*, London, 14 January 1985.

15 Louis L. Knowles, *A Guide to World Hunger Organisations*, Seeds/Alternatives, USA, 1984, from figures based on ICA's own published accounts.
16 *Daily Mail*, London, 14 January 1985.
17 *The Plain Dealer*, Cleveland, Ohio, 21–7 December 1982.
18 *The Observer*, London, 9 November 1986.
19 B. E. Harrell-Bond, op. cit.
20 William Shawcross, *The Quality of Mercy*, Fontana, London, 1985.
21 B. E. Harrell-Bond, op. cit.
22 Ibid.
23 Personal communication from a World Vision supplier.
24 *The Plain Dealer*, op. cit.
25 From an unpublished paper by Sydney R. Waldron, a former American voluntary agency worker.
26 *World Vision* newspaper, November 1982.
27 Louis L. Knowles, op. cit., and report compiled by the West German charity Pax Christi International. In its own investigation of what happened World Vision discovered enough problems with its personnel that it dismissed and transferred a number of staff. The balance of probability is that the problem has had more to do with poor staff selection than with World Vision policy.
28 *Voluntary Funds Administered by the United Nations High Commissioner for Refugees: Audited Financial Statements for the Year Ended 31 December 1984*, UN General Assembly, New York.
29 Private communication from a UNHCR senior programme officer.
30 B. E. Harrell-Bond, op. cit.
31 Letter from Robin MacAlpine to Bishara Ali, 12 November 1987.
32 Letter from Bishara Ali to the author, 14 March 1988.
33 Sydney R. Waldron, op. cit.
34 Ibid.
35 Ibid.
36 *The Plain Dealer*, op. cit.
37 Ibid.
38 *Help Yourself: The Politics of Aid*, Third World First Links Magazine No. 20, Oxford, September 1984.
39 *The Independent*, London, 13 March 1987.
40 *One World News*, London, April 1988.
41 *The Plain Dealer*, op. cit.
42 Cited in Anders Wijkman and Lloyd Timberlake, *Natural Disasters: Acts of God or Man?* Earthscan, London, 1984.
43 Ibid.
44 *The Plain Dealer*, op. cit.
45 Ibid.
46 Dried skimmed milk, heavily marketed in the Third World during the early 1970s by multinational companies, is of much lower nutritional value than breast milk; however, the high-pressure advertising campaigns caused

many mothers in the developing countries to switch from breast to bottle feeding – a practice that resulted in large-scale infant deaths from malnutrition. Vitaminisation of skimmed milk can help reduce the problem; however, a complicating factor is that DSM must be mixed with water – and water supplies are often severely polluted. Mothers in poor communities frequently have neither the know-how, nor the means, to boil all water before mixing with DSM.

47 EEC Court of Auditors, *Special Report No. 1/87 on the Quality of Food Aid*, Official Journal of the European Communities No. C 219/1, Brussels, 17 August 1987.

48 Ibid.

49 Ibid.

50 Ibid.

51 *The Guardian*, London, 22 April 1986.

52 EEC Court of Auditors, *Special Report*, op. cit.

53 *The Times*, London, 6 February 1988.

54 *The Plain Dealer*, op. cit.

55 *The Independent*, London, 25 November 1987; *Spin* Magazine, Vol. 2, No. 2, New York, July 1986. See also Kurt Jansson et al., *The Ethiopian Famine*, Zed Books, London and New Jersey, 1987.

56 *The Independent*, London, 25 November 1987.

57 *The Plain Dealer*, op. cit.

58 Peter Gill, *A Year in the Death of Africa*, Paladin, London, 1986.

59 Quoted in *The Plain Dealer*, op. cit.

60 Confidential report produced in April 1985 by the Australian Council of Churches.

61 Personal communications with the author.

62 *The Plain Dealer*, op. cit.

63 Ibid. See also *Crusade* magazine, Christian Aid, London, May 1981.

64 Ibid.

65 Ibid.

66 Quoted in B. E. Harrell-Bond, op. cit.

67 Letter in *The Independent*, London, 15 July 1987.

68 B. E. Harrell-Bond, op. cit.

69 Sydney R. Waldron, op. cit.

70 R. C. Kent, *Anatomy of Disaster Relief*, Pinter Publishers, London, 1987.

71 Ibid.

72 *The Times*, London, 21 August 1987.

73 Assistance to Refugees: Alternative Viewpoints, International Symposium held in Oxford, 1984.

74 *Evaluation of the Office of the United Nations Disaster Relief Co-ordinator*, Joint Inspection Unit of the United Nations, Geneva, October 1980.

75 Ibid.

76 Ibid.

77 Ibid.
78 Ibid.
79 Lloyd Timberlake, 'The Politics of Food Aid', in E. Goldsmith and N. Hildyard (eds), *Earth Report*, Mitchell Beazley, London, 1988.
80 Otto Matzke, *German Review of Foreign Affairs*, Stuttgart, April/June 1982.
81 Interviewed in the documentary *African Calvary*, BBC, Easter 1985.
82 B. E. Harrell-Bond, op. cit.
83 Ibid.
84 R. Chambers, *Rural Development: Putting the Last First*, Longman, New York, 1983. Emphasis added.
85 For anyone wishing to study the subject of development assistance, Somalia – with its heavily aid-dominated economy – represents a considerable fund of material. The country is also 'disaster-prone', which is why it figures so prominently in the analysis of emergency assistance presented in this chapter. In recent years Somalia has suffered from repeated severe droughts and famines (at least five since 1974, when more than a million dispossessed nomads had to be installed in resettlement camps). The Ogaden war in 1977–8 produced a huge influx of refugees into Somalia, and periodic fighting along the border since then has created new refugee populations. Plagues of locusts are common, as are cholera epidemics. Perhaps unsurprisingly, the last case of smallpox in the world occurred in Somalia.
86 Personal communications during 1987 from Samuel Montague and Co. Ltd, then financial advisers to the Somali government.
87 Personal communication from former USAID employee in Somalia.
88 Joint Inspection Unit, *Staff Costs and Some Aspects of the Utilisation of Human and Financial Resources in the United Nations*, New York, 26 September 1984.
89 Ministers in the Somali government are remunerated at a rate of below 10,000 Somali shillings per month. This is equivalent to US$100 per month at the official rate of exchange, i.e. $1,200 per year – thus it would take a Somali Minister slightly more than forty-five years to earn the amount that a typical UN employee can expect to receive in just one year. At the *unofficial* (black market) rate of exchange, which reflects the real purchasing power of the Somali shilling, a ministerial salary is worth just $50 per month – i.e. $600 per annum. Middle-level Somali civil servants (for example, departmental directors, many of whom have university degrees), earn just 2,600 shillings per month. At the black market rate they would therefore have to work for 352 years to match a UN employee's annual income.
90 From which, I am proud to say, I was banned in February 1988. 'It is not obligatory that any reason is given,' I was told in the pompous letter that terminated my membership. This was amusing because, at the time, I was not in fact a member of any kind (although I had visited the club occasionally and had earlier held a temporary membership). The message of the 'banning' was clear: because I had sided with the Somalis over the issue of the drought I was

to be ostracised by the close-knit and xenophobic expatriate community in Mogadishu.

91 For a detailed account, see Graham Hancock, *Ethiopia the Challenge of Hunger*, Victor Gollancz, London, 1985, and Peter Gill, op. cit.

92 Tony Vaux, Oxfam Disasters Unit, quoted in Peter Gill, op. cit.

93 For a detailed account see Hal Sheets and Roger Morris, *Disaster in the Desert: Failures of International Relief in the West African Drought*, Special Report, Humanitarian Policy Studies, The Carnegie Endowment for International Peace, Washington, DC, 1974.

94 Ibid.

95 *The Independent*, London, 5 August 1987.

PART TWO

1 Address by Barber B. Conable to the Board of Governors of the World Bank and International Finance Corporation, Washington, DC, 30 September 1986.

2 *Washington Post*, 28 September 1986. For detailed accounts of the meeting see this issue of the *Post* and also the issue of 1 October 1986. See also *New York Times*, 30 September 1986.

3 Computed from figures in Ruth Leger Sivard, *World Military and Social Expenditures 1987–88*, World Priorities, Washington, DC, 1987.

4 *Wall Street Journal*, New York, 18 July and 27 September 1985.

5 *The Guardian*, London, 18 May 1987; *The Independent*, London, 11 August 1987; *South*, London, September 1987.

6 Computed from figures in Ruth Leger Sivard, op. cit.

7 Address by Barber B. Conable to the Board of Governors of the World Bank and International Finance Corporation, Washington, DC, 29 September 1987.

8 Ibid.

9 Quoted in Hal Sheets and Roger Morris, *Disaster in the Desert: Failures of International Relief in the West African Drought*, Special Report, Humanitarian Policy Studies, The Carnegie Endowment for International Peace, Washington, DC, 1974.

10 Anders Wijkman and Lloyd Timberlake, *Natural Disasters: Acts of God or Man?* Earthscan, London, 1984.

11 *Twenty-Five Years of Development Co-operation: A Review*, OECD, Paris, 1985.

12 From the United Nations Charter, 1945.

13 This definition of ODA is the one used by the Development Assistance Committee of the OECD and accepted by the aid industry as a whole. It is quoted in *Twenty-Five Years of Development Co-operation: A Review*, op. cit.

14 *World Bank Annual Report 1987*, World Bank, Washington, DC; *British Overseas Aid 1986*, Overseas Development Administration, London, summer 1987; *The Independent*, London, 3 September 1987.

15 General figures on military expenditure from Ruth Leger Sivard, op. cit.

16 *The Independent*, London, 24 October 1987.

17 The British government's 1988 Defence White Paper gave details of a budget of £19 billion for that year – approximately fourteen times larger than the aid budget. See *The Independent*, London, 23 May 1988.

18 *Sunday Times*, London, 19 July 1987.

19 *Time* magazine, New York, 1986, special supplement on duty-free shopping.

20 William U. Chandler, *Improving World Health: A Least Cost Strategy*, Worldwatch Institute, Washington, DC, 1984.

21 *Time* magazine, New York, 17 August 1987.

22 *Guinness Book of Records*, Guinness, London, 1986.

23 *The Independent*, London, 17 October 1986.

24 *Sunday Times*, London, 11 October 1987.

25 *The Independent*, London, 24 July 1987.

26 *United Nations: Image and Reality*, United Nations Department of Public Information, New York, 1986.

27 Ibid.

28 Ibid.

29 Figure calculated from information in Derrik Mercer, *Rural England*, Queen Anne Press, London, 1988.

30 The World Bank defines GNP as: 'the market value of the final output of all goods and services produced by the residents of a country in a year'. See *World Bank Atlas 1987*, World Bank, Washington, DC.

31 General Assembly Resolution No. 1522 (XV).

32 The Algiers Charter of the Group of 77, adopted at UNCTAD II, Algiers, 1967.

33 Reported in *Twenty-Five Years of Development Co-operation: A Review*, op. cit.

34 Ibid.

35 *World Development Report 1987*, World Bank, Washington, DC. The 1987 figure for British aid (0.28 per cent of GNP) was given in a parliamentary written answer by Christopher Patten, Minister for Overseas Development, in response to a question asked in the House of Commons by Joan Lestor, MP, Labour Party Spokesperson for Development (quoted in literature from *One World: Just 0.7 Campaign*, London, 1988). It is worth noting, meanwhile, that the main Arab oil-exporting countries give considerably more aid as a percentage of GNP than do the industrialised countries of the West. In 1986 Saudi Arabia gave 4.5 per cent and Kuwait gave 3 per cent. Despite rapidly falling oil revenues the 1986 average for all OPEC member states was still 0.9 per cent of GNP given as ODA (*World Bank Annual Report 1987*, World Bank, Washington, DC).

36 It is also smaller than British Petroleum and Texaco and much smaller than Shell and Exxon. For detailed figures on the earnings and profits of multinational corporations, see Axel Madson, *Private Power*, Abacus, London, 1981.

37 This is the case in the USA, for example, and in Britain. See *Facts About Aid*, US Agency for International Development, Washington, DC, 1986. In Britain total public expenditure runs at around £155 billion (*The Independent*, London, 24 July 1987); the aid budget, at around £1.4 billion, is just below 1 per cent of this. See *British Overseas Aid 1986*, op. cit.

38 *British Overseas Aid 1986*, op. cit.

39 Ibid. See also *Real Aid: Missed Opportunities*, Report by the Independent Group on British Aid, London, 1986.

40 *The Economist Development Report*, London, June 1985.

41 *British Overseas Aid 1986*, op. cit.

42 Ibid. See also *Ten Years of Lomé: A Record of EEC–ACP Partnership*, Report of the Directorate General for Development of the Commission of the European Communities, Brussels, 1986. Figures on EDF and Title 9 aid are from *ODA Flows and Prospects*, restricted-distribution report prepared by the World Bank for the meeting (3 September 1986) of the Joint Ministerial Committee of the Boards of Governors of the World Bank and the International Monetary Fund on the Transfer of Real Resources to Developing Countries.

43 *United Nations: Image and Reality*, op. cit.

44 Ibid.

45 Ibid. See also *ODA Flows and Prospects*, op. cit.

46 *United Nations Development Programme: 1985 and towards the 1990s*, UNDP, New York, 1986.

47 Ibid.

48 Ibid.

49 The exact number of FAO staff is not known and is complicated by distinctions between 'permanent' employees – who are included on official registers – and those hired on contracts typically of two or three years' duration (who are not always counted). The problem is the extreme secretiveness of the organisation itself; as one senior official puts it: 'We are so secretive that nobody knows what we are doing.' According to critic Rosemary Righter, whose estimates I accept: 'The FAO's Personnel Director says the organisation employs about 7,000 people. But the FAO's computer says 8,279. The true figure is thought to be 9,730.' *The Sunday Times*, London, 26 August 1984.

50 *Wall Street Journal*, New York, 18 December 1986.

51 *FAO: What It Is, What It Does*, FAO, Rome, 1984.

52 Ibid.

53 Ibid.

54 Douglas Williams, *The Specialised Agencies and the United Nations*, C. Hurst, London, 1987. See also Christopher Stevens, *Food Aid and the Developing Countries*, Croom Helm for the Overseas Development Institute, London, 1979.

55 Douglas Williams, op. cit.

56 Ibid. (quote).

57 Ibid.
58 Ibid.
59 *UNICEF Annual Report 1986*, UNICEF, New York.
60 Ibid.
61 From Article 1 of the UNESCO Constitution, adopted in London, 16 November 1945.
62 Douglas Williams, op. cit.
63 *The Guardian*, London, 4 October 1985 and 6 December 1985.
64 Douglas Williams, op. cit.
65 Ibid. See also *UNIDO: Programme and Budget 1986–87*, UNIDO, Vienna, January 1988.
66 *United Nations: Image and Reality*, op. cit.
67 See *British Overseas Aid 1986*, op. cit., and Douglas Williams, op. cit.
68 *British Overseas Aid 1986*, op. cit.
69 *World Bank Annual Report 1987*, op. cit.
70 Ibid.
71 Ibid.
72 Ibid.
73 *IDA in Retrospect*, Oxford University Press for the World Bank, 1982.
74 *World Bank Annual Report 1987*, op. cit.
75 *World Bank Atlas 1987*, op. cit. These thirty-five countries all have annual per-capita incomes of $400 or less.
76 *World Bank Annual Report 1987*, op. cit., and *World Bank Annual Report 1986*.
77 *British Overseas Aid 1986*, op. cit. See also *World Bank Annual Report 1987*, op. cit.
78 *World Bank Annual Report 1987*, op. cit.
79 Ibid.
80 Ibid.
81 Ibid.
82 Ibid.
83 Ibid.
84 *Asian Finance*, 15 September 1987. See also *The Economist*, London, 27 September 1986.
85 Morris B. Goldman, 'Multilateral Institutions and Economic Development', in Doug Bandow (ed.), *US Aid to the Developing World*, Heritage Foundation, Washington, DC, 1985.
86 *The World Bank and International Finance Corporation*, World Bank, Washington, DC, 1986.
87 Ibid.
88 Ibid.
89 *World Bank Annual Report 1987*, op. cit.
90 Ibid.
91 Ibid.
92 Ibid.

93 Ibid.
94 Ibid.
95 *The World Bank and International Finance Corporation*, op. cit.
96 *The Economist*, London, 27 September 1986.
97 *World Bank Annual Report 1987*, op. cit.
98 *The Economist*, London, 27 September 1986.
99 See, for example, James Bovard, *The World Bank vs. the World's Poor*, Cato Institute Policy Analysis No. 92, Washington, DC, 28 September 1987.
100 *World Bank Annual Report 1987*, op. cit.
101 Address to the Board of Governors, 29 September 1987, op. cit.
102 Speech at the Royal Institute of International Affairs, Chatham House, London, 18 March 1987.
103 *Facts About AID*, US Agency for International Development, Washington, DC, November 1986.
104 *IMF Annual Report 1987*, International Monetary Fund, Washington, DC.
105 *The Rôle and Function of the International Monetary Fund*, International Monetary Fund, Washington, DC, 1985.
106 *The IMF and the Debt Crisis*, Zed Books, London, 1986.
107 *IMF Annual Report 1986*, International Monetary Fund, Washington, DC.
108 Ibid., and also *IMF Annual Report 1987*, op. cit.
109 Caleb M. Fundanga, paper on Zambia and the IMF presented at the Institute for African Alternatives conference on the 'Impact of IMF and World Bank Policies on the People of Africa'. Held at City University, London, 7–10 September 1987.
110 Speech at the Royal Institution of International Affairs, op. cit.
111 Figures from Susan George, *A Fate Worse than Debt*, Penguin Books, London, 1988.
112 *Structural Adjustment Lending: An Evaluation of Programme Design*, Staff Working Paper No. 735, World Bank, Washington, DC, 1985.
113 *Brazil: A Paradise Lost*, Institute for Food and Development Policy, San Francisco, 1987.
114 Susan George, op. cit.
115 This was one of the points that came out most strongly from the range of authoritative papers presented at the 1987 IFAA conference, op. cit. See in particular Vali Jamal, 'Somalia: Economics for an Unconventional Economy'.
116 Giovanni Andrea Cornia, Richard Jolly and Frances Stewart (eds), *Adjustment with a Human Face: Protecting the Vulnerable and Promoting Growth*, Oxford University Press for UNICEF, 1987.
117 Ibid.
118 Ibid.
119 Ibid.
120 Ibid.
121 Ibid.

122 Ibid.
123 Ibid.
124 Cornia et al., op. cit.
125 Ibid.
126 Ibid.
127 *Food Monitor* (World Hunger Year), No. 37, summer 1986. See also Susan George, op. cit.
128 Cornia et al., op. cit. See also papers from 1987 IFAA conference, op. cit.
129 Speech at the Royal Institution of International Affairs, op. cit.
130 *Structural Adjustment Lending: An Evaluation of Programme Design*, op. cit.
131 *Structural Adjustment Lending*, Report No. 6409, World Bank, Washington, DC, 1986.
132 *Structural Adjustment Lending: An Evaluation of Programme Design*, op. cit.
133 Ibid.
134 *Structural Adjustment Lending*, Report No. 6409, op. cit.
135 *Washington Post*, 26 September 1985.
136 Staff Regulations of the United Nations, Article I, Regulation 1.5.
137 See Patricia Adams, 'The World Bank: A Law Unto Itself', in *The Ecologist*, Vol. 15, No. 5/6, 1985. The USA is the only member country to have passed a law which states that no funds will be provided to 'any international financial institution whose US representative cannot upon request obtain any document developed by the management of the international financial institution'.
138 Ibid.
139 *International Monetary Fund Annual Report 1987*, op. cit. Emphasis added. It seems to me quite bizarre that the Board of Governors of an international financial institution is allowed by its members to abrogate national sovereignty in this way.
140 Ruth Leger Sivard, op. cit.
141 Quoted in D. Seers and G. M. Meir (eds), *Pioneers in Development*, OUP, Oxford, 1984.
142 Quoted in Cheryl Payer, *The World Bank: A Critical Analysis*, Monthly Review Press, New York and London, 1982.
143 *Generation: Portrait of the United Nations Development Programme 1950– 1985*, UNDP, New York, 1985.
144 Ibid.
145 Ibid.
146 Quoted in P. T. Bauer, *Equality, the Third World and Economic Delusion*, Weidenfeld & Nicolson, London, 1981.
147 Ibid.
148 Quoted in Maggie Black, *The Children and the Nations*, UNICEF, New York, 1986.

149 Quoted in Teresa Hayter, *The Creation of World Poverty*, Selectbook Service Syndicate, New Delhi, 1982.
150 Quoted in Susan George, *How the Other Half Dies*, Penguin Books, Harmondsworth, 1976.
151 Quoted in Teresa Hayter, op. cit.
152 Ibid.
153 Ibid.
154 Kwame Nkrumah, *Africa Must Unite*, Heinemann, London, 1963.
155 *Sunday Times*, London, 23 February 1969.
156 Quoted in P. T. Bauer, op. cit.

PART THREE

1 US International Development Co-operation Agency, Congressional Presentation, Fiscal Year 1988, Washington, DC, May 1987.
2 *United Nations: Image and Reality*, UN Department of Public Information, New York, 1985.
3 Ibid. See also David Pitt and Thomas G. Weiss (eds), *The Nature of United Nations Bureaucracies*, Croom Helm, London and Sydney, 1986. The bulk of the $5.5 billion that the UN has to spend comes in voluntary contributions from governments as opposed to assessed contributions to the regular budget.
4 *United Nations: Image and Reality*, op. cit.
5 Richard Hoggart, *An Idea and Its Servants: UNESCO from Within*, Chatto & Windus, London, 1978.
6 *The Times*, London, 10 August 1987.
7 Interviewed in 'Mister Famine', a documentary in the 'This Week' series which was broadcast on Britain's ITV, 5 November 1987. The incident was also reported in *The Times*, London, 5 November 1987. For a more detailed account, see Dawit Wolde-Giorgis, *Red Tears*, The Red Sea Press, Trenton, NJ, 1989.
8 Reported in *The Independent*, London, 30 October 1987.
9 Ibid.
10 *The Observer*, London, 21 June 1987.
11 Ibid.
12 *The Independent*, London, 30 October 1987.
13 Otto Matzke, *German Review of Foreign Affairs*, Stuttgart, April/June 1982.
14 Ibid.
15 See *FAO Dossier*, published by the *Daily American*, Rome, 20 May 1983. See also *African Business*, London, August 1982; *The Sunday Times*, London, 26 August 1984, and Marcus Linnear, *Zapping the Third World*, Pluto Press, London and Sydney, 1985.
16 *Africa Is Starving and the United Nations Shares the Blame*, Heritage Foundation, Washington, DC, 14 January 1986.

17 *Sunday Times*, London, 26 August 1984; *African Business*, London, August 1982; *Globe and Mail*, Toronto, 5 November 1986.

18 *Sunday Times*, London, 26 August 1984.

19 *The Times*, London, 10 November 1987.

20 *The Times*, London, 10 August 1987.

21 *Sunday Times*, 26 August 1984; Marcus Linnear, op. cit.; *African Business*, op. cit.

22 *The Times*, London, 10 November 1987.

23 FAO press handout sent to author, 4 January 1989.

24 According to information supplied to the author on 4 January 1989 by Richard Lydiker (the Director of FAO's Information Division), Mr Saouma's annual remuneration package inclusive of post adjustment and representation allowances is $135,546.

25 Raymond Lloyd, 'Memorandum of Resignation from FAO', 10 December 1979.

26 *FAO Dossier*, op. cit.

27 *New York Times*, 18 June 1986.

28 Section 143 of the Foreign Relations Authorisation Act, Fiscal Years 1986 and 1987, p. 21. The Amendment reads as follows:

'*Subsection A:* The Congress finds that the United Nations and its specialized agencies which are financed through assessed contributions of member states have not paid sufficient attention in the development of their budgets to the views of member governments who are major financial contributors to these budgets. *Subsection B:* In order to foster financial responsibility in preparation of the budgets of the United Nations and its specialized agencies, the Secretary of State shall seek the adoption . . . of procedures which grant voting rights to each member state on matters of budgetary consequence. Such voting rights shall be proportionate to the contribution of each member state to the budget of the United Nations and its specialized agencies. *Subsection C:* No payment may be made for an assessed contribution to the United Nations or its specialized agencies in excess of 20 per cent of the total annual budget of the United Nations or its specialized agencies (respectively) for the United States fiscal year 1987 and following years unless the United Nations and its specialized agencies have adopted the voting rights referred to in Subsection B.'

Traditionally organised on the basis of one vote per member state, irrespective of the size of its contribution, the United Nations responded to the Kassebaum Amendment at the end of 1986 by forming a Committee on Programme Co-ordination with twenty-one members including all the main donors as well as representatives of the Third World. Charged with drafting the UN budget and setting spending priorities (subject to final approval by the General Assembly) the CPC is obliged to operate by consensus – i.e. the USA and other main donors are now theoretically able to veto budget decisions they oppose. In practice, however, they have had little success in doing so.

29 *Congressional Record*, Washington, DC, 7 June 1985.

30 *The Times*, London, 4 December 1987.
31 *The Guardian*, London, 29 April 1986 and 10 May 1986.
32 *The Independent*, London, 9 December 1986, and *APS Newsletter*, Rome, December 1986/January 1987.
33 *The Guardian*, London, 10 May 1986.
34 *Sunday Times*, London, 16 March 1986.
35 *The Guardian*, London, 10 May 1986.
36 Ibid.
37 *The United Nations Continues to Duck Needed Reforms*, Heritage Foundation, Washington, DC, July 1987.
38 Ibid.
39 One UN consultant I talked to regarded per diems as a useful supplement to his earnings. By economising on hotels and avoiding expensive restaurants he estimated that he could save between $40 and $50 per day: 'That's up to $500 on a ten-day trip.' In an average year, he told me, he could expect to clear about $3,000 in this way: 'Not bad if you consider that this is income that doesn't have to be accounted for to the tax-man.'
40 *How the UN Spends Its $1 Billion from US Tax-payers*, Heritage Foundation, Washington, DC, 1984.
41 *FAO Dossier*, op. cit.
42 *How the United Nations Can Be Reformed: The Recommendations of Four Former Ambassadors to the UN*, Heritage Foundation, Washington, DC, August 1986.
43 David Pitt and Thomas G. Weiss, op. cit.
44 *Follow-Up Report on Organisation and Methods of Official Travel*, Joint Inspection Unit, United Nations General Assembly, New York, 25 February 1986.
45 Ibid.
46 Ibid.
47 David Pitt and Thomas G. Weiss, op. cit.
48 *Follow-Up Report on Organisation and Methods of Official Travel*, op. cit.
49 Ibid.
50 *Standard of Accommodation, Travel Time and Rest Stopovers*, United Nations Secretariat, New York, 15 August 1983.
51 UNICEF is a persistent offender; UNDP and UNFPA have also been extremely dilatory in applying the rule. See, for example, *Proceedings of the Committee on Administrative and Budgetary Questions*, 4 October 1985 (UN Document A/C.5/40/SR.7).
52 *Standard of Accommodation, Travel Time and Rest Stopovers*, op. cit. There are exceptions to the nine-hour rule, however. For example: 'When designated to represent the Secretary General on ceremonial occasions these staff members shall be provided with first-class travel irrespective of the duration of the flights involved.' The Secretary General himself always flies first class and also uses Concorde from time to time.
53 Ibid.

54 Ibid.
55 Ibid.
56 *New York Times*, 30 April and 2 May 1986.
57 *Daily Telegraph*, London, 4 October 1986; *New York Times*, 5 October 1986; *The Guardian*, London, 6 October 1986.
58 *FAO Dossier*, op. cit.
59 David Pitt and Thomas G. Weiss, op. cit.
60 *The United Nations: Its Problems and What to Do About Them*, Heritage Foundation, Washington, DC, September 1986.
61 Joint Inspection Unit, *United Nations Common System: Staff Costs and Some Aspects of Utilisation of Human and Financial Resources in the United Nations Secretariat*, United Nations General Assembly, New York, 26 September 1984.
62 Ibid.
63 From enclosures included in personal correspondence sent to the author by Mr E. J. Freeman, dated 26 October 1987.
64 *APS Newsletter*, Rome, May/June 1987.
65 UNESCO estimate, cited in Paul Harrison, *Inside the Third World*, Penguin Books, Harmondsworth, 1985.
66 UNICEF, *State of the World's Children: 1987*, Oxford University Press, Oxford and New York, 1987.
67 Joint Inspection Unit, *Staff Costs and Some Aspects of Utilisation of Human and Financial Resources in the United Nations Secretariat*, op. cit., paragraph 30.
68 Ibid., paragraph 31.
69 Ibid., paragraph 32.
70 Ibid., paragraph 29.
71 Ibid., paragraph 51 and table II.
72 Ibid., paragraph 28.
73 Ibid., paragraph 42.
74 Ibid., paragraph 92(b).
75 Javier Pérez de Cuéllar, *Report of the Secretary General on the Work of the Organisation*, United Nations, New York, 1986.
76 Maurice Bertrand, *Some Reflections on Reform of the United Nations*, Joint Inspection Unit of the United Nations, Geneva, 1985, paragraph 39.
77 Ibid., paragraph 37.
78 Ibid., paragraph 38.
79 Joint Inspection Unit, *Personnel Questions, United Nations Common System: Follow-Up Report on Staff Costs in the United Nations Secretariat*, United Nations General Assembly, New York, 18 September 1985.
80 Ibid.
81 Ibid. In 1986, following a review of the UN's efficiency, a high-level group of intergovernmental experts recommended strongly that staff unions and associations should in future 'finance all their activities from their own funds'. To date this recommendation has not been acted upon.
82 Richard Hoggart, op. cit.

83 Joint Inspection Unit, *Staff Costs and Some Aspects of Utilisation of Human and Financial Resources in the United Nations Secretariat*, op. cit.

84 *Proceedings of the Committee on Administrative and Budgetary Questions, 12 November 1985*, UN Document A/C.5/40/SR.30.

85 Advisory Committee on Administrative and Budgetary Questions, *First Report on the Proposed Programme Budget for the Biennium 1986–1987*, United Nations, New York, 1985.

86 UN Doc A/C.5/40/SR.30, op. cit.

87 Richard Hoggart, op. cit.

88 *Report of the Group of High-Level Intergovernmental Experts to Review the Efficiency of the Administrative and Financial Functioning of the United Nations*, General Assembly, New York, 1986. See also *First Report on the Proposed Programme Budget for the Biennium 1986–1987*, op. cit.

89 *FAO Dossier*, op. cit.

90 *Report of the Group of High-Level Intergovernmental Experts*, op. cit.

91 *United Nations Reform: Where's the Beef?* Heritage Foundation, Washington, DC, 10 March 1987.

92 UN Document A/C.5/40/SR.45, United Nations, New York, 4 December 1985.

93 Raymond Lloyd, op. cit.

94 *UNICEF Annual Report 1986*, UNICEF, New York.

95 *The Star*, London, 19 June 1987; *New York Times*, New York, 25 June 1987; *Newsweek*, 6 July 1987. Also conversations with UNICEF, Belgium and New York.

96 *UNICEF's Mounting Troubles*, Heritage Foundation, Washington, DC, 1 September 1987. In October of the same year Australia suspended its voluntary contributions to UNICEF because of 'concern over its financial mismanagement' – *The Independent*, London, 24 October 1987.

97 *United Nations Conferences and Special Observances*, UN Reference Paper No. 26, Department of Public Information, New York, January 1987.

98 Ibid.

99 Ibid.

100 Figures from Maurice Bertrand, op. cit.

101 See Johan Galtung in David Pitt and Thomas G. Weiss (eds), op. cit.

102 Maurice Bertrand, op. cit.

103 *How the UN Spends Its $1 Billion from US Tax-payers*, op. cit.

104 *The UN Department of Conference Services*, Heritage Foundation, Washington, DC, 20 June 1986.

105 Ibid.

106 *Problems of Storage and Its Costs in Organisations of the United Nations System*, Joint Inspection Unit, New York, 1986.

107 *Wall Street Journal*, New York, 27 August 1974.

108 *Globe and Mail*, Toronto, 1 September 1980.

109 *United Nations Conferences and Special Observances*, op. cit.

110 Richard Hoggart, op. cit.

111 *The Guardian*, London, 8 January 1988.

112 *Daily Telegraph*, London, 8 October 1986.

113 *Report of the Group of High-Level Intergovernmental Experts*, op. cit., p. 7.

114 Maurice Bertrand, op. cit.

115 See Paul Streeten in David Pitt and Thomas G. Weiss (eds), op. cit.

116 Maurice Bertrand, op. cit.

117 Douglas Williams, *The Specialised Agencies and the United Nations*, C. Hurst, London, 1987.

118 *The United Nations: Its Problems and What to Do About Them*, op. cit.

119 Maurice Bertrand, op. cit.

120 Maurice Bertrand, op. cit. Emphasis added.

121 Ibid.

122 Ibid.

123 *Report of the Group of High-Level Intergovernmental Experts*, op. cit.

124 Ibid.

125 Ibid.

126 Ibid., page 7, Recommendation 8 (1).

127 See *United Nations Reform: Where's the Beef?*, op. cit.

128 Ibid.

129 Ibid. See also *Proposed Programme Budget for the Biennium 1988–1989: Revised Estimates under Section 32, Construction, Alteration, Improvement and Major Maintenance of Premises*, United Nations General Assembly, New York, 14 September 1987. Document No. A/C.5/42/4.

130 *The UN Department of Public Information*, Heritage Foundation, Washington, DC, 23 February 1984.

131 Maurice Bertrand, op. cit.

132 Quoted in the *International Herald Tribune*, Paris, 6 February 1987.

133 *The UN Department of Public Information*, op. cit.

134 *New York Times*, 28 May 1982.

135 *The UN Department of Public Information*, op. cit.

136 *The GAO Renders Its Verdict*, Heritage Foundation, Washington, DC, 9 June 1986.

137 Letter from the journalist in question to *The Times*, London, 2 December 1986.

138 *Development Forum*, UN Division for Economic and Social Information, Geneva, March 1987.

139 *Generation: Portrait of the United Nations Development Programme*, UNDP Division of Information, New York, 1985.

140 *UNICEF News*, Issue 123/1986, UNICEF Division of Communication and Information, New York, 1986.

141 This phrase, originally quoted by Cheryl Payer in relation to the World Bank, is borrowed from Furnival who said of the British Colonial Office that it 'concealed itself, like a cuttlefish, in a cloud of ink'. John S. Furnival, *Colonial Policy and Practice*, New York University Press, New York, 1956.

142 *United Nations: Image and Reality*, op. cit.

143 See Paul Streeten in David Pitt and Thomas G. Weiss (eds), op. cit.
144 Maurice Bertrand, op. cit.; see paragraphs 100 and 101.
145 Ibid., paragraph 51.
146 Ibid., paragraph 19.

PART FOUR

1 *Sunday Times Magazine*, London, 3 April 1988.
2 *New York Times*, 29 September 1987. For accounts of Filho's assassination, see, for example, *The Independent*, London, 24 December 1988 and (obituary) 27 December 1988.
3 *Survival International Urgent Action Bulletin*, London, 3 January 1985.
4 Gustavo Esteva, 'Development: Metaphor, Myth, Threat', in *Seeds of Change*, Vol. III, Washington, DC, 1985.
5 *Famine: A Man-Made Disaster*, Report for the Independent Commission on International Humanitarian Issues, Pan Books, London and Sydney, 1985.
6 E. S. Ayensu, 'Aid to Africa', paper presented to the World Commission on Environment and Development, third meeting, Oslo, Norway, 21–8 June 1985.
7 Johan Galtung, 'An Anthropology of the United Nations System', in David Pitt and Thomas G. Weiss (eds), *The Nature of United Nations Bureaucracies*, Croom Helm, London and Sydney, 1986.
8 *International Daily News*, 1 April 1982.
9 Paul Streeten, 'The United Nations: Unhappy Family', in David Pitt and Thomas G. Weiss (eds), op. cit.
10 *1985 – And Towards the 1990s*, United Nations Development Programme, New York, October 1986.
11 Ibid.
12 *Twenty-Five Years of Development Co-operation: A Review*, OECD, Paris, 1985.
13 Robert Cassen and Associates, *Does Aid Work?*, Oxford University Press, Oxford and New York, 1986.
14 Maurice Bertrand, *Some Reflections on Reform of the United Nations*, Joint Inspection Unit of the United Nations, Geneva, 1985.
15 See Part Two for figures on Official Development Assistance.
16 Robert Cassen and Associates, op. cit.
17 See V. S. Baskin, *Western Aid: Myth and Reality*, Progress Publishers, Moscow, 1985.
18 Harka Gurung, 'Economic Implications of Foreign Aid', *The Motherland*, Kathmandu, 30 June 1970.
19 Bihari K. Shresta, 'Technical Assistance and Growth of Administrative Capability in Nepal', paper presented at a Seminar on Foreign Aid and Development held in Kathmandu, Nepal, 4–5 October 1983.
20 Hari Mohan Mathur, 'Experts of the United Nations in Third World

Development: A View from Asia', in David Pitt and Thomas G. Weiss (eds), op. cit.

21 V. S. Baskin, op. cit.

22 Quoted in Bernard Lecomte, *Project Aid: Limitations and Alternatives*, Development Centre of the OECD, Paris, 1986.

23 Ibid.

24 Ibid.

25 Robert Cassen and Associates, op. cit.

26 *UN Special*, New York, October 1985.

27 Bernard Lecomte, op. cit.

28 Warren C. Baum and Stokes M. Tolbert, *Investing in Development: Lessons of World Bank Experience*, Oxford University Press for the World Bank, Oxford, December 1985.

29 *Rural Development: World Bank Experience, 1965–86*, Operations Evaluation Department, World Bank, Washington, DC, April 1988, pp. 33–4.

30 Bernard Lecomte, op. cit.

31 Hari Mohan Mathur in David Pitt and Thomas G. Weiss (eds), op. cit.

32 V. S. Baskin, op. cit.

33 Robert Chambers, *Rural Development: Putting the Last First*, Longman Scientific and Technical, Harlow, 1983.

34 *Sunday Times*, London, 26 August 1984.

35 Ibid.

36 Ibid.

37 Personal communications with Douglas W. Cross, BSc., CBiol., MIBiol., CEd. Cross, a professional ecologist, teaches aquaculture studies at UK universities and colleges and works as an aquaculture policy and technology adviser in developing countries. He lives as a smallholder fish-farmer in the UK.

38 Interview with David Deppner, former USAID official, Washington, DC, 2 October 1987.

39 When one of my researchers visited the ODA library on 27 June 1988 to get copies of evaluation reports (including those on the Victoria Dam and the Nepal road), she was given access to very little material, the bulk being either 'classified' or 'unavailable'. She notes: 'I was allowed to look at a small file containing a brief précis of each evaluation. In the précis, criticism was kept to a minimum and the more successful parts of particular projects were emphasised . . . Of the very few evaluations I was able to look at in more detail, those which did criticise a particular aid project had second parts which were classified.'

40 *The Lessons of Experience: Evaluation Work in ODA*, HMSO, London, 1983.

41 Ibid.

42 Warren C. Baum and Stokes M. Tolbert, op. cit. This book, written by senior members of staff and intended to synthesise and make accessible 'the principal *lessons* learned by the World Bank' from its field experience, relegates

the whole subject of 'social analysis' to a small chapter very near the end, and tells us: 'The Bank is still in the process of devising appropriate techniques of social analysis.' Such techniques will, however, be confined to 'people-oriented projects' (sic). What sort of projects, exactly, are *not* people-oriented – and why?

43 *The World Bank and International Finance Corporation*, World Bank, Washington, DC, April 1986.

44 Adrian Adams, 'An Open Letter to a Young Researcher', *African Affairs*, 78, No. 313, London, October 1979.

45 Guy Gran, 'If Africans Are to Eat: Whose Knowledge Matters?', paper presented at the Annual National Meeting of the International Association of Political Psychology, 19 June 1985.

46 *The World Bank and International Finance Corporation*, op. cit. See also Warren C. Baum, *The Project Cycle*, World Bank, Washington, DC, 1983, and *The World Bank*, World Bank, Washington, DC, January 1985.

47 *The World Bank and International Finance Corporation*, op. cit.

48 Ibid.

49 Ibid.

50 Ibid.

51 Guy Gran, op. cit.

52 *Rural Development: World Bank Experience, 1965–86*, op. cit., p. 60.

53 Teresa Hayter and Catherine Watson, *Aid Rhetoric and Reality*, Pluto Press, London and Sydney, 1985.

54 Ibid.

55 Warren C. Baum, op. cit.

56 Cited in Hayter and Watson, op. cit.

57 Ibid.

58 *Rural Development: World Bank Experience, 1965–86*, op. cit., p. 57.

59 Cited in Cheryl Payer, *The World Bank: A Critical Analysis*, Monthly Review Press, New York and London, 1982.

60 *The Economist*, London, 27 September 1986.

61 *The World Bank*, op. cit.

62 *Institutional Development in Africa: A Review of World Bank Project Experience*, World Bank, Washington, DC, May 1984 (two vols, unpublished).

63 Hayter and Watson, op. cit.

64 Guy Gran, op. cit.

65 James E. Austin, *Confronting Urban Malnutrition: The Design of Nutrition Programmes*, Johns Hopkins University Press for the World Bank, Baltimore, Md, 1980.

66 *Poverty and Hunger: Issues and Options for Food Security in Developing Countries*, World Bank, Washington, DC, February 1986. Emphases added.

67 Cheryl Payer, 'Effects of World Bank Project Lending on Borrowing Countries', paper presented at the Centro de Estudios Economicos Y Lociales del Tercer Mundo, Mexico City, April 1982. Emphasis added.

68 *Toward Sustained Development in Sub-Saharan Africa*, World Bank, Washington, DC, August 1984.
69 Ibid. See in particular pp. 40 and 44.
70 Ibid. See Foreword.
71 See Guy Gran, op. cit., p. 12.
72 See Cheryl Payer, *The World Bank: A Critical Analysis*, op. cit., Chapter One, for a detailed discussion of World Bank co-financing and intellectual hegemony in the donor community. In its publication *The World Bank* (Washington, DC, January 1985), the Bank itself is happy to tell us that:

'Under special co-operative agreements, four of the United Nations specialised agencies provide staff support for Bank operations in their fields of expertise. These are the Food and Agriculture Organisation of the United Nations (FAO), the United Nations Educational, Scientific and Cultural Organisation (UNESCO), the World Health Organisation (WHO) and the United Nations Industrial Development Organisation (UNIDO).

'The World Bank has almost continuous contact and close working relations with other UN agencies and commissions, regional development banks, the Organisation for Economic Co-operation and Development (OECD), regional organisations such as the European Communities and the Permanent Executive Committee of the Inter-American Economic and Social Council of the Organisation of American States, and most of the national agencies that provide development finance and technical assistance. In addition closer links are being forged with many non-governmental organisations engaged in development activities.

'The Bank plays a leading rôle in efforts to co-ordinate assistance from a variety of sources to individual countries. For this purpose, it has organised and currently serves as chairman of a number of co-ordinating groups of national and international organisations . . . *For all such groups, the Bank's country studies and analyses of need serve as part of the basic documentation.*' (Emphasis added.)
73 Testimony of Bruce Rich, Senior Attorney, Environmental Defense Fund, before the House Subcommittee on International Development Institutions and Finance. Hearing on the Environmental Performance of Multilateral Development Banks, Washington, DC, 8 April 1987.
74 Ibid.
75 See Cheryl Payer, *The World Bank*, op. cit. For details of loan size, see *Statement of Loans 94,101 (31 December 1984)*, IBRD, Washington, DC.
76 *The New York Times*, 11 May 1987; *Christian Science Monitor*, 7 May 1987. See also Bruce Rich, *Ecology Law Quarterly*, Vol. 12, No. 4, University of California, Berkeley, 1985.
77 Bruce Rich, *Ecology Law Quarterly*, op. cit.
78 Bruce Rich, Senior Attorney, Environmental Defense Fund, quoted in *The Orlando Sentinel*, 10 March 1987. See also *Bankrupting the Environment*, Central Independent Television, Birmingham, 1987.

79 *The Independent*, London, 22 September 1987.
80 *Brazil: A Paradise Lost?*, The Institute for Food and Development Policy, San Francisco, 1987.
81 Ibid.
82 Cheryl Payer, *The World Bank*, op. cit. See p. 346.
83 *Washington Post*, 15 May 1986.
84 *Brazil: A Paradise Lost*, op. cit.
85 *Bankrupting the Environment*, op. cit.
86 *Polonoroeste Information Packet*, Environmental Defense Fund, Washington, DC (updated regularly).
87 Testimony of Bruce Rich, op. cit.
88 See the following: (1) *Wall Street Journal*, New York, 24 December 1986 (4.3 million people had been moved by this date); (2) *Indonesia, Transmigration Sector Review*, Report No. 6508-IND, World Bank, Washington, DC, 24 October 1986. The resettlement target for financial year 1986–7 was reduced from 100,000 fully sponsored families to 36,000 fully sponsored families; (3) *Jakarta Post*, Jakarta, 6 January 1988. An increase of 56 per cent in the government's transmigration budget was announced and the resettlement target for financial year 1987–8 was raised to 160,000 families.
89 *Indonesia, Transmigration Sector Review*, op. cit., executive summary, paragraph 83.
90 Ibid., p. 156.
91 *The Ecologist*, Vol. 16, No. 2/3, Bodmin, Cornwall, 1986.
92 Basic Forestry Act, Clarification Act No. 2823 of 1967.
93 *The Ecologist*, Vol. 16, No. 2/3, 1986, op. cit.
94 *Indonesia, Transmigration Sector Review*, op. cit., executive summary, paragraph 62.
95 Ibid.
96 *The Ecologist*, Vol. 16, No. 2/3, 1986, op. cit., quoting relief workers and UNHCR sources.
97 Speech of 20 March 1985, reported in *The Ecologist*, Vol. 16, No. 2/3, 1986, op. cit.
98 Kenneth Davidson, writing in *The Melbourne Age*, Melbourne, 1 June 1986.
99 Ibid.
100 Ibid.
101 Reported by James Bovard in *The World Bank vs. the World's Poor*, Cato Institute Policy Analysis, Washington, DC, 29 September 1987.
102 *Wall Street Journal*, New York, 30 September 1985.
103 *Indonesia, Transmigration Sector Review*, op. cit., Chapter 5, paragraph 23.
104 *Forest Policies in Indonesia: The Sustainable Development of Forest Lands* (four vols), Government of Indonesia/International Institute for Environment and Development, Washington, DC, 1985.
105 Ibid.

106 *Five Year Plan 1984–1989.* See Graham Searle, *Major World Bank Projects*, Wadebridge Ecological Centre, Camelford, Cornwall, 1987.
107 Letter to the Honourable M. Peter McPherson, Administrator, USAID, Washington, DC, 11 June 1986.
108 Graham Searle, op. cit., p. 151.
109 *Information Packet on World Bank Financed Transmigration in Indonesia*, Environmental Defense Fund, Washington, DC (regularly updated).
110 *Forest Policies in Indonesia*, op. cit.
111 Interview with David Deppner, op. cit.
112 *Indonesia, Transmigration Sector Review*, op. cit., executive summary, paragraph 44(a).
113 Ibid., paragraph 44(b).
114 Ibid., paragraph 10.
115 Ibid., paragraph 6.
116 Ibid., paragraph 44(b).
117 *List of Upcoming MDB Projects with Possible Environmental Issues*, The Bank Information Center, Washington, DC (enclosure in letter to Friends of the Earth, UK, dated 22 March 1988).
118 Letter dated 6 May 1988 to Stephen Corry, Director, Survival International, from Russel J. Cheetham, Director, Country Department 5, Asia Region, World Bank.
119 Telex (Ref. AS 5AG) from World Bank to author, dated 30 June 1988. The Bank took more than a month to reply to my repeated telexed requests for clarifications of the scope and purpose of the Indonesia transmigration loans.
120 Ibid.
121 Letter dated 6 May 1988, op. cit.
122 *Indonesia: World Bank Maintains Support for Transmigration*, Survival International Occasional Report No. 8, London, January 1988.
123 *Indonesia: News and Views VI (21)*, Indonesian Embassy, Washington, DC, 1986.
124 Ibid.
125 *Jakarta Post*, 15 December 1987, plus various statements cited in Survival International Occasional Report No. 8, op. cit.
126 Letter from Russel Cheetham, World Bank, dated 6 May 1988, op. cit. In the classic tradition of digging holes, and then filling them in again, the World Bank decided in April 1988 to provide $34 million to assist a 'Natural Resource Conservation Project' in Indonesia. One of the main purposes of this project is to mitigate the 'forest depletion' caused by the transmigration programme – which, of course, the Bank also supports. The loan announcement comments on the 'movement' of large numbers of Javanese 'to the outer islands' and the damage done by subsequent 'settler encroachment' into forested areas. See News Release No. 88/63, World Bank, Washington, DC, 6 April 1988.
127 Survival International Occasional Report No. 8, op. cit.
128 Ibid.

129 Ibid.
130 Ibid.
131 Ibid.
132 Letter from Russel Cheetham, World Bank, op. cit.
133 *Indonesia: Transmigration Sector Review*, op. cit., p. 95, paragraph 5.18.
134 Quoted in Bruce Rich, *Ecology Law Quarterly*, op. cit.
135 Barber B. Conable, Address to the World Resources Institute, Washington, DC, 5 May 1987.
136 Ibid.
137 Thomas Fuller, MD, *Gnomologia*, 1732.
138 *The Independent*, London, 3 January 1989. It is also worth noting that a loan of $500 million for the Brazilian electric-power sector was signed in 1986 between the Bank and the government. This project has the potential to continue the destruction of the Amazonian forests well into the twenty-first century. According to Bruce Rich, Senior Attorney with the Environmental Defense Fund: 'Most of the funds from this loan are going to complete a series of hydroelectric projects in the Amazon basin and elsewhere, some of which even in Brazil are acknowledged to be ecological disasters and economic débâcles.' See Testimony before House Subcommittee on International Development Institutions and Finance, op. cit.
139 *Financing Ecological Destruction: The World Bank and the International Monetary Fund*, booklet prepared by an international group of non-governmental environmental organisations for presentation at the World Bank/IMF Annual Meeting, Washington, DC, 29 September–1 October 1987.
140 Ibid., and *Washington Post*, 29 May 1986.
141 *Financial Times*, London, 3 September 1986.
142 Cheryl Payer, *The World Bank*, op. cit., Chapter 9.
143 Figures from D. Hart, *The Volta River Project*, Edinburgh University Press, 1980.
144 See in particular E. Goldsmith and N. Hildyard (eds), *The Social and Environmental Effects of Large Dams* (two vols), Wadebridge Ecological Centre, 1984 and 1986. See also Brent Blackwelder and Peter Carlson, *Disasters in International Water Development*, Environmental Policy Institute, Washington, DC, September 1986.
145 Robert Repetto, *Skimming the Water*, World Resources Institute, Washington, DC.
146 E. Goldsmith and N. Hildyard (eds), op. cit.
147 Ibid.
148 Ibid.
149 Ibid.
150 Ibid. See also Blackwelder and Carlson, op. cit.
151 Blackwelder and Carlson, op. cit.
152 *Financing Ecological Destruction*, op. cit.
153 Ibid.
154 Testimony of Bruce Rich, 8 April 1987, op. cit.

155 Ibid., enclosure with testimony.

156 *Express Magazine*, India, 22 September 1985.

157 *Financing Ecological Destruction*, op. cit. According to some estimates, cost escalation of the project is in the region of $2.5 million *per day*. See also Graham Searle, op. cit.

158 Ioid.

159 *Structural Adjustment Lending: A First Review of Experience*, World Bank (Report No. 6409), Washington, DC, 1986. See Part Two, 'Development Incorporated', for fuller details on structural adjustment loans.

160 *The Future of the World Bank*, Report of the Conference Presented by the Overseas Development Council, Washington, DC, 23–4 June 1986. Panel III, 'The World Bank and Poverty'.

161 *Le Monde*, Paris, 25 July 1987. Emphasis added. As noted in Part Two, total commitments of the Bank in fiscal year 1987 were $19.207 billion (including the commitments of IDA, IFC and the Special Facility for Sub-Saharan Africa, as well as those of the IBRD). See *World Bank Annual Report 1987*, World Bank, Washington, DC.

162 *The Twelfth Annual Review of Project Performance Results*, Operations Evaluation Department, World Bank, Washington, DC, June 1987, paragraph 2.50.

163 Ibid., paragraph 2.51.

164 Ibid., paragraph 2.51.

165 Ibid., paragraph 2.52.

166 Ibid., paragraph 2.52.

167 Ibid., paragraphs 1.16 and 1.19.

168 Ibid., paragraph 1.62.

169 Ibid., paragraph 2.13.

170 *Project Performance Results for 1986*, Operations Evaluation Department, World Bank, Washington, DC, May 1988, paragraph 1.08.

171 *Rural Development: World Bank Experience, 1965–86*, op. cit., p. 35.

172 *Project Performance Results for 1986*, op. cit., paragraphs 1.18 and 1.45.

173 R. Ehrhardt, *Canadian Development Assistance to Bangladesh*, Canadian International Development Agency, Ottawa, 1983.

174 Interview with David Deppner, op. cit.

175 *Audit of AID Renewable Energy Projects*, Audit Report No. 9-00-86-3, Regional Inspector General for Audit, Washington, DC, 21 February 1986.

176 Ibid.

177 Ibid.

178 *Audit of Safaga Grain Silos Complex*, Audit Report No. 6-263-87-1, Regional Inspector General for Audit, Cairo, 27 October 1986.

179 *Audit of USAID/Peru Integrated Rural Development Project*, Audit Report No. 1-527-86-18, Regional Inspector General for Audit, Tegucigalpa, 18 June 1986.

180 Barbara Dinham and Colin Hines, *Agribusiness in Africa*, Earth Resources Research, London, 1983.

181 Ibid. See also Jon Bennett and Susan George, *The Hunger Machine*, Polity Press, Cambridge, 1987.

182 Bennett and George, op. cit.

183 Ibid.

184 Ibid.

185 Ibid.

186 *Real Aid: Missed Opportunities*, The Independent Group on British Aid, London, 1986. The Department of the Bank involved in the project was the International Finance Corporation which specialises in private-sector industrial ventures.

187 *The Ecologist*, Vol. 13, No. 5. Bodmin, Cornwall, 1983, and Vol. 15, No. 5/6, 1985. In several places peasants uprooted eucalyptus seedlings and inserted tamarind seeds in their place. See also John Clark, *For Richer, for Poorer*, Oxfam, Oxford, 1986.

188 John Clarke, op. cit.

189 *Christian Science Monitor*, 1 May 1987.

PART FIVE

1 *The Ecologist*, Vol. 14, No. 2, Bodmin, Cornwall, 1984.

2 Ibid.

3 Jon Bennett and Susan George, *The Hunger Machine*, Polity Press, Cambridge, 1987.

4 *British Overseas Aid 1986*, Overseas Development Administration, London, summer 1987.

5 Jon Bennett and Susan George, op. cit.

6 See J. Michael Luhan, 'Too Much Aid, Too Little Development', in *Development International*, Vol. 1, No. 4, Arlington, Virginia, July/August 1987.

7 Ibid.

8 See Penny Lernoux, *Cry of the People: The Catholic Church in Conflict with US Policy in Latin America*, Penguin, Harmondsworth, 1982.

9 *AID Highlights*, United States Agency for International Development, Washington, DC, winter 1987.

10 Ibid.

11 Ibid.

12 *British Overseas Aid 1986*, op. cit. See p. 11.

13 See *British Overseas Aid 1986* (p. 47) as well as previous and subsequent annual reports of the Overseas Development Administration, London.

14 *Real Aid: Missed Opportunities*, Report by the Independent Group on British Aid, London, 1986.

15 *The Aid and Trade Provision: Guidelines for Applicants*, Department of Trade and Industry, London, October 1986.

16 *Financial Times*, London, 24 May 1985. The suppressed report on ATP analysed six projects and concluded: 'You can't use the same fork to eat your

dinner and to dig your garden with.' In other words aid should either be for exporters or for developing countries, but should not attempt to be both things at the same time.

17 *Bilateral Aid: Country Programmes (Second Report, Session 1986–87),* House of Commons Foreign Affairs Committee, London, 22 April 1987. See in particular Appendix 11, memorandum by Graham Clark and Professor John Toye.

18 *Press Release: £21 Million Increase in ATP,* Overseas Development Administration, London, 1 September 1986.

19 *British Overseas Aid 1985,* Overseas Development Administration, London, 1986.

20 *British Overseas Aid 1984,* Overseas Development Administration, London, 1985.

21 *British Overseas Aid 1986,* op. cit. See also *Some Aid and Development Issues,* Background Information Paper, February 1986, and *The British Overseas Aid Programme: Some Basic Facts,* November 1986, both also published by the Overseas Development Administration, London.

22 *UNDP: The Development Connection,* Centre for World Development Education, London, July 1983.

23 Ibid.

24 *African Business,* London, August 1982.

25 Ibid.

26 *United Nations: Image and Reality,* UN Department of Public Information, New York, April 1986.

27 Ibid.

28 *New York Times,* 24 September 1985.

29 *United Nations: Image and Reality,* op. cit.

30 *World Bank Annual Report 1986,* World Bank, Washington, DC. See in particular p. 32.

31 Ibid. See p. 31, table 1.13.

32 *World Bank Annual Report 1987,* World Bank, Washington, DC. See p. 38, table 2.10.

33 See, for example, Richard T. Montoya, 'The Foreign Aid Cancer', lecture given at the Heritage Foundation, Washington, DC, 28 May 1987. Montoya was at the time Assistant Secretary for Territorial and Internal Affairs at the US Department of the Interior.

34 James Bovard, *The World Bank vs. the World's Poor,* Cato Institute Policy Analysis No. 92, Washington, DC, 28 September 1987.

35 Letter and enclosure from Joel A. Kurtzman, editor, *Development Business,* United Nations, New York, 9 March 1987.

36 *Aid Highlights,* winter 1981, op. cit.

37 *British Overseas Aid 1983,* Overseas Development Administration, London.

38 Address to the Board of Governors of the World Bank and the International Finance Corporation, Washington, DC, 30 September 1986.

References

Statement of Secretary of State Cyrus Vance before the Senate's Foreign Relations Committee on the Administration's foreign assistance programmes for fiscal year 1979, Washington, DC, 2 March 1978.

40 *Congressional Presentation Fiscal Year 1988*, United States International Development Cooperation Agency (of which AID is a constituent part), Washington, DC, May 1987.

41 *British Overseas Aid 1984*, op. cit.

42 *The Changing Emphasis in British Aid Policies: More Help for the Poorest*, 1975 White Paper (HMSO, London). There has been no subsequent White Paper on British overseas aid and the British government remains formally committed to the implications of this 1975 document.

43 Quoted in *AID Highlights*, winter 1987, op. cit.

44 Speech to the Royal Institute of International Affairs, London, 18 March 1987.

45 *Some Aid and Development Issues*, op. cit.

46 P. T. Bauer, *Equality, the Third World and Economic Delusion*, Weidenfeld & Nicolson, London, 1981.

47 P. T. Bauer and B. S. Yamey, *Development Forum*, Vol. XIV, No. 3, United Nations, Geneva, April 1986.

48 Testimony of Bruce Rich, Senior Attorney, Environmental Defense Fund, before the House Subcommittee on International Development Institutions and Finance. Hearing on the Environmental Performance of Multilateral Development Banks, Washington, DC, 8 April 1987.

49 Roger C. Riddell, *Foreign Aid Reconsidered*, Johns Hopkins University Press, Baltimore, Md, 1987.

50 Ibid.

51 *Bilateral Aid: Country Programmes*, op. cit. See p. 158. Despite the contract, Willowbrook International went into receivership shortly after the bus bodies had been delivered to Zambia

52 B. E. Cracknell, *Evaluation of ODA's Cofinancing with IBRD for Cargo-Handling Equipment in Port Sudan*, ODA, London, October 1984.

53 *The Times*, London, 19 March 1987.

54 *Bilateral Aid: Country Programmes*, op. cit. See pp. 101–2.

55 *Daily Telegraph*, London, 3 May 1985.

56 Ibid.

57 *Overseas Development*, No. 102, Overseas Development Administration, London, March 1986.

58 *Real Aid*, op. cit.

59 *The Guardian*, London, 14 December 1987; *The Independent*, London, 12 August 1988.

60 *The Guardian*, London, 14 December 1987.

61 Ibid.

62 *Overseas Development*, No. 102, op. cit.

63 *Bilateral Aid: Country Programmes*, op. cit. See Annex 11.

64 *Financial Times*, London, 26 August 1986.

65 Ibid.
66 *Financial Times*, London, 17 December 1986.
67 Ibid.
68 Ibid.
69 *Bilateral Aid: Country Programmes*, op. cit. See p. 160.
70 *The Guardian*, London, 13 February 1987.
71 *Bilateral Aid: Country Programmes*, op. cit. See pp. 106–7.
72 *British Overseas Aid 1985*, op. cit.; *British Overseas Aid 1986*, op. cit.
73 *British Overseas Aid 1986*, op. cit.
74 Jon Bennett and Susan George, op. cit. See also *British Overseas Aid 1986*, op. cit.
75 Christopher Flavin, *Electricity for a Developing World*, Worldwatch Institute, Washington, DC, June 1986.
76 Tom Learmouth and Francis Rolt, *Underdeveloping Bangladesh*, War on Want, London, 1987.
77 Christopher Flavin, op. cit.
78 Minister of Health Mohamed Abdul Matin, quoted in *The Independent*, London, 4 June 1988.
79 *The Independent*, London, 14 June 1988.
80 Ibid.
81 R. Young, *Canadian Development Assistance to Tanzania*, North-South Institute, Ottawa, 1983.
82 Derek Warren, 'Aid Grows a Crop of Problems', *The Guardian*, London, 2 December 1983.
83 Ibid.
84 *Africa Guide 1986*, World of Information, UK, 1986.
85 *The Ecologist*, Vol. 14, No. 2, op. cit.
86 *USAID Highlights*, US agency for International Development, Washington, DC, spring 1987.
87 *AID Highlights*, US Agency for International Development, Washington, DC, winter 1987.
88 Ibid.
89 *USAID Highlights*, spring 1987, op. cit.
90 J. Tendler, *Inside Foreign Aid*, Johns Hopkins University Press, Baltimore, Md, 1975.
91 *Washington Post*, 12 March 1975.
92 See Frances Moore Lappe, Joseph Collins and David Kinley, *Aid as Obstacle*, Institute for Food and Development Policy, San Francisco, 1980, p. 95.
93 Ibid., p. 97.
94 *Audit of PL480 Title I Programme in Somalia*, Audit Report No. 3-649-87-2, Regional Inspector General for Audit, Nairobi, 26 January 1987.
95 Ibid.
96 Ibid.
97 Ibid.

References

98 Jonathan Kwitny, *Endless Enemies*, Congdon & Weed, New York, 1984. See also discussion in Susan George, *A Fate Worse than Debt*, Penguin Books, London and New York, 1988.

99 Jonathan Kwitny, op. cit.

100 *Christian Science Monitor*, 1 May 1987.

101 Ibid.

102 Ibid.

103 *Washington Post*, 26 July 1986.

104 Betsy Hartman and James Boyce, *Bangladesh Aid to the Needy?* Washington Center for International Policy, May 1978.

105 *Audit of USAID/Jamaica Agricultural Development Foundation* (Project No. 532-0105), Regional Inspector General for Audit, Tegucigalpa, 11 July 1986.

106 Rehman Sobhan, *The Crisis of External Dependence: The Political Economy of Foreign Aid to Bangladesh*, Zed Press, London, 1982.

107 Ibid.

108 The researchers were Betsy Hartmann and James Boyce. Reported in Lappe et al., op. cit.

109 Ibid.

110 *Christian Science Monitor*, 1 May 1987.

111 Ibid.

112 *Wall Street Journal*, New York, 10 November 1977.

113 *Financial Times*, London, 26 October 1986.

114 For further details, see in particular Walden Bello, David Kinley and Elaine Elinson, *Development Débâcle: The World Bank in the Philippines*, Institute for Food and Development Policy, San Francisco, 1982.

115 *The Independent*, London, 22 July 1987.

116 See R. T. Naylor, *Hot Money*, Unwin Hyman, London and Sydney, 1987.

117 Ibid.

118 *The Independent*, London, 12 November 1987.

119 Ibid.

120 Lappe et al., op. cit.

121 Ibid. See also Walden Bello et al., op. cit.

122 Five-year forward projection of the Philippines Ministry of Finance, reported in *Financial Times*, London, 20 October 1986. A year later debt service stood at 42 per cent of export earnings and accounted for 36 per cent of the entire national budget – money that could otherwise have been used for economic development. See Richard Gourlay, 'Philippine Politicians Attack Deal on Debt', *Financial Times*, London, October 1987.

123 Quoted in David Lamb, *The Africans*, Vintage Books, New York, May 1985.

124 Ibid.

125 Ibid.

126 Ibid.
127 *The Guardian*, London, 10 May 1985.
128 Peter Korner et al., *The IMF and the Debt Crisis*, Zed Books, London, 1986. See pp. 97-105. See also *Fiche d'Information du CRI*, No. 3, Centre de Recherche et d'Information, Brussels, 1985.
129 *World Bank Atlas 1987*, World Bank, Washington DC, 1987.
130 Peter Korner et al., op. cit. See also David Lamb, op. cit.
131 Ibid.
132 *Info Zaire* No. 36, October 1982. Published by the Comité Zaire, Brussels, Belgium.
133 Peter Korner et al., op. cit.
134 See Ghislain Kabwit, 'The Roots of Continuing Crisis', in the *Journal of Modern African Studies*, No. 3, 1979.
135 *Info Zaire*, op. cit.
136 *Financial Times*, London, 31 October 1986.
137 Ibid.
138 Susan George, op. cit.
139 *Financial Times*, London, 31 October 1986.
140 Giovanni Andrea Cornia, Richard Jolly and Frances Stewart (eds), *Adjustment with a Human Face: Protecting the Vulnerable and Promoting Growth*, Oxford University Press for UNICEF, 1987.
141 *Le Monde diplomatique*, Paris, 21 and 22 May 1983. See also Peter Korner et al., op. cit. Some of these incidents are additionally cited in Riddell, op. cit., and in *Haiti: Family Business*, a special brief published by the Latin America Bureau, London, 1985. I sent the IMF a lengthy telex on 8 July 1988 requesting either further details of the vanishing $20 million, or a refutation. Graham Newman of the Fund's External Relations Department replied on 25 July 1988 in the following ambiguous terms: 'As I am sure you are aware, the Fund makes its financial resources available to members for general balance-of-payments support while they are undertaking corrective measures to alleviate their payments problems. As the Fund's financial assistance is "untied" in that the resources released to members are not earmarked or designated for any specific purpose, it is impossible, given that money is fungible, to determine the end-use of the funds supplied. Any time there is a misappropriation of public monies in a country drawing on the Fund's resources it could, I suppose, be claimed that IMF Funds were involved . . .'
142 From data cited in Riddell, op. cit.
143 Ibid.
144 Ibid.
145 Ibid.
146 C. Zuvekas, *Agricultural Development in Haiti*, USAID, Washington, DC, 1978.
147 Riddell, op. cit.
148 Ibid.
149 Quoted in *Arab News*, London, 28 October 1983.

References

150 *Christian Science Monitor*, Boston, 9 September 1985; *The Economist*, London, 24 October 1986.
151 *Chicago Tribune*, 31 March 1987.
152 *Wall Street Journal*, 27 May 1986.
153 Ibid.
154 *Financial Times*, London, 23 February 1987.
155 Quoted in James Bovard, *The World Bank and the World's Poor*, Cato Institute Policy Study No. 92, Washington, DC, 28 September 1987.
156 *Ecology Law Quarterly*, Vol. 12, No. 4, School of Law, University of California, 1985.

CONCLUSION

1 Guy Arnold, *Aid and the Third World*, Robert Royce, London, 1985.
2 *Twenty-Five Years of Development Co-operation: A Review*, OECD, Paris, 1985.
3 Ibid.
4 Ibid. ODA from DAC members was $28.7 billion in 1984.
5 *British Overseas Aid 1987: Annual Review*, Overseas Development Administration, London, summer 1988.
6 P. T. Bauer, *Equality, the Third World and Economic Delusion*, Weidenfeld & Nicolson, London, 1981.
7 *One World*, Just 0.7 Campaign, April and July 1988.
8 *North–South: A Programme for Survival*, Report of the Independent Commission on International Development Issues under the Chairmanship of Willy Brandt, Pan Books, London and Sydney, 1980.
9 *Common Crisis*, Pan Books, London, 1983.
10 UN–DIESA 1986. Quoted in table 1.2 of Giovanni Andrea Cornia, Richard Jolly and Frances Stewart (eds), *Adjustment with a Human Face*, Oxford University Press for UNICEF, 1987.
11 From figures prepared by the Catholic Fund for Overseas Development, London, together with seven other non-governmental organisations. See *The Times*, London, 26 September 1988.
12 Ibid.
13 Ibid.
14 *Christian Aid News*, London, July–September 1987.
15 Calculated from *British Overseas Aid 1986*, Overseas Development Administration, London, 1987, and *World Bank Atlas 1987*, World Bank, Washington, DC.
16 House of Commons Foreign Affairs Committee, *Bilateral Aid: Country Programmes*, HMSO, London, 1987.
17 *North–South: A Programme for Survival*, op. cit.
18 *Financial Times*, London, 24 May 1988.
19 *World Bank Atlas 1987*, op. cit. See also Michael Prowse, *Financial Times*, London, 15 October 1987 and 25 November 1987.

20 Michael Prowse, *Financial Times*, London, 15 October 1987 and 25 November 1987.
21 *The Independent*, London, 12 August 1987.
22 Michael Prowse, op. cit.
23 *Financial Times*, London, 23 June 1987.
24 John Clark, *For Richer, for Poorer*, Oxfam, Oxford, 1986.
25 Laurence Harris, *The Bretton Woods System and Africa*, paper presented to the IFAA Conference, 'Africa, the IMF and the World Bank', City University, London, 7 September 1987.
26 *The Times*, London, 26 September 1988.
27 *The Independent*, London, 29 January 1987.
28 Richard Gott, *The Guardian*, London, 1987.
29 *The Guardian*, London, 13 February 1987.
30 Dianna Melrose, *Nicaragua: The Threat of a Good Example?*, Oxfam, Oxford, 1985. See also Jon Bennett with Susan George, *The Hunger Machine*, Polity Press, Cambridge, 1987.

Index

Acre, 132
Addis Ababa, 85, 106, 119–20
advertisements, fraudulent, 17–18
'advice', 110, 114–15
Afar nomads, 113
Afghanistan, 52
Africa: expatriates, 114; failure of aid, 191–2; famine, 103; structural adjustment loans, 129; see also individual countries
Africare, xiii
African Development Bank, 51, 129
agriculture: FAO and, 48; and food aid, 168–70; IFAD, 50; misdirected aid, 22–3
AID see United States Agency for International Development (USAID)
aid personnel: consultants, 99–100; Directors General, 84–8; disaster relief, 7–9; 'experts', 110, 114–19; failure to consult local people, 23, 124–8; fraud, 93; fringe benefits, 80, 88, 90–91; lifestyle and remuneration, 31, 32, 74, 79–80, 93–6; motivation, 79–84; quality, 96–100; travel, 90–92
Aid-Trade Provision (ATP), 157, 162–3, 164
Akosmobo Dam, 140–1
Ali, Bishara, 10
Amazon basin, 113, 131–3, 138–9
American Hospital Supply Corporation, 15
'Amerika' (television show), 108
Amin, Mohamed, 17
Amnesty International, 102–3
Anderson, Graeme, 164
Andra Pradesh, 141
Angola, 178–9
Annis, Sheldon, 143
Anti-Slavery Society, 134
Antilles, 70
aquaculture, 122–4
Arab Bank for Economic Development in Africa, 39, 51

Argentina, 182
Artibonite River, 141
Asian Development Bank/Fund, 51
Assab, 15, 121
Australia, 43, 45
Australian Council of Churches, 17
Austria, 43, 45, 158
Ayari, Dr Chedly, 39

Balfe, Robert, 12
Balfour Beatty, 157
Balsells, Robert, 151, 172, 175
Band Aid, xiii, 4, 7, 15
Bangalore, 150
Bangladesh, 53, 127, 162, 166, 174, 192
Bangladesh Agricultural Development Corporation, 155
Barber, Martin, 18
Bati, 121
Bauer, Lord, xiv–xv, 69, 161, 187
Bazin, Marc, 180
BBC, 17
Beirut, 10
Belet Weyne, 10, 11
Belgium, 43, 44, 45, 100, 158
Belize, 124
Benin, 127
Bertrand, Maurice, 97, 99, 101, 104, 108
Better Business Bureau (US), 6
Bhai, Prem, 165
bilateral aid, 46, 161, 162–3
Biwater Group, 157
Black, Eugene, 70, 71
Blumenthal, Erwin, 178, 179
Bokassa, Jean Bedel, 176–7
Bolanos, Rafael, 175
Bolivia, 127, 192
Bonnist, Steve, 18
Botswana, 13, 139–40
Bousquet, Jacques, 115–16, 119
Brandt, Willy, 188
Brandt Commission, 188, 189–90

Brazil, 53, 54, 60, 63, 68, 113, 117, 131–3, 138–9, 142, 182, 183
Bretton Woods conference (1944), 68
Britain: aid to Bangladesh, 155, 156; Aid-Trade Provision, 157, 162–3, 164; bilateral aid, 46; economic benefits of foreign aid, 156–8, 159, 160–1, 162–7; Hunger Project, 6; and the IMF, 58; motives for giving aid, 71–2; multilateral aid, 46, 47, 51; net receipts from Third World, 189; Official Development Assistance, 43–5; withdraws from UNESCO, 49; and the World Bank, 52, 53, 54; World Vision's fund-raising, 16–17; *see also* Overseas Development Administration
British Leyland, 158, 162
British Refugee Council, 18
Buerk, Michael, 32
Bula Hoyos, Gonzalo, 86–7
Burkina Faso, 114–15, 127
Burma, 70
Burundi, 127

Cafod, 17
Cajamarca, 150
Calcutta, 165
Cambodia (Kampuchea), 4, 13, 16, 70, 189
Cambridge University, 72
Cameroons, 70, 127
Canada, 43, 45, 85, 167–8
Canadian International Development Agency (CIDA), 45, 145, 167, 180–1
Cape Verde, 52
capital flight, 181–2
Caracas, 102
CARE Incorporated, 4
Caribbean, 70, 173–4
Caribbean Development Bank, 51
Catholic Relief Services, xiii, 133
cattle ranches, 139–40
CBS, 16
Central African Republic, 177
Central Intelligence Agency (CIA), 178–9
Central Rangelands Development Project (Somalia), 25–6, 27
Ceylon, 70
Chad, 53, 104
Chambers, Robert, 121
Channel 4, 30
charities: administration costs, 6–7; emergency relief aid, 3–6; evangelism, 9; fund-raising methods, 15–18; relief workers, 7–9; wasted aid, 11–15
Charities Aid Foundation, 7
Cheetham, Russel, 136
Chernobyl, 13

Chile, 63, 68
China, 14, 141, 142
Chixoy Dam, 150–1, 172, 175
Christian Aid, 4, 17–18, 81
Christianity, 9
Colchester, Marcus, 134
Cold War, 71
Colombia, 18, 127
Colomoncagua, 9
Commission on International Development, 188
Committee of Eighteen, 106–7
Conable, Barber, 38, 41, 57, 137–8, 139, 144, 160
conferences, 101–2
Connolly, Cyril, 71–2
Conservative Party, 187–8
Copenhagen, 49
Cordillera Mountains, 114
corruption, 174–83
Corry, Stephen, 137–8
Costa Rica, 56
Cross, Douglas W., 122–3, 124

dams, 140–3, 150–1, 175
Davy McKee, 157
debt-service ratio, 24
'defence' spending, 43
deforestation, 131–3, 135, 137, 138–9
Denmark, 43, 45, 46, 68, 162
Department of Commerce (US), 160, 180
Department of Trade and Industry (Britain), 157, 160, 163
Deppner, David, 145–6
Development Assistance Committee (OECD), 45, 50, 71, 115
development banks, 50–1
Development Business, 159
development industry, 41–75; bureaucratic survivalism, 72–5; motivation, 69–72; structural adjustment loans, 56–7, 59–66; UN agencies, 46–50; World Bank, 51–7
Dewey, Arthur E., 18
Dhaka, 166
Diaz, Ramon, 176
disaster relief, 3–33, 42
Disasters Emergency Committee, 17
Djibouti, 14, 87
Dominican Republic, 146
Draper, Beverly, 12
Draper, William, 109
Drought Action Committee (Somalia), 30–1
drugs, 12
Duvalier, Jean-Claude, 179–81
Duvalier, Michèle, 179
Dyaks, 137

East Africa, 10, 17
East Timor, 134–5
Economic Commission for Africa, 129
Egypt, 46, 70, 122–3, 147, 163
Ellis, Jeff, 38
Engstrom, Ted, 9
Environmental Defense Fund, 142
Eritrea, 15, 70
Esteva, Gustavo, 114
Ethiopia, 8, 22, 70, 127; Afar nomads, 113; Band Aid, 15; bilateral aid, 46; famine, 4, 6, 7, 15–17, 31–2, 85, 119–21; proposed UN conference centre, 89, 106
European Development Fund (EDF), 46–7, 117
European Economic Community (EEC), 46–7, 129; bilateral aid, 46; Court of Auditors, 13, 14; Directorate General for Development, 5; food aid, 12–13, 21; food surpluses, 14, 44; and the Indonesian transmigration programme, 133; Somalian roads, 171; wasted aid, 13–14
European Investment Bank, 47
evangelism, 9
'experts', 109–10, 114–19

Falkland Islands, 189
Federation of the British West Indies, 70
Feldman, Edward, 16
Finland, 43, 45
fish-farming, 121–4
FNLA, 179
Food and Agriculture Organisation (FAO), 5, 19, 103, 129; 'advice', 109; Britain benefits from aid, 157–8; consultants, 99; Director General, 84–8, and the Ethiopian famine, 120; fish-farming, 122–3; funding, 48; Indonesian transmigration programme, 133; objectives, 48; public relations, 109; satellite bodies, 103; and the Somalian drought, 25, 30; staff, 81–2, 91, 93–5; Technical Co-operation Programme, 87
food-aid, 12–15, 25–33, 48, 168–70, 181
Food for Hungry Inc., 13
Food for Peace programme, 168–70
Foran, Richard, 90
Foreign Relations Authorisation Act (USA, 1985), 89, 106
France: aid to Bokassa, 177; economic benefits of foreign aid, 158; and the IMF, 58; Indonesian transmigration programme, 133; Ministry of Development Co-operation, 45, 46, 71; Official Development Assistance, 43, 45; and the World Bank, 52, 53, 54, 68

Freeman, Ed, 94–5
fund-raising methods, charities, 15–19

Galgaduug, 26, 27, 28
Galkaio, 30
Galloway, George, 7
Gandhi, Rajiv, 142
Geldof, Bob, xiii, 15, 18, 116
General-Electric, 157, 171
Generation, 109
Geneva, 49, 50, 82, 91, 102, 158
German Development Corporation, 45
Ghana, 70, 127, 140–1
Gibraltar, 189
Goldberg, John, 40
Gordon, General, 166
Goyder, Hugh, 20
Gramm-Rudman Act (USA, 1985), 89
greenhouse effect, 132
Guardian, 108
Guatemala, 15, 126, 150–1, 172, 175
Guinea, 70

Haiti, 141, 144, 169, 179–81, 182
Hamburg, 44
Harrell-Bond, Barbara, 22
Haryana, 191
health care, 48–9
health centres, prefabricated, 11–12
Helms, Jesse, 93
Heston, Charlton, 120
Hiraan, 26, 27, 28
Hocke, Jean-Pierre, 103
Hoggart, Richard, 98–9
Holman, William, 38
Honduras, 9, 10, 13, 91
Hoover, Herbert, 70, 71
Hubei province, 14
Hume, Cardinal Basil, 120
Humphrey, Hubert, 71
The Hunger Project, 6
hydroelectric power, 140–3, 150–1, 172, 175

INDE, 172
The Independent, 28
India, 30, 70, 127, 189; bilateral aid, 46; British aid, 163–5; capital flight, 182; continuing poverty, 190–1; famines, 13; hydroelectric dams, 141, 142–3; IBRD loans, 54; Karnataka project, 150; Singrauli Power and Coal Mining Complex, 130–1, 162, 165; solar power, 146
Indian Council of Science and Technology, 142–3
Indians, Amazonian, 132

Indonesia, 70, 124, 127, 175; capital flight, 182; food aid, 14; IBRD loans, 53, 54; transmigration programme, 113, 133–8, 139, 143, 183
Inga-Shaba Power Project, 171–2, 178
Institute of Development Studies, Sussex University, 121
Inter-American Development Bank, 51, 150
Intermediate Technology Development Group, 18–19
International Bank for Reconstruction and Development (IBRD), 51, 52–5, 68, 144, 159, 188
International Christian Aid (ICA), 6, 8–9, 17
International Commission of the Red Cross (ICRC), 7, 19, 116
International Conference on Disarmament (1987), 101
International Development Association (IDA), 51, 52, 53, 159
International Finance Corporation (IFC), 51
International Fund for Agricultural Development (IFAD), 50
International Golf and Tennis Club, Mogadishu, 25
International Institute for Environment and Development, 135
International Labour Office (ILO), 49–50, 73, 84, 103
International Monetary Fund (IMF): co-operation with World Bank, 37–40, 58; creation of, 68; loans to Haiti, 179–80; loans to Zaire, 179; net receipts from Third World, 188; secrecy, 67; structural adjustment loans, 62–6
International Telecommunication Union, 92
Ireland, 43, 45
Irian Jaya, 133–4, 135–6, 137
irrigation projects, 140, 142, 144, 155
Israel, 20, 189
Italy, 43, 45, 46, 158, 171
Ivory Coast, 65, 115–16, 119, 127, 191

Jakarta, 124
Jamaica, 63, 173–4
Jamaica Agricultural Development Foundation, 173–4
Japan: economic benefits of foreign aid, 159, 167; funding for UN, 47; and the IMF, 58; Official Development Assistance, 43, 45; and the World Bank, 52, 54
Java, 133, 134, 136, 138, 183
Jayapura, 136
Jonglei Canal, 149
Jordan, 70

Kalahari, 139
Kalimantan, 133, 137
Kampala, 177
Kampuchea (Cambodia), 4, 13, 16, 70, 189
Karnataka, 150
Kashoggi, Adnan, 176
Kasinthula, 123
Kassebaum Amendment, 89, 106
Kasten, Robert, 135
Kathmandu, 156
Kenana sugar complex, 148–9
Kennedy, Edward, 120
Kennedy, John F., 71, 156
Kenya, 30, 46, 65, 127
Khartoum, 5, 8, 12, 166
Kismaayo, 171
Koh, Tommy, 91
Korem, 32, 119, 121
Kuwait, 15

Labour Movement (Britain), 187
LAMI consortium, 172
Land O'Lakes Inc. (LOL), 173–4
Laos, 70
Laoying Reservoir, 141
Lawson, Nigel, 39
Lazard Frères, 144
Lebanon, 20, 70
Libya, 14, 46, 70
Limones, 9
Live Aid, 18
Lloyd, Raymond, 87, 100
Lommatzch, Martin, 172
Los Angeles, 16
Lucas Garcia, General Romero, 175
Luxembourg, 68

MacAlpine, Robin, 10
McCloy, John J., 68
McGovern, Senator, 70, 71
Madagascar, 127, 144
Mahaweli River, 124
Makalle, 121
Malawi, 123, 191
Malaya, 70
Malaysia, 157, 182
Mali, 123–4, 127, 147
Maluku steel mill, 171
Mamdani, Dr Mahmood, 177–8
Mani, Ramaswamy, 93
Manzalah, Lake, 122–3
Map International Inc., 15
Marcos, Ferdinand, 62, 175–6
Marcos, Imelda, 175–6
Marlowe, Tony, 14
Mathur, Hari Mohan, 117, 119
Mato Grosso, 131–2

Index

Mauritius, 13, 14
Mayor, Federico, 49, 85
M'Bow, Ahmadou Mahtar, 49, 85
Médecins Sans Frontières, 4
Mendes Filho, Francisco, 113
Mensah, Moise, 86, 87
Mexico, 54, 68, 114, 117, 127, 144, 182, 183
military expenditure, 43
Mobutu Sese Seko, 64, 172, 178–9
Mogadishu, 12, 24–5, 26, 29, 30, 31, 171
Morgan Guaranty Trust Company, 182
Morocco, 14, 70
Morondova Irrigation and Rural Development Project, 144
Morrison-Knudsen, 171–2
Mosley, Maurice, J., 18
Mozambique, 14, 15
MPLA, 179
Mudug, 27, 28, 30
multilateral aid, 42–51
Murphy, Steve, 40
Mysore, 150

Nairobi, 50, 127
Namarigounou, 155
Namibia, 91, 100
Narmada River, 142–3
NASA, 131
National Catholic Reporter, 17
Negash, Tessema, 85
Nepal, 13, 116, 124, 127, 155–6
Netherlands, 43, 45, 46, 68, 104, 133, 158
New England Journal of Medicine, 192
New Internationalist, 83
New York, 40, 44, 49, 82, 83, 91, 92, 97, 102, 158–9
New York Times, 40
New Zealand, 43, 45
Nicaragua, 192
Niger, 14, 127
Niger River, 155
Nigeria, 117–18, 127, 142, 182
Nile, River, 5, 148–9, 166
Nixon, Richard, 71
Nizamsagar Dam, 141
Nkrumah, Kwame, 71
Noblemaire, Georges, 95
Northern Engineering Industries (NEI), 157, 164–5
Norway, 43, 44, 45
Nykindi, Joseph, Bishop of Wau, 12

Obote, Dr Milton, 178
OECD, 45, 50, 71, 115, 118, 187
Office for Emergency Operations in Africa (OEOA), 103–4

Official Development Assistance (ODA), 42–5, 47, 52, 53, 180, 188
Official Secrets Act (Britain), 157
Oil and Natural Gas Commission (India), 163–4
oil price rises, 60
Operation California, xiii, 17
Organisation of African Unity, 87
Organisation of Petroleum Exporting Countries (OPEC), 43, 45, 50, 187
Ottawa, 145
Overseas Development Administration (ODA), xiii, 5, 45, 71, 165; aid to Egypt, 163; Aid-Trade Provision (ATP), 157; disaster relief, 19; economic benefits of foreign aid, 158, 160–1; failure to talk to local people, 124, 150; secrecy, 67; and the Somalian drought, 30; staff, 46, 81; tsetse eradication plan, 23; withdraws loan to Zambia, 59
Overseas Development Council, 143
Oxfam, xiii, 20, 42; Disasters Emergency Committee, 17; and the Ethiopian famine, 4, 32; Kampuchean appeal, 3–4; and the Somalian drought, 26, 29, 30; staff, 25, 81, 82

PADCO, 156
Pakistan, 56, 64, 70, 91, 127, 141, 142, 191
Palestinians, 20
Papaloapan Integrated Rural Development Project, 144
Papua New Guinea, 134
Paraguay, 53, 142
Paris, 49, 82
Paris Club, 179
Patten, Christopher, 57, 59, 64, 161, 163, 164
Peace Corps, 81
Peligre Dam, 141
Pérez de Cuéllar, Javier, 89, 90, 96
Peru, 62, 127, 148, 150
Philippines, 70, 142; bilateral aid, 46; capital flight, 176, 182; high technology projects, 146, 147; IMF agreement, 62–3; local opposition to development programmes, 114; Marcos régime, 176–7, 182; oil price rise, 60
Phnom Penh, 7
Phuket, 149–50
Polonoreste project, 131–3, 138–9
Poverty and Hunger, 128
Priority One International, 6, 18
Project Hope, 4
public relations, xiv, 107–9, 189
Puerto Rico, 70
Punjab, 191

231

Racal Decca, 158
Rahman, Al Haj Nugdalla, 6
rainforests, 131–3, 135, 137, 138–9, 142
Raison, Timothy, 163
Raoni, Chief, 113
Rapti Area Rural Development Project, 156
Reagan, Ronald, 161
Red Crescent Society, 5, 28
Red Cross, 7, 17, 121, 177
Red Sea, 13
Reed, Joseph, 103
Regan, Donald, 181
religion, 9
renewable energy projects, 146–7
reservoirs, 140–3
Rich, Bruce, 130
Ridgewells (catering company), 38–9
Rihand, 165
Ripert, Jean, 93
Ristoro, Al, 94
Rolls-Royce, 163
Rome, 48, 50, 82, 88, 94
Rondônia, 131–3, 139
Roosevelt, Franklin D., 68
Rothberg, Herb, 39
Rwanda, 127

Safaga, 147
Sahara Desert, 16
Sahel, 32, 142
El Salvador, 9
San, 123–4
Sanmenxia Reservoir, 141
Saouma, Edouard, 85–8, 104
Sardar Sarovar Dam, 142–3
Saudi Arabia, 127
Save the Children Fund, xiii, 7, 17, 81
Schwartz, Harriet, 39
Seaman, Dr John, 32
Seibu Group, 44
Senegal, 65, 125, 127
Seoul, 40
Shebelle River, 11
Sheraton-Washington Hotel, 39–40
Shoreham Hotel, Washington, 39
Simon, Larry, 13
Singrauli Power and Coal Mining Complex, 130–1, 162, 165
Smith, Robert, 8
Sobhan, Rehman, 174
Somalia, 18, 70, 127, 191; bilateral aid, 46; debt-service ratio, 23–4; drought, 23–31; evangelism, 8–9; food aid, 169–70; roads, 171; wasted aid, 10–12; and the World Bank, 52
Somoza, General Anastasio, 192
Sorong, 136

South Korea, 40, 128–9, 168, 169, 182
Soviet Union, 13, 43, 45, 144, 187
Special Facility for Sub-Saharan Africa, 51, 52
Sport Aid, 18
Sri Lanka, 63, 64, 124, 127, 142, 191
State Department (US), 6, 18, 85, 100, 172
State of the World's Children Report, 99
Streeten, Paul, 115, 117
structural adjustment loans (SALs), 56–8, 59–66, 129, 143, 182
Sudan, 10, 70, 127; famine, 8, 12, 20; floods, 5–6; Jonglei Canal, 149; Kenana sugar complex, 148–9; power stations, 165–6; Ugandan refugees, 22; wasted aid, 15, 162–3
Sudan People's Liberation Movement, 149
Sulawesi, 133, 135, 137
Suleiman, Ahmed, 29
Sumatra, 135, 137
Surla, Sean, 40
Survival International, 137
Sussex University, 121
Sweden, 43, 44, 45, 46
Switzerland, 43, 45, 158
Syria, 70

Tamil Nadu, 191
Tamils, 127
Tanzania, 8, 114, 127, 158, 167–8
Thailand, 7, 65, 89, 127, 149–50
Thatcher, Margaret, 22, 157
Tigre, 15, 17, 32
Togo, 70, 87, 127
Tokyo, 44, 49
Tonton Macoutes, 181
tourism, 119–21
Toye, John, 164
'Trucks for Hope', 16
Truman, Harry, 69, 70, 71
tsetse flies, 23
Tsutsumi, Yoshiaki, 44
Tunisia, 14, 70
Turkey, 65

Uganda, 22, 127, 178
UNICEF News, 109
UNIDO, 129
United Nations (UN):
    accountability, 88–9; 'advice', 109–10, 114–15; agencies, 47–50; aid targets, 44, 187; calendar events, 100–1; committees, 103; conferences, 101–2; consultants, 99; duplication of effort, 19; economic benefits of foreign aid, 158–9; and the Ethiopian famine, 120; 'experts', 117; financial crisis, 89–90;

fortieth anniversary, 40; funding, 47; Joint Inspection Unit, 94, 105; need for streamlining, 104–7; objectives, 68–9; public relations, 107–9; quality of staff, 96–9; Second Development Decade, 44; secrecy, 66; staff lifestyle, 7, 31, 88, 90–1, 93–6; staff motivation, 81–4; staff travel, 90–2; and the World Bank, 51

United Nations: Image and Reality, 108

United Nations Centre for Human Settlements, 50

United Nations Children's Emergency Fund (UNICEF), 5, 19, 73; child sex ring scandal, 100; conflict with WHO, 103; consultants, 99; and the Ethiopian famine, 120; funding, 49; objectives, 49; public relations, 109; in Somalia, 25, 26, 29, 30; staff, 81–2, 97

United Nations Conference on Trade and Development (UNCTAD), 44, 50, 101

United Nations Development Programme (UNDP), 19, 50, 129; 'advice', 110; Britain benefits from aid, 158; 'experts', 115; funding, 50; Indonesian transmigration programme, 133; objectives, 47; public relations, 109; satellite bodies, 103; and the Somalian drought, 25, 26; staff, 40, 81

United Nations Disaster Relief Office (UNDRO), 20–1, 50

United Nations Educational, Scientific and Cultural Organisation (UNESCO), 129; 'advice', 109; and Amnesty International's conference on torture, 102; Director General, 84–5; 'experts', 116, 119; funding, 49; objectives, 49; public relations, 108–9; quality of staff, 98; satellite bodies, 103; secrecy, 66; staff travel, 90–2

United Nations Environment Programme (UNEP), 19, 50

United Nations Fund for Population Activities (UNFPA), 50, 83

United Nations High Commissioner for Refugees (UNHCR), 5, 9–11, 18, 19, 50, 82, 103, 109

United Nations Industrial Development Organisation (UNIDO), 50

United Nations Office for Emergency Operations, 19

United Nations Relief and Rehabilitation Administration (UNRRA), 68

United Nations University, 93

United States of America: aid to Haiti, 180–1; bilateral aid, 46; charitable donations, 4; defence spending, 43; demands more accountability from UN, 88–9; economic benefits of foreign aid, 156, 158, 159, 160–1; Food for Peace programme, 168–70; funding for UN, 47; Hunger Project, 6; and the IMF, 58; motives for aid, 69–72; Official Development Assistance, 43–4, 45; Point Four Plan, 69; wealth, 43–4; withdraws from UNESCO, 49; withholds money from UN, 89; and the World Bank, 52, 54

United States Agency for International Development (USAID), xiii, 5, 15, 19, 45, 67, 73; economic benefits of foreign aid, 156, 160; Egyptian project, 147; fish-farming, 123–4; Food for Peace programme, 168–70; Indonesian transmigration programme, 133; Jamaica Agricultural Development Foundation, 173–4; lending targets, 145–6; Peruvian project, 148; Renewable Energy Programme, 146–7; and the Somalian drought, 24, 26–9, 30; staff, 31, 80, 81; structural adjustment loans, 57, 64

US Congress, 88–9, 100

US National Charities Information Bureau, 6

US Presidential Commission on World Hunger, 4

US Senate, 130

Uttar Pradesh, 191

vaccination programmes, 9

VALCO aluminium plant, 140

Valverde, Orlando, 139

Venezuela, 102, 182

Verbeek, Jos, 100

Victoria Dam (Sri Lanka), 124

Vienna, 50, 82, 158

Vietnam, 70

vitamin A, 38

Volta River, 140–1

Voluntary Service Overseas (VSO), 81, 155

Walden, Richard, 16

Waldron, Sydney, 11–12, 19

Walker, Mary Noel, 39

Wall Street Journal, 42

Wanle Weyn, 26

War on Want, 4, 7

Washington, 37–40

Washington Inc. (catering company), 39

Washington Post, 108

Watson, Catherine, 126, 127

Wau, 12

Weill, Michael David, 44

West Germany, 44; economic benefits of foreign aid, 159; funding for UN, 47; and

West Germany – *cont.*
  the IMF, 58; Indonesian transmigration programme, 133; Official Development Assistance, 43, 45; and UNHCR, 103; and the World Bank, 52–3, 54
Westland helicopters, 163–4
wheat, 167–8
Whelan, Eugene, 86
Williams, Douglas, 104
Williams, Maurice, 115
Willowbrook International, 162
Wimpey (George) International, 158
Wolde-Giorgis, Dawit, 32, 85
Wollo, 17, 32
World Bank, xiii, xiv, 5, 51–7, 150; aid to Haiti, 180; Akosmobo Dam project, 140–1; Botswanan livestock projects, 139–40; Britain benefits from aid, 158; co-operation with International Monetary Fund, 39–40, 58–9; creation of, 68; economic benefits of foreign aid, 159–60; 'experts', 115, 117; failure rates, 144–5; failure to consult local people, 124–8; fraud, 172–3; hydroelectric dams, 140–1, 172, 175; Indonesian transmigration programme, 133–8, 143; lending targets, 143–6; loan commitments, 51–2; local offices, 127;

opinion polls, 4; philosophy, 128–9; Polonoroeste project, 131–3, 138–9; project lending, 55–6; redundancy payments, 41; secrecy, 66–7; sector adjustment loans, 56; Singrauli Power and Coal Mining Complex, 130–1, 162; structural adjustment loans, 56–7, 58, 59–60, 62–6, 129, 143, 182
World Food Programme (WFP), 19, 104, 133; disaster relief, 21, 22, 120; objectives, 48; in Somalia, 25, 28, 29, 30; staff, 94
World Health Organisation (WHO), 5, 19, 73, 84, 129; conflict with UNICEF, 103; funding, 48–9; objectives, 48–9; public relations, 109; satellite bodies, 103; in Somalia, 25, 26, 30; staff, 7, 82
World Meteorological Organisation, 19
World Resources Institute, 141
World Vision, 4, 8, 9, 16–17

Xingu tribe, 113

Zaire, 14, 64, 127, 171–2, 178–9, 182
Zambia, 14, 46, 59, 65, 127, 162
El Zawiyah, 122
Zuniga, Mary de, 13